Berachos

Perek 1
Daf
2a-13a

The daf b'iyun
הדף בעיון

CONCISE NOTES THAT DEVELOP THE MAJOR TOPICS OF EACH DAF

Also featuring
Essays from the Bnei Chabura
—— קונטרס פרי עמלינו ——

A Project of the Hollywood Community Kollel Iyun Chabura

Hollywood Community Kollel

3670 Stirling Rd.

Ft. Lauderdale, FL 33312

info@hollywoodkollel.org

Rabbi Moshe Baruch Parnes, Rosh Kollel

Please direct questions or comments regarding these notes to the author at:

rabbirs@hollywoodkollel.org

Cover Design – Ethan Berner

Preface and Dedication

With tremendous joy and gratitude to Hashem, we present the fruit of our labor on the first Perek of Maseches Berachos. Under the guidance of our Rosh Kollel, Rav Moshe Baruch Parnes Shlit"a, the Hollywood Community Kollel has grown since its inception (only three years ago!) to become a bastion of Torah learning and teaching in our wonderful community. Along with providing an environment of serious Torah study throughout the day, the Kollel creates an atmosphere where all feel welcome to learn whenever they find a free moment amidst their busy schedules. The daily and nightly classes, chaburas, and chavrusas at the Kollel continue to enhance our thriving Torah community, as people from all backgrounds feel comfortable joining in and partaking of Toras Hashem.

Our Iyun Chabura began around ten months ago. Each week, every member of the Chabura learns that week's amud of Gemara on his own, and the Chabura meets every Sunday night in the Kollel to hear a shiur on the week's amud delivered by a rotation of Chabura members. The Chabura members create a remarkable "kol Torah" in the Kollel Beis Medrash as the shiurim evolve into lively, in-depth discussions. Each member treats his turn to deliver the shiur seriously and prepares thoroughly to ensure that he has substantive and thought-provoking material to offer his friends. The Chabura members consistently strengthen one another and provide the group at large with a "mechayiv" to continue working hard and growing in Torah learning. How beautiful it is to witness the Torah conversation amongst friends, the "pilpul chaveirim", not just on Sunday nights but often in shul and while walking the streets of the neighborhood. Each member of the Chabura deserves remarkable recognition for uplifting one another and our city at large!

This kuntrus would simply not have happened if not for the Chabura members. They keep me constantly on my toes with questions and comments on each page of the Gemara. They force me to work hard on each week's Gemara and to try to offer the ideas of the Gemara and its commentators in a precise, yet concise, fashion. It is my hope and prayer that readers find these notes helpful in enhancing their own Torah study. The notes incorporate many insights raised by the Chabura members during their shiurim, and I am personally indebted to each participant for his involvement and dedication.

In addition to the notes on each amud, we also present "קונטרס פרי עמלינו", essays (in both Hebrew and English) on various topics throughout the Perek. While working hard in various professions to provide for our families, our community, and Klal Yisroel at large, the members of the Chabura also toil fastidiously in Torah, and it is an honor to present the fruit of our labor. A number of Chabura members contributed essays to this volume, and we look forward to incorporating even more contributions from our participants in the future.

Along with our Chabura in Hollywood, a number of people throughout the country and the world have been learning the Gemara and keeping up with these notes long-distance. It is a privilege to learn with people both inside and outside of our community, and we welcome anyone, anywhere, who would like to join us.

On a personal note, I thank my parents, Dr. and Mrs. William and Avivya Stohl, who have guided me throughout my life and continue to lead by example. I thank my parents-in-law, Mr. and Mrs. Fred and Clarisse Schlesinger, who shower our family with constant love and support. I owe my Torah learning to my Rebbe, Rav Moshe Stav Shlit"a, as well as to all of my dedicated Rebbeim, chavrusas, friends, and students who always challenge me and propel me to new heights. I especially thank my dear brother, Shelly (Dr. Sheldon Stohl), for being my role model since I was young and for being my confidant and chavrusa throughout life. And, to be sure, everything that I will ever accomplish is credit to my extraordinary wife, Malki. Her wisdom beyond her years, her perfection of character, and her *mesiras nefesh* for Torah and our family are simply beyond words.

May Hashem give us strength to continue our spiritual growth on both personal and communal levels, and may the Hollywood Community Kollel Iyun Chabura be only one of many projects to spread Torah within our community and beyond. We welcome and encourage one and all to join our Chabura from near or far or to develop similar Torah study programs of their own, as we continue to spread Hashem's Torah throughout the world and deep within our souls.

- Raphael Stohl, Rosh Chabura (Tamuz 5776)

Sponsors

Rabbi Ranan and Dr. Rebecca Amster

Tzvi and Aliza Aronin

Daniel and Alyssa Barzideh

Joey and Russi Bohm

Will and Jen Coane

Dr. Jonathan and Dina Dobkowski

Josh and Gitty Levine

Drs. Jonathan and Ilana Mazurek

Yitz and Mor Taub

The Bnei Chabura

Rabbi Yosef Weinstock
Rabbi Yehuda Fensterszaub
Rabbi Yitzchak Marmormstein
Rabbi Gavriel Grossman
Rabbi Ranan Amster
Rabbi Doniel Bensoussan
Rabbi Aryeh Blum
Matis Adar
Tzvi Aronin
Dr. Eli Berman
Will Coane
Dr. Jonathan Dobkowski
Josh Levine
Dr. Jonathan Mazurek
Shlomo Schwartz
Shimon Segelman
Josh Seiden
Yitz Taub
Rami Zvida

Long-Distance Members

Daniel Barzideh
Joey Bohm
Buri Rosenberg
Jonathan Stieglitz
Dr. Sheldon Stohl

מכתב ברכה

אמרו חז"ל, פרקי אבות פ"א, ולא המדרש הוא העיקר אלא המעשה. ומה טוב ומה יפה היכא דהמעשה הוא המדרש.

קונטרס זה נערך ונכתב ע"י האי גברא רבה חבר כולל שלנו בהאליוואוד פלורידא ה"ה הרב רפאל סטוהל שליט"א, והוא מדרש וגם מעשה. הוא מדרש, ראשית פרי עמלו של בעלי בתים אשר נעדדו ע"י הרב רפאל הנ"ל לבוא ביחד כל שבוע להכין חבורות בתורה ולשמוע איש יגיעת רעהו, ועמל הרב רפאל עם כל אחד ואחד במסירה רבה כדי לסדר דבריו ע"פ האמת בתוך הסוגיא לפי פירושו של רש"י ותוספות.

והרי הוא גם מעשה, דכמה מבני החבורה שמו מחשבתיהם בכתב, איש כפי הבנתו והשגתו, והרב רפאל לקט כל עמלם ושם לילות כימים להעריך ולהכין תורתם כדי שתהיה ראוי לדפוס. חלק מהן ידפיס בתוך קונטרס זה וחלק מהם בתוך קונטרס שני אשר יבא לדפוס בתוך זמן קצר בעז"ה.

וגם ליקט וחיבר הרב רפאל דברי הראשונים וגדולי אחרונים על כל הסוגיות שלמד עם בני החבורה ושם עיונו לפרשם ולסדרם בכתב נעים וברור להראות בו עיקר הדיוקים ועמקות הסוגיות וליתן לחכמים כדי להחכים עוד.

והנה, עיקר העבודה של האדם היא היגיעה בתורה וכבר אמרו חז"ל, מגילה ו' ע"ב, אמר רבי יצחק אם יאמר לך אדם יגעתי ולא מצאתי אל תאמן, לא יגעתי ומצאתי אל תאמן, יגעתי ומצאתי תאמין. וכתב מהרש"א שם דזה הפירוש במה שאמר דוד המלך ע"ה בתהלים, האמנתי כי אדבר אני עניתי מאד, היינו מה שעניתי ויגעתי בתורה האמנתי, כלומר מה שאני אומר ביגיעה הוא נאמן, אבל מה שאני אומר בחפזי, דהוא בלי יגיעה, כל האדם כוזב. דהיינו מה שאדם אומר מעצמו הוא בודאי כוזב דאין אמת אלא התורה ואין להבין התורה בלי יגיעה.

ועל זה אמרתי בצחות לפרש מאמרם הנ"ל לא המדרש הוא העיקר אלא המעשה, דהיינו לא המדרש דאדם דורש בעצמו בלי יגיעה מרעיון שלו הוא העיקר, אלא המעשה, היינו התורה הבאה לו ע"י מעשה ויגיעה היא העיקר ולא זולת זה אמת כלל.

וע' מש"כ הרה"ג ר' אהרן קטלר זצ"ל במשנת רבי אהרן שלו, חלק א' שער שני בד"ה עמלה של תורה, מהגמ' מנחות דף ז'. אבימי מסכתא איתעקרא איתעקרא ליה ואתא לקמיה דרב חסדא לאדכורי גמריה. ולשלח ליה וליתי לגביה? סבר הכי מסתייעא מילתא טפי ע"ש. ופרש"י דאבימי נשתכחה הימנו (מסכת מנחות). והלך לגבי רב חסדא שיזכיר לו לימודו ולא רצה לשלוח לרב חסדא לבוא אליו משום דהכי מסתייעא מילתא טפי. ופרש"י משום יגעתי ומצאתי. ומפ' משנת ר"א וז"ל והיינו דע"י היגיעה זוכים גם לדברים כגון אלה שאין בכח האדם להשיגם ע"י העמל ע"ש.

ובודאי ע"י עמלם הרב כבר זכו בני החבורה, ובראשם הרב רפאל שליט"א למדרגת האמנתי כי אדבר, ודבר כוזב מפיהם ודאי לא יצאו חו"ש.

וע"ש עוד במשנת ר"א דכתב וז"ל מעובדא זו אנו למדים שלא רק היגיעה בעצם הלימוד מביאה לידי השגה, אלא גם הטורח עבור הלימוד בדבר שאין לו שייכות לגוף הלימוד, וכגון ההליכה ללימוד, ג"כ גורם להשגה יתרה ע"ש אריכות דבריו בזה.

ופשוט דבני החבורה הגיעו להשגות גדולות בתורה יותר מכדי לימודם ע"י טירחתם המיוחדת לבוא לבית המדרש ללמוד תורה במקום ובזמן שאין מי לעזר ולתמוך אותם.

וגם פשוט וברור דע"י יגיעת נשי בני החבורה הקד' אשר שלחו ועדדו לבעליהם ללמוד וללמד ונשארו בבתיהן בודדות בלי עוזר זכו בעליהן להבנות והשגות בתורה. וכבר אמרו חז"ל, מסכת ברכות דף י"ז ע"א נשים במאי זכיין וכו' ובאתנויי גברייהו בי רבנן ונטרין לגברייהו עד דאתו מבי רבנן.

ונ"ל להעמיס גם זה בתוך מאמרם הנ"ל לא המדרש הוא העיקר אלא המעשה, דהיינו לא המדרש של נשים הוא העיקר, אלא המעשה שהוא שלוחות בעליהן ללמוד תורה וממתינות להם עד דאתו מבי רבנן הוא העיקר. ובודאי זכו גם הן למדרגות גדולות.

והנני מסיים בברכתי, ברכת הדיוט, שיזכו בני החבורה וראשם הר"ר רפאל סטוהל שליט"א להמשיך בלימודם בגפ"ת וע"י עמלם ויגיעתם יעלו מעלה מעלה בהשגת התורה וביראת שמים ויזכו זרעם אחריהם לשתות בצמא ממימי התלמוד תדיר.

בכבוד רב ואהבה רבה

משה ברוך בן הרב יהושע פרנס

ראש הכולל, האליוואוד פלורידא

Short Notes on the Daf

Berachos Perek 1 (2a-13a)

1. *What is the meaning of the word "maseches" (commonly referred to as "tractate")?* – R. Dovid Cohen (Z'man Nakat ch. 5) cites various explanations for the origin of the word "maseches". Some commentators (see Sefer Chasidim #928) show that the word refers to the Mishnah's culling information about a specific topic and offering it in an organized and clear fashion. Others (see intro. to Tos. Yom Tov) refer to the fact that the Mishnah's teaching of the Oral Torah provides us with a deeper connection to the Written Torah. Yet others (Mekor Chaim) explain that the word indicates that the Oral Torah is based on a strong tradition. See Z'man Nakat further, along with Chadashim Gam Yeshanim on Berachos (Pesicha 2:1). (Chadashim Gam Yeshanim 2:3 further notes that the Gemara is referred to by different names: "Gemara" or "Talmud" refer to its in-depth study, while "Shas" refers to either the "six sedarim" of Mishnah and Gemara or "sixty masechtos" (but see Z'man Nakat ch. 2 for various opinions regarding the exact number of Masechtos). Some scholars (see "Printing the Talmud" pg. 3) point out that Christian censors opposed the term "Talmud", therefore the term "Gemara" became much more widespread – for example, see "The Censorship of Hebrew Books" (pgs. 52; 90) regarding the 16th century edicts "Index of Trent" and "Index Librorum Prohibitorum".)

2. *Is Berachos the first maseches in Shas?* – R. Yonasan Steif (Chadashim Gam Yeshanim on Berachos, Pesicha 1:3) cites Dikdukei Sofrim who posits (based on an old manuscript of the Gemara) that Seder Zera'im truly begins with Maseches Pe'ah and not with Berachos. But R. Steif disagrees, pointing to a number of sources (e.g. Bamidbar Rabba 13:16 that expounds why Shas begins with the letter "מ" of the word "מאימתי" of Maseches Berachos). He explains (1:5, based on the Meiri) that some old manuscripts place Maseches Berachos along with Seder Mo'ed since those tractates were studied regularly as opposed to the rest of Seder Zera'im which was not studied by the general populace. But he notes (1:10-11) that some Midrashim indeed seem to order the sedarim of Mishnayos differently than the standard sequence (of Zera'im, Moed, Nashim, Nezikin, Kodshim, Taharos), but he posits that all agree that Zera'im (and thus Berachos) really comes first, and the various Midrashim are teaching other additional lessons; see there. R. Reuven Margaliyos (Yesod HaMishnah Va'Arichasa pg. 28-29) contends that before the time of R. Yehuda HaNasi, Seder Zera'im did not constitute its own seder but was recorded in various places throughout the other sedarim. He also writes that there was a seventh seder of Mishnah which included Masechtos on Tefillin, Mezuza, Tzitzis etc., and Berachos was original part of that seder. For further discussion see Z'man Nakat (ch. 7).

3. *Why does Shas begin with Maseches Berachos and the laws of Keriyas Shema?* – a) Rambam (Hakdama to Peirush HaMishnah, pg. 108 in back of the standard Gemara Berachos) explains that we begin with Seder Zera'im because food sustains us and thus forms the physical foundation for our service of Hashem, we begin with Maseches Berachos because we may not eat from Hashem's food without reciting a beracha. Since we need to discuss berachos, we first discuss the berachos which we say every day, i.e. the berachos of Keriyas Shema. And before discussing berachos of Keriyas Shema, we need to first discuss Keriyas Shema itself. b) Rabbenu Yeshaya (note on Rambam ibid.) explains that we discuss Keriyas Shema first in order to begin our learning of Shas with the fear of Heaven, which is the basis for understanding true wisdom. Shema also includes the Torah's most fundamental ideas: the oneness of Hashem, the mitzvah to learn Torah, and the importance of keeping mitzvos. And it is constant, as we say it every morning and night. Meiri (toward the end of his intro., ד"ה והוא אצלי) similarly writes that the recital of berachos is most fundamental to our religious growth as it forms an ongoing connection between us and our Creator, and the mitzvos mentioned in Maseches Berachos apply numerous times throughout each day. c) Tiferes Yisroel explains that learning Torah is the source of all Mitzvos, as Chazal state that "learning leads to performance". Since the mitzvah of learning Torah is mentioned in Keriyas Shema ("ושננתם לבניך"), and Keriyas Shema itself serves as Talmud Torah (Menachos 99b), we therefore begin our study with Keriyas Shema. See also Chadashim Gam Yeshanim (Pesicha #9) who elloborates on this idea. (Commentators further point out that Chazal include laws of purity, Teruma, and Kodshim in our Mishnah to remind us that the acceptance of Mitzvos must be done with purity etc. See note from Sefer Hon Ashir quoted on the side of Mishnah Yachin U'Boaz here.) d) Chadashim Gam Yeshanim (ibid. 1:6) explains that we begin the Oral Torah in same way that Hashem began the Written Torah, with the letter "ב" which hints to (beracha); see Bereishis Rabba (1:10). (He continues to explain that the next tractate, Maseches Pe'ah begins with the letter "א" just as the Ten Commandments begin with "א".) He adds (ibid. 3:2-8) that Shas begins with Keriyas Shema just as the Written Torah begins with hints to Keriyas Shema (see there) and because Shema hints to the Ten Commandments (as mentioned in Yerushalmi 1:5, quoted in Tosafos 12b) which were the first words that Bnei Yisroel heard from Hashem at Har Sinai.

4. *Why does the Mishnah preface the law with a question rather than simply state the various opinions?* – R. Yonasan Steif (Chadashim Gam Yeshanim, Pesicha #8) answers by referring to a fundamental idea mentioned in a number of commentators: most issues discussed in the Mishnah and Gemara throughout Shas do not refer to the most rudimentary laws but to various details (often uncommon details) of each particular law or mitzvah, for the most basic laws are either explicit in the Written Torah or widely known and unnecessary to be recorded by Chazal. Therefore our Mishnah *assumes* that Shema must be recited since the mitzvah is well-known and practiced; the only relevant question

is "from when" it may be recited. Chadashim Gam Yeshanim (beg. of 2a) further notes that there are some variant texts of the Mishnah, but he concludes (based on Bamidbar Rabba 13:16) that our text is the correct one. He adds that the Mishnah begins with the letter "מ" in order to illustrate that the Mishnah is a continuation of the Written Torah which ends with the previous letter in the alef-beis ("ל"). Furthermore, the first letter of the Torah ("ב") when joined with the first letter of the Mishnah ("מ") forms the word "בם", referring to the mitzvah to learn Torah ("ודברת בם"), for both the Written and Oral Torahs are necessary when studying Hashem's word. See there for further hints found in the letter "מ" in our Mishnah.

5. *Does one need to recite Shema himself or can he hear it from someone else?* – The Gra (Sh'nos Eliyahu on our Mishnah and 3:3 ד"ה ומתפילין) writes that the Mishnah uses the plural form ("קורין") because we must all read the Shema ourselves. R. Yehuda ben Yakar (quoted in Shitos Kamai 11b pg. 230) writes this as well, explaining that Keriyas Shema is a form of Torah study (see above and our notes on 11b) and therefore requires personal involvement, as opposed to Torah Reading and Tefilla which can be fulfilled through listening to another. He adds (as does Maharam Al Ashkar #10 ד"ה ואין מי) that the source of the mitzvah, "ודברת בם", implies speech ("ודברת"). R. Shlomo Wahrman (Sh'eiris Yosef vol. 7 end of #26) and R. Tzvi Schachter add a further idea, noting that Keriyas Shema entails "accepting the yoke of Heaven" which is inherently personal and must be done by oneself. But others disagree with these contentions and opine that one can indeed fulfill the mitzvah of Keriyas Shema by listening to another person read it (see argument of Pri Chadash 62:1 and his explanation of Ritva Rosh Hashana 29a ד"ה תני, but see wording of Ritva here 21a ד"ה והרי תפלה). (For further sources see Einayim LaMishpat here; Piskei Teshuvos 62 note 13; Dvar Shaul Sotah 59:12 ד"ה ובדברי.)

6. *Until when may one recite Keriyas Shema at night?* – The Torah commands that you say Shema "when you lie down (sleep)". That is, timing for Shema depends on "sleep", not necessarily on "night" (see Rashi on the Mishnah, but see our notes on 2b for further discussion). Therefore, the first opinion in the Mishnah holds that it must be recited in the first third of the night, based on when we *go* to sleep. The other opinions hold that it can be recited all night, when we are *sleeping*. The Tannaim further disagree whether or not one must recite Shema before midnight in order to ensure that he does not forget to recite it altogether. The Rishonim debate whether or not everyone agrees that it should ideally be said before midnight and whether one can fulfill his obligation (at least "bedi'eved") after midnight. See our notes on 9a for this discussion. The Shulchan Aruch paskens (235:3) that it should ideally be read before midnight, but "bedi'eved" it could be read all night.

7. *Can we fulfill the mitzvah of Keriyas Shema in shul before nightfall?* – It is clear from the Mishnah that Keriyas Shema must be recited after nightfall. But a prevalent custom in the time of the Rishonim was (and still exists today in many congregations) to daven Maariv with Shema while it was still day. (They did this due to practical concerns, since it was hard to gather a minyan for a later Maariv). The Rishonim disagree why this practice was allowed. a) Rashi explains that they recited Shema in shul in order to enhance the davening (see Meiri here ד"ה ולגוף that we find a parallel concept in "somech Geula l'Tefilla"; see also Yerushalmi quoted in Tos. here, and quote from R. Soloveitchik in our notes on 11b), but they only truthfully fulfilled their obligation of Shema through reciting Shema before bed. (It seems that Rashi understands that it is enough to recite just the *first* paragraph before bed, while the final two paragraphs of Shema and Birchos Keriyas Shema were enacted as a part of *Tefilla* but not as an integral part to one's fulfillment of the mitzvah of Keriyas Shema. But Ritva 3a quotes a number of Rishonim that said to recite Birchos Keriyas Shema before reciting Shema before bed.) b) Rabbenu Tam in Tosafos explains that in fact we do not practice in accordance with the Tanna of this Mishnah. He explains that according to R. Yehuda (on 27a) Keriyas Shema can be recited after "Plag HaMincha" just like Maariv, and we act in accordance with that opinion. Even though Shema is not based on "night" but on "the time for sleep", the Bach (235:4) explains that Rabbenu Tam understands that just as the period after Plag HaMincha is "night" for the sake of Tefilla, so too it is "the time for sleep" for the sake of Shema, for "the time for sleep" *is* "night". (See our notes further on 2b.) And even though it is not yet "night" for all matters, nonetheless, it seems that R. Tam equates timing for Tefilla and Keriyas Shema because of their similarities in purpose. An alternative understanding of R. Tam can be gleaned from Tosafos (end of 2b) who explain that R. Yehuda does not require Shema to be said when "going to sleep", but rather at "night". R. Tam, assuming like R. Yehuda, could thus sidestep the problem altogether, for R. Yehuda bases Shema on "night" which begins for matters of prayer at Plag HaMincha. (The Bach, however, rejects Tosafos's opinion on 2b, explaining that Shema is certainly based on "the time for sleep". Regardless, the Bach's explanation is necessary to explain the Ri's and Rosh's opinion (below) who disagree with Tos. 2b but nonetheless equate the time for Maariv and Shema.) R. Tam further holds that even though we daven Mincha *after* Plag HaMincha in accordance with the opinion of the Chachomim who disagree with R. Yehuda, we can nonetheless daven Maariv and recite Shema at that time in accordance with R. Yehuda's opinion. He seemingly opines that we can act like one opinion for one Tefilla and like an opposing opinion for the next Tefilla in accordance with the dictum "elu v'elu divrei Elokim Chayim", that both opinions are valid. (The Acharonim discuss R. Tam's opinion at length, and many Rishonim disagree with R. Tam and hold that one cannot

daven both Mincha and Maariv after Plag HaMincha before nightfall; see Rosh and Maadanei Yom Tov on Rosh #4. Nonetheless, Aruch HaShulchan 235:1-3 justifies the custom with his own novel approach, explaining that Maariv can be recited during the day and is not a contradiction to Mincha, for the fats of the korbanos were offered both during the day and night, and Maariv follows the laws of those fats. But most Poskim write that one should ideally refrain from this leniency; see Shulchan Aruch 333:1 with Mishnah Berurah.) c) Ri (quoted in Tosafos) and Rosh write that we rule (because of the difficulty to get a late minyan) like the Tannaim (on 2b) who disagree with our Mishnah and hold that Shema can be recited even before nightfall. Meiri (ד"ה מעתה) writes that we don't officially "rule" this way, but we rely on this opinion because of necessity ("עת לעשות לה' וכו"). (Practically, the Poskim write that someone who davens Maariv early should ideally repeat Shema after nightfall. The Aruch Hashulchan 235:6-8 agrees with this ruling as well, for his novel explanation cited above only applies to Tefilla, not to Keriyas Shema.)

8. *What comes first - the day or the night?* – The Gemara originally questions why the Mishnah discusses Keriyas Shema of the night before Shema of the day. But the Gemara then bouts face and explains that the Torah itself mentions the Shema of night before the Shema of the morning. Moreover, the night came before day during the Creation of the world. This give-and-take points to a more general discussion whether the night precedes the day or vice versa. On the one hand, Tosafos here point out that the Torah mentions the morning korban Tamid before the one in the afternoon. Similarly, commentators note that the night follows the day in the Beis HaMikdash. It is possible to explain (see Tzidkas Hatzadik pg. 2a #11) that our general service of Hashem begins at night because we first need to put our trust in Hashem as represented by the darkness and uncertainty of night, and only then can we experience the glory of the day. But in the Beis HaMikdash the Shechina is more clearly felt, and we therefore do not need the same level of faith and trust (represented by night) to begin our Avodas Hashem. But Emes L'Yaakov (Berachos 4b) notes that the Gemara there describes the morning Shema as the first of the day, seemingly contrary to the order described in the Torah and in our Gemara. We can reconcile these apparent contradictions by explaining that the day indeed begins in the morning on an *experiential level* (and therefore our day is "sandwiched" by Shema, as expressed on 4b), but the *spirituality* (kedusha) of the day truly begins at night (and therefore Shabbos and holidays begin at night). (See Emes L'Yaakov here who discusses this idea and a possible halachic ramification whether the obligation to recite 100 berachos each day begins in morning or at night.) We can add that it is possible that spirituality begins at night only in today's world, but in the end of days the world will constantly shine like the day, and thus spirituality will begin during the day as well. (See our notes on 26a beg. of Perek 4 for a fuller discussion of the topic of night/day. See also our notes on 11b.)

Short Notes on Berachos 2b

1. *At what point during the evening does a Kohen become pure and thus permitted to eat teruma?* – Rashi and Tosafos (see also Tos. HaRosh end of 2a) disagree how to explain the possibility that the Gemara initially raises, but according to both of them the Gemara concludes that a Kohen only becomes pure once "tzeis hakochavim" arrives. But R. Hai Gaon (quoted in Tos. HaRosh end of 2b) explains according to R. Eliezer that a Kohen becomes pure at the beginning of the night (like the initial thought of the Gemara according to Tosafos). (But see footnote 90 in R. Nissan Zak's ed. of Tos. Rabbenu Yehuda here who asks a strong question on R. Hai Gaon's explanation of the Gemara.)

2. *Various opinions in the Gemara regarding the earliest time for Keriyas Shema at night* – See our notes on 2a that the mitzvah of Keriyas Shema does not depend on "night", but on the "time when you sleep". The Gemara here records more opinions regarding the exact timing. For instance, R. Meir opines that one may recite Keriyas Shema from the time that a poor person begins eating until the point when such a person gets up from his meal. Rashi explains that R. Meir understands that Keriyas Shema must be recited during the *beginning* of the time when people go to sleep". This point is baffling, however, for people do not yet go to sleep before they eat their dinner, so why does the beginning of the dinner hour constitute the first time that one may recite Keriyas Shema? It seems that the "time when you go to sleep" does not necessarily mean "sleep" literally; it could mean the time when one puts his daily activities to rest and begins his nightly routine, "resting" from his workday. (The other opinions in the Beraisa here can be understood in a similar vein.) Based on this understanding we can gain further insight into the fact that the Gemara learns the timing for Keriyas Shema from Pesukim in Nechemia which refer to the definition of "night". The Gemara understands that it makes sense that the "time when you sleep" is tantamount to "night", for even though people do not sleep immediately when night hits, nonetheless, "night" begins the period of rest. Indeed, Tosafos (ד"ה אע"פ) point out (see also Tosafos HaRosh here and Tosafos in Megilla 20b for further clarification) that the Pesukim in Nechemia are not clear proof regarding the timing for Keriyas Shema, for Keriyas Shema depends on the "time when you sleep" whereas these Pesukim refer to the time of "night". But nonetheless, the Gemara understands that it is sensible to understand that "night" helps define "when you sleep", as we explained. (See also our notes on 2a where this idea is already expressed to a degree in the opinion of Rabbenu Tam as explained by the Bach. And see R. Hai Gaon quoted in Tos. HaRosh end of 2b who also explains that some Tannaim hold that Keriyas Shema depends on "night". Some Acharonim also understand the Rambam this way; see Rambam beg. of hilchos Keriyas Shema along with the letters in the beginning of Mishnas Chaim on Bereishis by R. Chaim Steinberg where he disagrees with R. Chaim Kanievsky Shlit"a regarding this point - whether Keriyas Shema according to the Rambam depends upon "nighttime" or upon "when you sleep" and whether they are one and the same. See also wording of Rashi end of 8b and our notes on 9a, 9b, 10b, and 11a.)

3. *When do "day" and "night" begin according to the Torah?* – The Gemara learns from a Pasuk in Nechemia that the day begins at "alos hashachar" and ends at "tzeis hakochavim". The Ran (on Bereishis 1:14, quoted in Otzar Haz'manim pg. 114) writes that the "nations of the world" understand that "night" begins at sundown and "day" begins at sunrise, but the Torah teaches that it is considered "day" whenever the light of the sun provides light to the earth. Nonetheless, there is proof that even according to the Torah, the time between sunset and "tzeis hakochavim" as well as the time between "alos hashachar" and sunrise have aspects of both night and day. See below for some discussion regarding the time between sunset and "tzeis hakochavim" and our notes on 9a regarding the time between "alos hashachar" and sunrise.

4. *When is "bein hashemashos"?* – "Bein hashemashos" is the time between that which is certainly "day" and that which is certainly "night". Some commentators explains that it is simply a "safek" - we do not know exactly when night begins. Others, however, explain that it is not a classic "safek", a simple lack of knowledge. Rather, it is a time period which is a "safek" by definition; it is a "grey area". See Ritva in Yoma 47b and Aruch HaShulchan (OC 455:3). The Gemara in Shabbos (34b-35b) discusses the argument between R. Yehuda and R. Yosi regarding "bein hashemashos". They disagree about two points: a) R. Yehuda opines that bein hashemashos covers a large period of time (anywhere between around 20 minutes to well over an hour; the exact timing is highly debated amongst the commentators and Poskim; see Otzar Haz'manim and many others), whereas R. Yosi holds that bein hashemashos is a much shorter period, "like the blink of an eye". b) R. Yehuda's bein hashemashos ends before R. Yosi's bein hashemashos even begins. Regarding the statement that R. Yosi holds that bein hashemashos is "like the blink of an eye", Tosafos (Shabbos top of 34b and clarified further in Tos. HaRosh there) explain that both R. Yosi and R. Yehuda agree that there is a distinct moment in time when it switches from "day" to "night", but R. Yehuda has a much longer time during which he is unsure, as opposed to R. Yosi who is only unsure for a very short period of time. Tosafos further point out that even according to R. Yosi there is some amount of time during bein hashemashos. That is, the time it takes to "blink an eye" is some small amount of time, enough time for a "zav" to have an emission (see there). But this time is obviously very short, and it occurs when it is already almost completely dark, right before the time which is "certainly night". (Rosh in Shabbos 2:23 notes that we do not know exactly when this "blink of an eye" occurs, and

he calculates the latest time that night could possibly begin according to both R. Yehuda and R. Yosi. Otzar Haz'manim pg. 202 calculates that R. Yosi's bein hashemashos is certainly over by around 30 seconds after R. Yehuda's bein hashemashos, even according to R. Tam's opinion; see there.)

Short Notes on Berachos 3a

1. *What are the halachic ramifications of the various Mishmaros during the night?* – a) Based on our Gemara, the Shulchan Aruch rules (OC 1:2-3) that it is proper to rise early from bed and bemoan the destruction of the Beis HaMikdash (just as Hashem does each night, kaviyachol) and to daven at the end of each Mishmar, for those times are especially opportune for such Tefilla. The Arizal (quoted in Poskim on Shulchan Aruch ibid.) writes that it is ideal for one to daven at midnight (chatzos) rather than at the end of each Mishmar. This is the basis for the custom to recite "tikkun chatzos". (The Poskim disagree how exactly chatzos should be calculated for this halacha; see Magen Avraham on Shulchan Aruch ibid.) The Arizal's opinion has roots in our Gemara as well, for one opinion describes the sign for the middle Mishmar as occurring in the middle of that Mishmar; i.e. chatzos. The Gemara on 3b also describes Dovid rising at chatzos to learn Torah, and it brings proof from a Pasuk in Tehillim. (See also Piskei Teshuvos on Shulchan Aruch ibid. note 73 for hints in other Gemaras to the Arizal's opinion.) Poskim further explain that it is proper to learn Torah during this time (from chatzos to morning). Indeed, the Gemara (Tamid 32b) quotes the Pasuk "קומי רוני בלילה" as the source for the unique greatness of learning Torah at night, while this same Pasuk serves as a source for rising in the night to daven about the destruction of the Beis HaMikdash (see Rosh here end of 1:2). Hashem is especially "close" to us at that time, and therefore it is a particularly opportune time to both daven and learn Torah (see notes on 3b further). The Poskim debate how much time should be spent for davening and how much for learning during those hours. Some write that young talmidei chachomim should focus much more heavily on learning Torah during those hours (see Piskei Teshuvos ibid. notes 82 and 95). Some Poskim urge those who aspire to grow in Avodas Hashem to get up early enough to learn at least during the final Mishmar, for the Gemara records the unique impact that the Torah has on one's soul (not just on his mind) during those hours (see Shevet HaLevi vol. 6 #1). Nonetheless, some great Talmidei Chachomim remained awake until very late at night, accomplishing this unique learning and davening during the first half of the night as opposed to the second half (see Piskei Teshuvos ibid. #13 and adjacent footnotes). b) The Tiferes Yisroel (beg. of Maseches Tamid) writes a novel idea that the Kohanim and Leviim who would guard the Beis HaMikdash throughout the night would guard in shifts. Each shift would guard for the length of one Mishmar.

2. *How is the spiritual nature of night unique in comparison to that of day?* – The Gemara describes that there are either three or four Mishmaros during the night, and each contains a unique time for Tefilla where even Hashem Himself (kaviyachol) bemoans the destruction of the Beis HaMikdash, as described above. These times may correlate to the three tefillos recited during the day, as the Gemara relates (end of this amud) that Hashem similarly bemoans the destruction of the Beis Hamikdash during each Tefilla of the day (see Hagahos Yaavetz end of amud here and Rashba in Chidushei Hahagados 6b beg. of his piece on Tefillas Mincha). There is also a correlation between studying Torah during the day and studying at night. The learning during the day provides clarity and structure to the Torah learned at night, but the Torah learned at night provides "soul" and a deep religious experience to the learning along with a measure of depth not easily attainable during the day (see Shevet Levi above and our notes on 3b). The Maharsha further describes the spiritual nature of the night: the first Mishmar is comparable to the neighing of a donkey (a donkey represents physicality) because the body is tired and heavy after its long day, and this physicality makes the person less cognizant of his soul. During the second Mishmar most bodies are sleeping, so this an opportune time for the non-physical soul to rise (represented in the fierce cries of dogs). By the end of the third Mishmar, the soul is well charged from a night of spirituality (from residing in Heaven), and the soul "nurses" from the holiness of the Torah just as a baby nurses from its mother. It should be noted that these occurrences during the night span a shorter period of time than those of the day: the Mishmaros of the night span from tzeis hakochavim until alos hashachar (even according to Gra on OC 458:2; see Demesek Eliezer there regarding Tosafos here), whereas halachos of the "day" span from alos hashachar (well before sunrise) until shekiya (sundown), and sometimes even until tzeis hakochavim (well after sundown). That is, one has more time to accomplish his duties of the day, whereas the highly-spiritual night is more compact. And more, some of the night itself is utilized to round off "daytime" activities (the third Tefilla of the day; Keriyas Shema). (Even though those tefillos contain some of the unique status of the night as explained by commentators regarding Birchos Keriyas Shema of Maariv, they are nonetheless also closely linked to the mitzvos of the day, whereas the unique spirituality of the Mishmaros begins later.) Based on the above, it is possible to give a deeper reason for the opinions in the Mishnah that Keriyas Shema must be recited before the end of the first Mishmar or before midnight. One can explain that the first half of the night finishes off the workings of the daytime, whereas from the end of the first Mishmar or chatzos the unique spirituality of the night is in full force, and it is no longer the proper time to finish daily activities. And more, those later points in the night actually lead into the next day. That is, even though the day halachically begins at night, it is possible to explain that the beginning of the night is also focused on finishing the previous day whereas the second part of the night focuses more heavily on the next day's avoda. Indeed, the night was a time to burn the fats from the *previous* day's korbanos, but it was also utilized by the Kohanim to rise early while it was still night to ready themselves for the *next* day's avoda (see beginning of Maseches Tamid

and our notes on 26a, beg. of Perek 4 at length.) Hence the night is an extension of the day, but it also contains its own unique kedusha, and it is man's job to tap into that spirituality.

3. *What is a "bas kol"?* – Einayim LaMishpat quotes an argument regarding the meaning of a "bas kol": Rashi explains that it is some sort of voice; Tosafos explain that it is an echo of a voice; Rambam explains that is a low-level quasi-prophecy.

4. *What is the proper way to recite Kadish and what is its meaning?* – Tosafos quote an understanding of "Yehei Shmei Raba etc." as a request for the time of Mashiach when Hashem's Name and throne will be "complete" once again (kaviyachol). But Tosafos reject this explanation based on the wording of our Gemara and explain that kadish simply praises Hashem's great Name without mention of its "incompleteness" and its "fix" in the future. The Poskim (on OC 56:1) explain the halachic difference between the two understandings: according to Tosafos there is no need for a "mapik hei" in the word "שמיה", whereas according to the other explanation the word "שמיה" indeed requires a "mapik hei" in order to accentuate the letters of the word and thus refer to the current incompleteness of Hashem's Name. There is also a difference regarding where one may pause while reciting the sentence. Practically, the Pri Megadim (on Taz 56:1) writes that we can have both meanings in mind; we should therefore not pause at all and we should use a "mapik hei" to cover both meanings. (It is quite possible that even those who explain that kadish refers to the time of Mashiach agree with the conclusion of the Pri Megadim, for the simple meaning is as Tosafos explain from our Gemara, but there is also a hint to the time when Hashem's Name will be complete.)

Short Notes on Berachos 3b

1. *When did Dovid wake up each day?* – a) The Gemara initially assumes (and is corroborated by Gemara 4a), based on a Pasuk in Tehillim, that Dovid woke up at midnight (chatzos). The Gemara then calculates (according to various opinions) how chatzos corresponds to his awaking "before two remaining Mishmaros", as clear in another Pasuk in Tehillim. b) Rashi on that Pasuk in Tehillim (119:148, see also Maharsha and Rashash here) adds another explanation based on the Gemara below on this very page: he arose after only one mishmar (after one third of the night) and learned Torah until chatzos when he began to sing praises etc. to Hashem (see below). c) Y'feh Einayim (hagahos in back of Gemara) points to the Yerushalmi and various Midrashim that offer yet another explanation: Dovid rose at different times each day - when he previously "ate the meal of a king" he rose later (chatzos); when he ate "his own meal" he rose earlier (after the first 3rd of the night); and he sometimes did not rise until shortly before alos hashachar. Based on this understanding, it may stand to reason that although it is most ideal to awake before chatzos (see notes on 3a regarding "tikun chatzos"), nonetheless, there are times that one may rise earlier or later depending on various circumstances. (Many Poskim quoted in Piskei Teshuvos on 3a already point out that most people today do not feel capable of rising so early, but it is nonetheless important to realize the greatness of doing so.)

2. *When did kings arise (and until when can Keriyas Shema be recited)?* – Our Gemara seems clear as Rashi writes here: kings rise in the beginning of the third hour. The Mishnah (9b, quoted here) states that Keriyas Shema can be recited until the third hour because that is when the kings rise. Most Meforshim (see list in Einayim LaMishpat 10b #4) explain the Mishnah as referring to the end of the 3rd hour, seemingly contradicting our Gemara. Meleches Shlomo (on Mishnah there, 1:2) answers that *most* kings rise at end of the 3rd hour, but some rise at beginning, so Dovid made sure to wake up well before even the minority of kings awoke. Nonetheless, since most kings did not rise until the end of the 3rd hour, we may recite Keriyas Shema all the way until then. Nonetheless, Meleches Shlomo quotes that a few Rishonim indeed explain that Keriyas Shema must be recited by the beginning of the 3rd hour, as implied by the simple understanding of our Gemara.

3. *What is allowed to be spoken in the presence of a dead body?* – There is a disagreement in the Gemara, Rishonim, and Poskim here pertaining to many different details (see Einayim LaMishpat). Some explain that the main problem with speaking in the presence of the deceased is "lo'eig l'rash" (mocking the poor); that is, since the deceased can no longer perform mitzvos, it is improper to speak Torah in the deceased's presence for this is a form of "mockery". Others explain that there is a more general problem of "bizayon ha'meis" (disrespecting the deceased); speaking about anything in the presence of the deceased other than the deceased himself displays a lack of care for the loss. Some explain (see Shita Mekubetzes) that the deceased even feel a sort of pain when one does so. (See Shabbos top of 152b and Taz YD 344:1 quoting Yerushalmi for a similar idea. See also Shabbos 13b which seems to state clearly that dead bodies feel physical pain when decaying. But see Sefer Chasidim #1163 and Kol Bo #114 who explain that the soul feels pain, not the body. Tos. Yom Tov on Avos 2:7 explains this way as well, but he quotes Medrash Shemuel who writes that neither the deceased nor its soul feel pain from decay. See also Teshuvas HaRashba vol. 1 #369; Radvaz vol. 1 #484; Shevus Yaakov vol. 2 #97; Chasam Sofer vol. 6 #37; Nachalas Shimon on Shemuel 1 vol. 2 59:6 with note 4. See also our notes on 18b below.) Some Poskim make a distinction regarding the proximity to the deceased, writing that speaking within 4 amos of the deceased is more of a "mockery" or "embarrassment". Einayim LaMishpat argues that during a funeral procession all attending are considered within "4 amos" of the deceased and may not speak, whereas speaking in the presence of the deceased at other times may only apply within 4 amos. (For various explanations as to why the Torah requires such great sensitivity towards the deceased, see Hebrew essay printed in the back of this kuntrus.)

4. *What did Dovid do when he rose early and what is unique about nighttime in this regard?* – The Gemara initially records that Dovid would learn Torah until chatzos and then recite songs and praises of Hashem. The Gemara later records (at the end of the amud) that Dovid would rise at midnight and learn Torah until morning. It would seem that his recital of songs and praise was itself considered learning Torah, as he infused his praises with deep meaning (see Radak on Tehillim 119:148; Medrash Tehillim 1:2, 1:8, 78:1; Kohelles Raba 3:12). Hence, during the night hours, we see a blending of Tefilla and Torah study. Indeed, the learning during the night is referred to as "rina shel Torah" (see Rambam hil. Talmud Torah end of ch. 3 and Gra there), while "rina" itself often refers to a sort of Tefilla (see Malbim's Sefer HaCarmel under "ranan" and "rina, tefilla, techina"). Similarly, Gemara Tamid 32b instructs us regarding the learning of Torah at night by quoting Pesukim ("kumi roni balayla"; "shifchi kamayim libeich") which refer also to Tefilla (as explained further in our notes on 3a). And Gemara Eruvin (bottom of 18b; see Rashi there ד"ה ולא אמר) refers to "the song of Torah at night". (For further sources that Torah study is itself a form of praise and song to Hashem, see also "Birkas HaMazon V'Nuschah" pg. 28-29 as well as Daf al HaDaf Avoda Zara 32b and Sdeh Tzofim Beitza 24a explaining the phrase "גמרא גמור זמורתא תהא".) This idea can be explained by the sources quoted in Shevet haLevi (vol. 6 #1) that the neshama of a person is particularly close to Hashem during the night hours, and a

person who learns Torah feels this closeness. He therefore feels a deep longing for Hashem as he learns, and this longing is itself a sort of Tefilla (see Michtav Me'eliyahu vol. 4 pg. 61 that the crux of Tefilla is the "she'ifa", the deep desire of the individual). Another idea is explained in Ze'ev Yitrof (Shavuos ch. 89, pg. 369) who quotes Pesukim in Tehillim, Yeshaya, and Zecharia that in the time of Mashiach the night will be light like the day, and thus someone who learns at night is utilizing the night as day just like it will be in the end of days, as he treats the night as a time of "work" (*Avodas* Hashem) rather than a time for rest. (But see Daf al HaDaf on 9a that even during times when the night shines like day, such as the night of Pesach in Egypt, it is still not considered "day", but "night which shines like day".) So in a sense, learning Torah at night (i.e. using the night as a time for "work" and learning) is a sort of prayer for the times of Mashiach when the night will indeed shine like the day. Similarly, Pachad Yitzchak (36:8-11) writes that true "ameilus b'Torah" (diligence in Torah study) is achieved when one finds "rest" through "working hard" in the study of Torah, when one "rests" by *not* sleeping. Through learning during the wee hours of the night, one yearns for true ameilus b'Torah. R. Chaim Volozhiner (Ruach Chaim on Avos 6:6 on "mi'ut sheina") writes that since sleep is similar to death, thus one literally adds time to his life by remaining awake at night and learning Toras *Chaim* (the Torah which *is* life). Hence learning at night has an added component of requesting life itself. (Nonetheless, note 78 on Ruach Chaim adds from the Gra that sleep also has its place in *adding* to one's wisdom: that which a person cannot comprehend during his waking hours because his neshama is "attached" to his body is sometimes revealed to him during his sleeping hours when the soul is detached from the body and more pristine.) Sefer Chareidim (38:24) adds a halachic ramification for the fact that we refer to learning during the night as "rina": one should learn aloud during the night (similar to Tefilla). Even though Chazal write that it is always preferable to learn out loud (see Megilla 32a), night-learning should be done with "*haramas* kol", seemingly in an even louder fashion. (Similarly, see Shl"a HaKadosh quoted in Piskei Teshuvos 238 note 8 that the *voice* of Torah at night restrains other forces.)

5. *Similarities between day and night* – Based on the above (and our notes on 3a), we can further understand that which the Gemara explains here that the same word ("*neshef*") is used for both day and night. We have seen this phenomenon earlier as well (top of 2b) regarding the wording for the setting and rising of the sun and at the beginning of Gemara Pesachim regarding the word "אור" in the Torah. The night and day run somewhat parallel and have the ability to be one and the same, but we will only experience this once again during the days of Mashiach.

6. *Was Moshe the wisest person to ever live?* – The Gemara here assumes that it is unimaginable that Dovid would figure something out that Moshe could not. See Mishmar HaLevi who quotes various commentators that Moshe was wiser than Shlomo HaMelech and others who disagree. See also Mishbatzos Zahav (Melachim 5:11) who quotes the Leshem that Moshe was certainly wiser. Nonetheless, it seems from our Gemara that everyone agrees that Moshe was wiser than Dovid.

7. *Ramification of the various winds* – Einayim LaMishpat (commenting on Rashi ד"ה כנור) notes that the order in which the lulav is shaken is patterned after the various winds of the day. The Ashkenazi custom follows Rashi's understanding, but others disagree.

8. *Explanation of the conversation between Dovid and the Chachomim* – Mishbatzos Zahav (Shemuel 2 7:29) explains that when the Chachomim initially informed Dovid that the nation needs sustenance, Dovid tried to teach his people that the wealthy members of the nation should support the poor and that G-d would provide them with further bounty due to their benevolence. When they did not accept Dovid's answer and expressed a degree of disbelief that Hashem would provide such bounty, Dovid then told them that they could wage war and Hashem would help them that way (although this path was possibly less ideal). Both of Dovid's responses were intended to teach his nation how to properly utilize human effort and open doors through which Hashem will send His Heavenly assistance.

9. *Who must be consulted before going to war?* – The Gemara records that before going to war, they would ask Achisofel, Sanhedrin, and the Urim V'Tumim. Rashi explains that they would ask Achisofel for military advice, Sanhedrin for their blessing and to daven for them, and Hashem through the Urim V'Tumim whether or not they would be successful. Other Rishonim write (see Einayim LaMishpat) that it is imperative that they ask *permission* from these authorities (whether or not they may and should go to war), not just for their blessing and advice. Einayim LaMishpat also discusses differences in this regard between a "milchemes reshus" (voluntary war) and "milchemes mitzvah" (obligatory war). See also Nachalas Shimon (Shemuel II #13:3-6). Also interesting is the Teshuvos HaRashba (vol. 1 #48) who writes that they would ask Achisofel for advice even though they would then ask Hashem Himself through the Urim V'Tumim. It seems that asking Achisofel was necessary so that they would better be able to understand Hashem's response.

1. *What were the Kreisi U'Pleisi?* – Rashi here and in Sanhedrin 16b explains that the term "Kreisi U'Pleisi" refers to the Umim V'Tumim worn by the Kohen Gadol. Tosafos disagree (based on other reasons, not because Kreisi U'Pleisi cannot refer to Umim V'Tumim) and explains that the Kreisi U'Pleisi here refers to the Sanhedrin. The Ralbag (Shemuel 2 15:18; 20:7,23) explains Kreisi U'Pleisi as referring to the families from which the Sanhedrin was comprised. Radak (Shemuel 2 15:18) writes that Chazal understood Kreisi U'Pleisi as referring to the Umim V'Tumim but that understanding is difficult in that Pasuk, so he prefers the explanation of Targum Yonasan that Kreisi U'Pleisi refers to various warriors; see also Rashi (Divrei HaYomim 1 18:17). (Ralbag ibid. 20:23 questions this explanation based on textual reasoning; see there.) Another twist is offered by Targum on Divrei HaYomim (1 27:34) who writes that they would ask the Urim V'Tumim by approaching Sanhedrin and then the Kohen Gadol. Based on this explanation, it is not surprising that "Kreisi U'Pleisi" can refer either to Sanhedrin or to the Umim V'Tumim, since even Sanhedrin may have been involved in the process of asking the Urim V'Tumim. (But this requires further research; see Ramban hil. Klei HaMikdash end of ch. 10 for further halachos regarding asking the Urim V'Tumim.)

2. *What does Ploni "ben" Almoni mean?* – According to the most obvious and most widespread understanding, this sentence means "Ploni the son of Almoni". But our text in the Gemara here quotes the Pasuk in Divrei HaYomim (1 27:34) as "Benayahu ben Yehoyada" when in truth the Pasuk reads "Yehoyada ben Benayahu". Tosafos point this out and change the text of the Gemara, but Rashi has our text. Binyan Shlomo on Sanhedrin 16b (quoted in Margaliyos HaYam there #1) explains Rashi based on Rashi's comments on Divrei HaYomim (1 2:50) that "Calev ben Chur" means "Calev's son was Chur". (But other commentators there explain differently.) We see that "Ploni ben Almoni" can sometimes mean "Ploni's son was Almoni". Hence, the Gemara here explains that although the Pasuk actually reads "Yehoyada ben Benayahu", it can be read as "Yehoyada's son was Benayahu", or more simply, "Benayahu ben Yehoyada" as quoted in the Gemara. (But see Binyan Shlomo further who explains that the Gemara's entire explanation of the Pasuk here is only homiletic and not in accordance with the simple explanation of the Pasuk as explained by Rashi and others on Divrei HaYomim 1 27:34.)

3. "למד לשונך לומר איני יודע שמא יודע תתבדה ותאחז" – It is clear from the Gemara that it is sometimes wise to say "I don't know" even in a situation when one indeed *does* know, such as in a case where the information will be misunderstood and the listener will look disparagingly upon him. (Orchos Yosher pg. 6 writes that this is not lying, for in all matters there are aspects that one indeed does not know.)

4. *Why did Dovid refer to himself as a chasid?* – The commentators on the Pasuk (Tehillim 86:2) explain that Dovid was not saying that he was great; he was merely pointing out that he would not stand up for himself against those who ridiculed him (as Chazal say, "נעלבין ואינן עולבין, שומעין חרפתן ואינן משיבין"), and therefore he was requesting that Hashem "stand up" for him. The Gemara here seemingly explains differently, that Dovid was indeed singing his own praises. Why would Dovid do this? Ben Yehoyada explains that Dovid was answering the scoffers who were saying that he was not fitting to be king due to his sin with Bas Sheva. Dovid responded that he truly was fitting to be king; he indeed made a mistake with Bas Sheva for which he repented at length, but he did not commit the heinous crime for which the scoffers were blaming him. He therefore pointed to the fact that his actions show that he is indeed more fitting for kingship than all other kings who rise late in the morning and do not involve themselves in degrading tasks (see Maharsha further). See also Ben Yehoyada.

5. *Can someone refer to his Rebbe by his first name?* – The Gemara records that Dovid referred to Mefiboshes as "Mefiboshes Rebbe". Einayim LaMishpat quotes the Rama that one can refer to his Rebbe by his first name as long as he precedes the name with the title "Rebbe". He cites a disagreement amongst the Poskim if one can refer to his Rebbe in such a fashion even in the presence of his Rebbe. Our Gemara indicates that this is permitted, but some explain that it is only permitted if the Rebbe gives permission (and it is possible that such was the case with Mefiboshes and Dovid). Others explain that Mefiboshes was not Dovid's "Rebbe muv'hak" (primary Rebbe), and it was therefore permitted. But some Poskim write that even permission does not suffice, and even a "talmid chaver" (a student who is also a semi-colleague) cannot refer to his Rebbe/colleague by his first name. Nonetheless, in Dovid's situation it was permissible because "Mefiboshes" was not his Rebbe's real name, but rather a name given to him out of honor for his Rebbe's great wisdom, as recorded in the Gemara.

6. *Mefiboshes's embarrassing Dovid* – The Gemara explains that Dovid's deep desire for truth brought him to belittle himself by asking Mefiboshes after ruling halacha. He was rewarded *mida keneged mida* when Hashem gave him a son even wiser than Mefiboshes. Why, however, was Dovid rewarded particularly with someone who "embarrassed" Mefiboshes and not simply with someone who was exceedingly learned? It seems from this language of the Gemara that Mefiboshes was indeed somewhat incorrect and thus liable to slight punishment for embarrassing Dovid (see Rambam hil. Talmud Torah 4:5 and 5:12 regarding when and how a Rebbe should scold or even embarrass a student),

and therefore Mefiboshes too was repaid *mida keneged mida* by eventually being humiliated by Dovid's son. (Sefer Mishbatzos Zahav on Shemuel 2 3:3 explains this way; a similar idea is found in Sefer V'lo Od Ela on Berachos here. Nonetheless, Chazal write that Mefiboshes was a great talmid chacham and tzadik - see Eruvin 53b and Yerushalmi Kedushin 42b. See also Mishbatzos Zahav ibid 9:6 and 19:31 bottom of pg. 469 for more on Mefiboshes's greatness as well as his mistakes. But it should be noted that Tosafos Yevamos top of 79a and Maharsha here explain that Mefiboshes here was not Mefiboshes the son of Yehonason, and therefore some of those sources may not apply to this Mefiboshes.) As to why Dovid was happy that his son *embarrassed* Mefiboshes, it is possible to explain that Dovid saw the *mida keneged mida* involved and was therefore joyous about Hashem's justice. (See HaMe'or Shebatorah by R. Yaakov Lesin zt"l vol. 3 on Sotah pg. 444 that the emotional responses of our great ancestors did not emanate from their sense of physical self but from their innate understanding of truth and sensitivity to the "image of G-d" within them.) Eitz Yosef on Ein Yaacov here explains further that Dovid's son was able to show that the very halachos about which Dovid was embarrassed were in fact correct.

7. *Can an auspicious prophecy be reversed?* – It is clear from the Gemara (see Meiri here) that an individual must always be careful to daven and act properly because "שמא יגרום החטא" (lest sin bring upon punishment). The Gemara states that this is true even in a case when someone was promised protection etc. by Hashem. The commentators ask from elsewhere (see bottom of 7a) where it seems clear that Hashem does not rescind propitious prophecy. They offer various details when this dictum is true vs. when Hashem indeed rescinds good tidings, distinguishing between one who is offered prophecy for himself as opposed to for someone else; a miraculous event and a natural event etc. See Einayim LaMishpat and Sefer Daf al HaDaf here and a lengthy discussion in Sefer Pi Kohen on Berachos (shaar 2 #10). See also Maharal (Vayishlach 32:7; Gevuros Hashem ch. 7) that "prophecy" is never rescinded, but a "promise" is. A "prophecy" is usually said in past-tense, a manner that indicates that it will surely occur, and it is usually said to the masses as opposed to an individual tzadik.

8. *Is redemption through the agreement of the other nations ideal?* – The Gemara states clearly (see also Rashi on Yechezkel 43:11) that it would have been more ideal if we would have merited grand miracles during the time of Ezra (similar to those of Yetziyas Mitzrayim) as opposed to the more "natural" course of events which in fact occurred. On the other hand, there are some sources that indicate that it was indeed ideal that the redemption was brought about through a non-Jewish king (Koresh) acting as a messenger of Hashem so that all of mankind would recognize Hashem. (Mishbatzos Zahav on Melachim 1 5:26 points out that non-Jewish nations assisted in the building of the first Beis HaMikdash for the same reason.) In fact, Ben Yehoyada and Rashba (Chidushei Hahagados) on Megilla 12a note that the redemption during Ezra's time could have been the final redemption if Koresh would have acted as a proper messenger. See also Ramban (Shir HaShirim 8:13 in Kisvei Ramban vol. 2 pg. 515) and Radak (Tehillim 146:3) who quote Yeshaya 66:20 to prove that the final redemption will come about through the permission of the other nations. (See further in HaTekufa HaGedola by R. Mendel Kasher ch. 7. Also possibly relevant are the words of the Rambam hil. Beis HaBechira 6:16 that Ezra's "kidush" was everlasting since it came about through "chazaka" as opposed to force.) But it is possible to reconcile these opposing ideas that it is truly best for all of the above to occur: Hashem will cause the nations to "send" Bnei Yisroel back to Eretz Yisroel, but after doing so, they will no longer rule over us at all (see Rashi here ד"ה אלא שגרם), and Hashem will also perform wondrous, open miracles.

Short Notes on Berachos 4b

1. *Eating and napping etc. before davening Mincha, Maariv, or Keriyas Shema* – Tosafos point out from the Gemara that one may not eat before reciting Keriyas Shema and davening Maariv. The Shulchan Aruch (OC 235:2) codifies that the same holds true regarding napping. The Mishnah Berurah adds (235:17, based on various Rishonim) that it is forbidden to engage in any activity that could cause one to be remiss in performing these mitzvos, just as recorded in Shulchan Aruch (232:2) regarding Mincha. The Poskim write, however, that one may engage in these activities if he has a regular minyan which he attends at a later point each night or if he appoints a "shomer" (someone to remind him to daven) or sets an alarm. (See details in Piskei Teshuvos 235:6-8 and notes 49-50 that relying on a "shomer" may only be permissible in a case of need.) It should be noted that there are differences between the necessary precautions for Mincha, Maariv, and Keriyas Shema. Keriyas Shema is a Torah obligation and therefore requires the most vigilance. Accordingly, the Shulchan Aruch (235:2) writes that one is required to pause his meal in order to recite Keriyas Shema, but for Maariv he may wait to daven until he finishes eating. Regarding Maariv, the Gemara explains that one could have thought that these precautions do not apply at all since the obligation to daven Maariv is not as strict as that of the other tefillos (i.e. Maariv has aspects of "r'shus"; see 27b). Although the Gemara concludes that this is not so, we nonetheless find some leniencies regarding Maariv pertaining to these halachos for different reasons: a) Aruch HaShulchan (235:16,18) argues on Mishnah Berurah (quoted above) and writes (based on various Rishonim) that only eating and napping are forbidden before Maariv since those actions induce lengthy sleep which can prevent one from fulfilling his obligation to daven, but other activities that are prohibited before davening Mincha are permitted before Maariv since one has more time to daven Maariv (i.e. the entire night) and there is therefore a much smaller chance that he will forget to do so. b) Some Poskim hold that one may daven Maariv the entire night even l'chatchila (see Aruch HaShulchan ibid. and Piskei Teshuvos 235:10), for we only have to be extra concerned regarding Keriyas Shema which is a Torah obligation, but not for Maariv. On the other hand, we find some stringencies regarding Maariv that do not apply to Mincha: a) The Gemara records that one has to be extra sensitive at night to the fact that he may fall asleep out of natural exhaustion. b) R. Akiva Eiger (on Mishnah Shabbos 1:2 #8) writes that one may not eat even a small amount before Maariv (see Einayim LaMishpat here) even though he *may* eat a small amount before Mincha (see Shulchan Aruch and Rama 332:2). c) One who readied himself to eat before davening Maariv but did not yet begin is required to pause and first daven Maariv, as opposed to Mincha where he is not obligated to pause (see Mishnah Berurah 235:24 and R. Akiva Eiger on Mishnah here #3). Since one has a longer amount of time to daven Maariv, he may end up being remiss and falling asleep before davening.

2. *Learning Torah SheBichsav at night* – Many Sefarim write (based heavily on kabbala; see Sha'ar HaTziyun 238:1 and Piskei Teshuvos 238:3) that one may not learn Torah SheBichsav (the Written Torah; i.e. Tanach) at night; nighttime hours are strictly for Torah SheBal Peh (Oral Torah; i.e. Mishnah, Gemara, etc.). Based on the above, Sefer Daf al HaDaf here quotes Maharsham who explains that our Gemara that states that someone who knows how to "read" (i.e. Tanach) should do so before reciting Keriyas Shema at night is referring to learning Tanach before nightfall completely arrives. But R. Ovadia Yosef (Yabea Omer OC vol. 6 #30 ד"ה ולכאורה) explains based on Chida that someone who knows how to learn only Tanach can indeed learn Tanach even at night. (It should be noted that many great people, including the Steipler Gaon quoted in Orchos Rabbeinu vol. 1 pg. 97, do not follow this custom and indeed learn Torah SheBichsav at night as well.)

3. *"Kol ha'over al divrei chachomim chayav misa"* – R. Akiva Eiger (Gilyon HaShas here) points to Gemara Eiruvin 21b and Tosafos Sotah 4b that write that this dictum is not specific to Keriyas Shema but to all Rabbinic laws. It seems, therefore, that our Gemara is only questioning why this statement is highlighted in this instance, but certainly it applies elsewhere as well. Sdei Chemed ("hei" end of #92 and P'as HaSadeh "ches" #15) explains differently: for most Rabbinic law, a transgressor is only deserving of death (which he explains as literal) if he acts out of disregard for the words of the Rabbis, but if he merely succumbs to his physical desires, his sin does not make him worthy of death. But in this instance and other instances where the Rabbis specifically write that someone who disobeys them is deserving of death, one is indeed culpable even when sinning due to physical desires. Maharal (Be'er HaGolah pg. 17) explains why "divrei chachomim" are more stringent: Rabbinic laws are "closer" to us, i.e. man-made and part of the "natural world". For this reason, someone who transgresses these commandments deserves to be punished more immediately and harshly in our natural world as opposed to in the afterlife (where a person is punished more severely for transgressing Torah law). He adds that the "fence around the Torah" (Rabbinic law) provides the form ("tzura") and boundary for the mitzvah. When someone breaks boundaries, the entire system begins to collapse.

4. *What is so special about being "somech Geula l'Tefilla"?* – Rabbenu Yonah explains that when a person davens in this fashion he displays that he understands that the reason that Hashem took us out of Egypt was in order that we serve Him, and he adheres to that directive by following his mentioning of the Exodus with davening to Hashem (*service* of the heart), illustrating that he is a servant of Hashem. A person who recalls the reason why he is "free" and

then acts upon that perspective by serving Hashem is indeed a "ben Olam Haba". R. Yonah adds another idea, explaining that davening demonstrates one's reliance upon Hashem which is one of the key lessons that we learned in the story of the Exodus. Someone who shows that he has inculcated this crucial idea gleaned from Yetziyas Mitzrayim is someone will lead a life that merits Olam Haba. Davening in this fashion of "somech Geula l'Tefilla" adds a spiritual dimension to one's Tefilla; it is silly *not* to utilize it (see Rashi here), while using this "tool" illustrates one's inculcation of the essential ideas gleaned from Yetziyas Mitzrayim.

5. *Which comes first at night: Keriyas Shema or Shemoneh Esrei?* – It seems that everyone is in agreement that mentioning "Geula" is appropriate at night, for everyone agrees that we certainly recite the beracha of Ga'al Yisroel (of birchos Keriyas Shema) at night as well. On the other hand, Einayim LaMishpat notes that everyone also agrees that "somech Geula l'Tefilla" at night is less important than it is during the day, and therefore someone who arrives late to shul should daven Shemoneh Esrei with the tzibur and recite Shema by himself afterwards. The argument to recite Keriyas Shema *after* Tefilla is also sensible, for the Torah implies that Keriyas Shema functions as the bookends of one's day. (Indeed, everyone acts this way to a degree through reciting "Keriyas Shema al ha'mita" right before going to sleep.) The argument in the Gemara comes down to which one of these two ideas trumps the other. The halacha (OC 236:2) follows R. Yochanon that it is more important to be "somech Geula l'Tefilla" even at night when the idea of Geula is less pronounced. (Ben Yehoyada adds that it is certainly important to mention Geula at night, for Maariv corresponds to the final Geula, while Shacharis corresponds to the first Beis HaMikdash and Mincha to the second. See our notes on 3b that in the end of days the night will shine like day; perhaps the final Geula corresponds to night because night itself will turn to day.) Moreover, besides for enhancing one's Tefilla (see Rashi and Emes L'Yaakov), Keriyas Shema also serves to prepare the individual for proper prayer as mentioned in Yerushalmi (quoted in Tosafos 2a end of ד"ה מאימתי). Similarly, Meiri (Magen Avos #11, top of pg. 111 in new ed.) writes that the opinion to recite Keriyas Shema before Tefilla makes more sense than the opposing opinion since the praise and themes of the berachos and of Keriyas Shema serve to properly introduce Tefilla.

6. *Explanation of berachos of Hashkivenu and Yir'u Eineinu* – The Gemara explains that "Hashkivenu" is an extension of the beracha for Geula. How so? Rabbenu Yonah (quoted in Beis Yosef OC 236) explains that Bnei Yisroel were nervous on the night of Yetziyas Mitzrayim and prayed to Hashem that He not strike them along with the Egyptians. "Hashkivenu" parallels their prayer and therefore serves to commemorate Geulas Mitzrayim. Ben Yehoyada explains completely differently: the very mention in this beracha of Hashem's protecting us and letting us rise the next morning hints to His protection during Galus and the "rising" of the final Geula. This explanation can indeed be deduced from the beracha itself, for one of the beracha's concluding sentences is patterned after a Pasuk in Tehillim (121:8): "Hashem yishmor tzeisecha uvo'echa me'ata v'ad olam". Radak (Tehillim ibid.) explains that that Pasuk is a reference to the Galus and the Geula, just as Ben Yehoyada explains here. This idea can also be deduced from the line "u'fros alenu succas shelomecha", seemingly asking for Hashem to "cover" us with His Shechina. The beracha of "Yir'u Eineinu" is also a longing for the Geula, and Tosafos therefore explain that it is also part of the main beracha about Geula. The Rosh (quoted in Beis Yosef 236:2) adds that this is also the reason why it is permitted to recite kadish before Shemoneh Esrei at Maariv, for kadish is also about Geula. (The Tur 236 seems to explain differently, that the beracha of "Yir'u Eineinu" was originally said in the place of Shemoneh Esrei and the custom therefore carried on to recite it at this point, before Shemoneh Esrei. See Poskim there that discuss whether or not someone should therefore stand during this prayer. See also Tos. HaRosh.)

7. *To what degree are "Hashem sefasai tiftach" and "yihe'yu l'ratzon imrei fi" part of the Shemoneh Esrei?* – See Einayim LaMishpat (#3) who discusses whether or not the Shliach Tzibur says these lines aloud in his repetition of Shemoneh Esrei and whether or not someone who needs to repeat Shemoneh Esrei (because he forgot a crucial part etc.) must repeat "Hashem sefesai tiftach" as well.

8. *Why is it so important to say Ashrei 3 times a day?* – The Gemara answers that Ashrei is organized according to the "alef beis" and includes a Pasuk that recognizes Hashem's sustaining us. The Maharsha explains that the "alef beis" hints to the Torah ("mazon hanefesh"; food for the soul) and "pose'ach es yadecha" to physical sustenance ("mazon haguf"). That is, we recall that they are both completely from Hashem. Pnei Yehoshua explains similarly and adds that through saying and remembering this idea, a person will certainly make his service of Heaven "ikar" (his main goal) and his mundane work only secondary, and his actions will therefore end up granting him a place in Olam Haba. Why 3 times a day? Some Rishonim write that it really only needs to be said once, but if we say it 3 times we will concentrate at least once (Eshkol quoted in Nesiv Bina on Tefilla pg. 203; see Einayim LaMishpat here #5). Others explain that the number "3" corresponds to the 3 Tefillos of the day (see Rashi) or to our 3 forefathers (see Rabbenu Yeshaya quoted in Shibolei HaLeket).

9. *What do the angels' pauses represent?* – Maharsha explains that Hashem causes Gavriel (who is in charge of judgement) and the Angel of Death to "pause" once/seven times before carrying out their tasks in order to offer more time for teshuva and therefore mercy from Heaven.

Short Notes on Berachos 5a

1. *What is the purpose of Keriyas Shema al ha'mita?* – It seems clear from the Gemara (and Yerushalmi quoted in the Rishonim) that the reason for Keriyas Shema al ha'mita is in order to gain protection from "mazikim" (damagers or evil spirits). Chazal write that sleep is similar to death where a person's soul is taken by Hashem (see language of Modeh Ani and Elokai Neshama), so one needs to merit to have his soul returned to him in the morning. (See Zohar quoted in Piskei Teshuvos 239:9 that the neshama is judged in Heaven when the body is sleeping). How does Keriyas Shema before bed protect from these "mazikim"? Besides for mystical ideas explained in various commentaries, it seems from the Gemara and its commentators that reciting Keriyas Shema is a form of engaging in Torah before sleeping (see our notes on 2a and 11b), and through its recital, a person shows that learning Torah is truly the bookend of his day. Furthermore, the involvement in Shema before bed elevates "sleep" to a loftier plane by showing that his sleep is part of his general service of Hashem, used to rejuvenate himself for another day of service (see Rambam hil. Dei'os 3:2). Reciting Shema also has lasting effects on a person's psyche as he sleeps, and its recital allows a person to be somewhat involved in Torah even while asleep, rather than remaining mere flesh bereft of spirituality during this period. (See Gra in notes on 3b who comments that there are even some aspects of wisdom which are revealed *only* while one is sleeping, when the neshama is detached from the body and more pristine.) These ideas can be gleaned from a number of sources: a) The Gemara quotes a Pasuk regarding Torah study as the source that "Keriyas Shema al ha'mita" protects from danger. Igros Moshe (EH vol. 1 #37) explains that the main protection comes from learning Torah, but the Chachomim required the recital of Shema because many people are unable to learn, whereas all people are able to "learn" Shema. b) Similarly, Einayim LaMishpat quotes from one of the Geonim that the Chachomim instituted Keriyas Shema al ha'mita so that each individual will fulfill the precept of "ובשכבך ובקומך" to its fullest, literally finishing his day with "Torah study" of Shema. Rashi (bottom of 4b) also mentions that this recital of Keriyas Shema is part of the fulfillment of "ובשכבך". (This is in addition to Rashi's opinion on 2a that if someone did not recite Keriyas Shema in shul at the correct time, that this recital is indeed a Mitzvah D'Oraysa; see below.) c) The Gaon explains that it is for this reason that a talmid chacham does not need to say Keriyas Shema al ha'mita, for he is anyway involved all day and night with learning Torah. Similarly, Rashi writes that the talmid chacham's constant review of Torah is enough to keep away the dangers of sleep. (Nonetheless, the Gemara states that even a talmid chacham must recite some minor Tefilla, seemingly to request that his Torah indeed help protect him. It should also be noted that Meiri 2a explains differently, writing that even a talmid chacham recites a verse "so that he doesn't go to bed like an am ha'aretz", i.e. he must indicate to some degree that his sleep is part of his overall service of Hashem. Nevertheless, Piskei Teshuvos 239 note 31 writes that all people today should recite Keriyas Shema before bed, for we are not great enough talmidei chachomim to rely on learning Torah alone.) d) Poskim write (Mishnah Berurah 239:7; Piskei Teshuvos 239 note 21) that learning Torah does not constitute a hefsek (unnecessary break) between reciting Shema/HaMapil and sleeping. e) Meiri explains that the "mazikim" refer to incorrect thoughts and opinions that may try to enter one's mind during his sleeping hours, and learning Torah or Shema before bed can occupy the psyche with pure and correct thoughts. Similarly, Metzudas Dovid on Tehillim 4:5 explains the simple meaning of the Pasuk "אמרו בלבבכם וכו' ודמו סלה", the source for Keriyas Shema al ha'mita, that people should rid their minds before they sleep of their evil and lies. A similar idea is expressed in the derasha on this Pasuk quoted in the continuation of the Gemara.

2. *How stringent is the obligation to recite Keriyas Shema al ha'mita?* – Siddur R. Amram Gaon (#94-95) mentions that immediately before reciting this Shema, one should "bless to accept the yoke of Heaven". It is not completely clear if he meant that a real beracha should be made for performing this mitzvah. Some Rishonim understand (see Tur OC 235; hagahos Magen HaElef on Siddur R. Amram Gaon) that R. Amram Gaon meant that this beracha is said only when one did not recite Keriyas Shema earlier at its proper time. Nonetheless, the Poskim write (Rama on OC 239:1) that one does not make any such beracha at this point. Indeed, R. Avraham ben HaRambam writes (responsa #79) that this Shema is a "r'shus" or "nedava" (voluntary mitzvah) and not completely obligatory, and Chazal therefore didn't institute a beracha. See also Teshuvos HaRashbash (#174; quoted in Beiur Halacha end of #239 mistakenly as #74).

3. *Various halachos regarding Keriyas Shema al ha'mita* – a) Many Poskim point out that it is more proper to say Keriyas Shema when not literally "on one's bed", but directly before going to bed, for this is a more honorable way to daven. Nonetheless, due to natural exhaustion, the fact that this Shema is not a complete obligation (see above), and the nature of this Shema that it is inherently connected to sleep, many Poskim permit one to say Shema even on one's bed, and according to some, even while lying down. See Piskei Teshuvos (239 note 42) and Einayim LaMishpat. b) Poskim discuss the order of "HaMapil" and Shema; see Einayim LaMishpat and Piskei Teshuvos 239:6. c) Regarding making a hefsek (break) between Shema and sleeping, see notes regarding HaMapil on 60b.

4. *Significance of the various parts of Torah* – The Gemara lists: "10 Commandments, Chumash (Mikra), Mishnah (Mitzvah), Nach, Gemara". The commentators point out that there is a clear order here: 10 Commandments are

mentioned first because all of the mitzvos in the Torah are hinted to in the 10 Commandments (see notes on 12a). Chumash is mentioned next because all of Torah Shebal Peh has its roots in the Chumash. Pnei Yehoshua explains that Mishnah is mentioned next because Mishnah existed even before the rest of Nach, for it contains the details of the mitzvos mentioned in the Chumash. Nach is mentioned next since it is part of the Written Torah and therefore a greater source of Hashem's wisdom than Gemara. Pnei Yehoshua explains that Gemara is mentioned last, for in truth Gemara was only necessary because Klal Yisroel were remiss in their transmission and learning of the Torah and allowed for halachic disagreement. Nonetheless, we learn elsewhere (see Tosafos Avoda Zara top of 19b) that Gemara comprises the bulk of Torah study, for ever since disagreement arose, we need the logic and wisdom of the Gemara in order to understand the halacha properly. But since Mishnah represents a more pristine encapsulation of the most fundamental precepts, there is still an obligation to toil in the understanding of the Mishnah as a work of its own (see Rashi).

5. *What was given at Sinai?* – The Gemara states that even Neviim and Kesuvim were given at Sinai, even though they were not authored until a much later time. That is, the basis of all truths are all already written in the Torah itself (explicitly, implicitly, or through various hints). The later Neviim and Chochomim expressed ideas that were already in the Torah, but in a manner in which their generation (and future generations) could understand them. Maharatz Chayes here similarly explains that the Mishnah, Gemara, and all later "chidushim" have their basis in the Torah, for Hashem provided us with the Torah and with the rules through which to expound its hidden wisdom.

6. *Are yissurin (hardships and suffering) positive or negative experiences?* – The Gemara first provides ways by which a person can protect himself from yissurin, but in the continuation of the Gemara the commentaries explain the greatness of yissurin! The Maharal writes (Nesivos Olam - Nesiv HaYissurin end of ch. 1) that indeed yissurin are exceedingly helpful in a person's religious growth, but it is also extremely difficult to properly accept and deal with yissurin, and if handled improperly, yissurin can have very negative consequences such as making a person upset with Hashem and question Him in a similar way that Iyov did (Heaven forbid). For this reason, we generally try to protect ourselves against yissurin so as not to bring this test upon ourselves. Nonetheless, there are circumstances where the Poskim have advised to punish oneself with moderate yissurin such as fasting etc. (For example, see customs regarding various forms of teshuva before Yom Kippur and OC 607:6.) Moderate yissurin can assist one's religious growth without the great danger of extraordinarily difficult yissurin. The commentators also explain that it is beneficial for a person to receive an abundance of minor yissurin, and therefore save himself from "major", truly terrible yissurin (Heaven forbid). (See Erchin end of 16b that even slight inconveniences are considered yissurin.) Chazal also stress the importance of "killing oneself" to learn Torah, and that the Torah learned with "messirus nefesh" is most impactful upon the individual (see Rambam hil. Talmud Torah 3:12). Indeed, the Gemara here writes that "Torah" is one of the 3 things that is acquired through yissurin. If an individual toils tirelessly in the study of Torah, his efforts can constitute the "yissurin" necessary to acquire Torah, and he will not need to suffer from worse yissurin. Similarly, Hagahos Marei Cohen here quotes Medrash Tehillim #94 that everyone needs to incur yissurin: one person won't be able to sleep because of an eye or toothache while another person won't sleep because he is heavily involved in the study of Torah. Hagahos Yaavetz here points to some great Chochomim who chose to live lives of yissurin, while others (as those described on 5b) chose to minimize yissurin. He also explains that the Torah originally "detracts" from one's strength but then offers extra strength.

7. *Does Hashem still "control" the Torah or did He "give it" to us?* – Hagahos R. Hurvitz notes that the Gemara implies that when Hashem gave us the Torah, He "relinquished" (kaviyachol) some control over it in a similar way to someone who sells an object to a friend. He explains based on Medrash Raba (Par. Re'eh 4:3) that indeed Hashem gave us the ability to define the fate of the world. Ben Yehoyada adds the precept "lo bashamayim hi": the Torah is out of Hashem's hands (kaviyachol) and given to us.

8. *What is the purpose of yissurin?* – As seen from the Gemara, yissurin are placed upon a person to awaken him to teshuva, to look deeply into his actions and change himself where necessary. In truth, we are told (Eruvin 13b) to live our entire lives with this outlook of "yefashfesh b'maasav" (investigating our actions), but it seems that yissurin are direct reminders that we have been remiss in that obligation and that we need to focus on doing so. Therefore, when something negative happens to a person, whether sickness or tragedy (Heaven forbid), a person's obligation is to look deeply into himself, not only deal with the natural ramifications of his yissurin (doctor visits, medicine, etc.). The commentators explain that Hashem punishes in a way that allows a person to understand how he should change. He therefore punishes mida keneged mida (measure for measure) and to a degree that is appropriate for the crime (see Rashi and Maharsha). But if a person cannot see how the punishment points to any sin, then he should understand that he has not worked hard enough to learn Torah. Ben Yehoyada (see also Daf al HaDaf from Or HaChaim Devarim 52:13) explains that the mitzvah to learn Torah depends on the amount of time that one needs to spend on earning a livelihood and other obligations and mitzvos. If one does not see another sin for which he deserves his punishment,

he must scrutinize his personal schedule to see if he is truly able to squeeze more time to learn Torah (i.e. sleep, relax, or work less). We also see this idea from our Gemara's derasha of Tehillim ch. 39 which seems to state that Dovid was punished with yissurin for being remiss in learning Torah. Even though Dovid is in fact famous for learning Torah under all circumstances (running away from enemies, dealing with obligations of leadership etc.), nonetheless, Chazal understood that he could still have done more and was therefore punished. In this sense, yissurin are meant not only to "punish" for blatant sin, but to push people to higher stages of religious growth. The next level of this same idea is "yissurin shel ahava". The Gemara states that the reason for these yissurin are to "purify" the individual. Maharal (Nesivos Olam - Nesiv HaYissurin ch. 1) explains that such yissurin cause a person to be less stooped in physical concerns and pleasures and more occupied with his everlasting, "truer" self, i.e. his mind and soul. (See also Living Inspired by R. Akiva Tatz ch. 4 who explains that challenges do not only reveal capabilities that already existed within a person, but they also serve as conduits through which Hashem *adds* more G-dliness to the individual.) Many commentators write that these yissurin are placed upon a person without any sin at all, simply to move an individual to a higher stage of spiritual living. Some Rishonim write, however, that even yissurin shel ahava only come because of some sort of sin, but the punishment does not "match" the crime and is brought to raise the individual. (See a discussion of the various opinions in Einayim LaMishpat and in Artscroll Gemara note 38.)

1. *Explanation of various mitzvos and yissurin and their consequences* – a) Maharal (Nesivos Olam – Nesiv HaYissurin ch. 2) explains that Eretz Yisroel, Torah, and Olam Haba are not "gashmi" (physical) in their essence and therefore require yissurin to remove one's close attachment to physicality before acquiring them. b) Tzara'as and infertility are not yissurin shel ahava because they distance a person from Hashem; they display a lack of broadening outward and closeness to others and G-d. On the other hand, Torah, Chesed, and burying one's child (chalila) detach a person from physicality (burying a child is tantamount to burying a part of oneself), and they therefore elevate the person.

2. *Tzara'as after destruction of Beis HaMikdash* – Einayim LaMishpat points out that it is clear from our Gemara (and explicit in Rambam etc.) that tzara'as applies even outside of Eretz Yisroel and even after the destruction of the Beis HaMikdash. It seems (see Chinuch end of #169) that the reason that we do not practice the laws of tzara'as today is because we are not experts in determining the exact status of tzara'as blotches, and our Kohanim therefore cannot declare a blotch as "tamei" (impure). But in the time of the Gemara they were still experts in these halachos, and they also had the special ashes of the "parah aduma" in order to purify themselves (see sources quoted in Shu"t Beis Dovid by R. Ze'ev Leiter, vol. 2 #64). Others answer slightly differently (see ibid.), explaining that we are not certain that our Kohanim are indeed Kohanim. He further quotes variant opinions in Chazal and some commentators that tzara'as does not apply when there is no Beis HaMikdash. (See also She'eilas Yaavetz #136. And see Einayim LaMishpat regarding "shiluach metzora" after the Churban.)

3. *Can a great tzadik receive yissurin that are not "shel ahava"?* – Rashi seems to write that such a phenomenon is impossible, whereas Tosafos write that even tzadikim are sometimes punished with yissurin which are not "shel ahava". But Rashi's opinion seems rather difficult, for the Pasuk states (Kohelles 7:20) that all people sin (at least to a degree, based on one's capabilities), so why is it impossible for a tzadik to receive yissurin as punishment? Perhaps Rashi agrees with this logic; he only means that the harsh yissurin of R. Yochanan must certainly have been shel ahava, for it is unimaginable that R. Yochanan deserved such harsh judgement (see our notes on 5a). (Indeed, Rashi ד"ה דהוו implies that there may well have been some sin in this instance.) Nonetheless, it is clear from the Gemara that infertility is not "yissurin shel ahava". Tzlach (on Tos.) and Rif (in Ein Yaakov) explain that infertility depends on "mazal" (Moed Katan 28a) and therefore not subject to criteria of "yissurin shel ahava". (But perhaps the Gemara there does not mean that fertility, life, and sustenance are always based solely on mazal, for indeed "mazal" can change [see Tos. there and R. Yonah here 3a in pgs. of Rif]. Rather, those things are often based largely on "mazal" and not subject to same criteria as other yissurin.)

4. *Is there an obligation to bury small parts of a corpse?* – Rashi explains that R. Yochanan walked around with a small bone from his deceased son. Einayim LaMishpat discusses why it was permissible to refrain from burying this part of the corpse. He explains (based on Acharonim) that Rashi holds that only the parts of the deceased that can cause tumaah need to be buried, whereas this bone was too small to cause tumaah. But he quotes others who disagree and write that all parts need to be buried in order to give complete honor to the deceased. They explain our Gemara differently than Rashi; see there.

5. *When is it proper to try to refuse yissurin?* – The Gemara recalls numerous great Rabbis who chose to put an end to their yissurin and thus forfeit the possibility of great reward for accepting the yissurin with love. The Maharal (cited on 5a) explains that it is extremely difficult to properly accept and live with yissurin, and therefore it is most wise and fitting to try to escape from this test altogether. The Mabit (Beis Elokim Teshuva ch. 9) similarly writes that the great Rabbis in our Gemara were davening to put an end to this test only because they saw that they were unable to handle the yissurin with love. But certainly, if the yissurin would have persisted they would have tried their hardest to accept them whole heartedly. R. Kook (Ein Aya on Berachos here #35) explains differently, writing that these great individuals did not want to accept any extra help from Above to better themselves (i.e. yissurin, which help "purify" one's personality); rather, they wanted to work hard on their own to achieve their spiritual heights. See Maharsha and Tzitz Eliezer (quoted in Sdeh Tzofim) for other approaches to our Gemara. It should be noted that it is only considered "kicking away" yissurin if one (chalila) questions Hashem's justice (see Michtav Me'Eliyahu vol. 3 pg. 329).

6. *Is wealth a blessing or a curse?* – See Rabbenu Bachya (beg. Parashas Vayetzei and Kad HaKemach "osher") that one should try to run from wealth because of the exceedingly difficult tests that come along with it (loss of focus from eternal matters, blindness in judgement, etc.). Yet, there are also great opportunities possible through wealth which make wealth a tremendous blessing. Hence, our Gemara refers to acquisition of wealth along with fear of Heaven as meriting "two tables". It seems that the most proper outlook on this matter is to indeed run from wealth and to focus on Heavenly pursuits (see Meiri Horios 10b), but if Hashem nonetheless bestows wealth, it is indeed a blessing and must be handled accordingly.

7. *Can one "steal" his own object back from a thief?* – Einayim LaMishpat quotes several opinions in Rishonim and Poskim regarding this issue based on various understandings of the parameters of the dictum, "עביד איניש דינא לנפשיה" (a man may carry out justice by himself). Some distinguish between a situation where one can *prove* one's case and a situation where one simply knows that he is correct but cannot prove it. Other distinguish between acting in a public fashion vs. giving the appearance of thievery by acting in a sneaky manner.

8. *How should one's bed be positioned?* – The Poskim write that these halachos apply to a person living with his wife, whereas the halacha of someone sleeping alone is more lenient (see MB 3:12). The Poskim disagree if the Gemara means that the bed should be stationed east-west or north-south. The Mishnahh Berurah (3:11) prefers the opinion of north-south, whereas other Poskim prefer east-west, based on an understanding of the Zohar. (See Halacha Berurah by R. Dovid Yosef vol. 1 pg. 43-4.) There is also a slight debate if there is a preference as to which direction the head of the bed should face; see Nekudos Or (on MB vol. 1, pg. 8). Poskim further point out (see Halacha Berurah ibid. and Aruch HaShulchan 3:13) that the general custom is not to be concerned with these halachos since every position has roots in various Poskim, as mentioned. According to Rashi, the reason for this halacha is to give extra honor to the Shechina. That is, Hashem displays Himself through the passage of time from east to west through the movement of the sun (see Mekor Chaim by R. Chaim HaKohen Maram Tzova on OC 3:5 and Kobetz Beis Aharaon V'Yisroel #66 pg. 107). Rabbenu Yonah (on Rif 3a) writes that it is in order to remind a person, before trying to conceive, to daven for one's child to have wisdom and a livelihood (which are connected to the north and south in the Mikdash; see there).

9. *Obstruction between person and wall during prayer* – Beis Yosef (OC 90:21) quotes Rambam that there should be nothing in front of an individual while praying as to not disturb his concentration. The Tur (98:4) explains differently, writing that there should be no "chatzitza" (obstruction) between the person and the wall (and floor) while praying just like there may not be any chatzitza surrounding the Kohen when offering a korban. The Poskim and Shulchan Aruch (90:21) seem to utilize the explanation of the Tur, for they write that small or stationary objects do not constitute a "chatzitza". (See Mishnah Berurah 90:68 and Einayim LaMishpat here who note this. But see Kaf HaChaim 90:131 who writes that we assume both explanations. See also Piskei Teshuvos 90:26 for a novel stringency based on the reasoning of the Tur.) Yet it still needs to be understood *why* a "chatzitza" between him and the wall is problematic. One can perhaps explain based on Shulchan Aruch (90:5) that it is most ideal to pray in a small, narrow area where one more fully feels the fear of Heaven. Here too, by confining oneself close to a wall one more keenly feels Hashem's presence. Indeed, Abudraham stresses that one should not stand in the "middle of the house"; seemingly the main point of the halacha is to be close to a wall. But perhaps we can explain differently based on Rabbenu Yonah (on Gemara 6b) who writes that the far wall in the direction that the tzibur davens has the status of the Heichal in the Beis HaMikdash (and therefore someone who finds himself standing behind that wall should turn around and face that wall, even though he faces the opposite direction of the tzibur; see notes on 6b). Seemingly, the shul ("small Mikdash") is patterned after the real Beis HaMikdash and we view the Shechina as being more present near the wall of the shul. This idea is also explicit in Yerushalmi Sanhedrin 51b (cited in Gilyon HaShas 10b below) that learns from the same Pasuk quoted in our Gemara that facing the wall of one's house (or shul) is tantamount to facing the wall of the Beis HaMikdash itself.

10. *Can one learn Torah before davening?* – Rashi explains that one may not learn Torah before davening (after alos hashachar), for he may lose track of time and forget to daven altogether. Tosafos write that only work is forbidden before davening, but Torah study is permitted. The Poskim (Shulchan Aruch 89:6) write that it is forbidden for someone to learn by himself at home etc. if he plans to daven there alone. But if he plans to stop and go to shul as usual, then he is allowed to learn and does not need to be concerned that he will forget. Indeed, it is often preferable to learn a little before davening (see Tosafos 2a). (Note that the Aruch, entry "תפל", and R. Chananel explain the Gemara completely differently than the above Poskim; see there.)

11. *Leaving another person alone in shul* – The Rishonim explain (Tos. top of 6a; see OC 90:15) that Chazal forbade leaving another person alone in shul because it was dangerous. Rashi (top of 6a) defines this as "chesed" (a kind act towards one's fellow). Aruch HaShulchan (90:19) explains that besides for providing a sense of protection, it also allows the other person to finish davening properly with peace of mind. Other Rishonim (R. Chananel) explain differently, that the Shechina is more intense when two people are present, and therefore when one leaves it causes the Shechina to "leave" as well, leaving his friend praying without the complete presence of the Shechina. (See Raavan note 26 that these Rishonim had a slightly variant text of the Gemara.)

Short Notes on Berachos 6a

1. *Notes about "Mazikin"* – Rashi (ד"ה לראות) refers to "mazikin" as "sheidim", and Rashi in Rosh Hashona (28a ד"ה התוקע לשיר) refers to sheidim as "ruach ra'ah"; seemingly all three concepts are the same. From our Gemara it seems that sheidim are a force in the world that hinder a person's peace of mind ("harchavas hada'as"). People do not like to feel crowded, and people's minds work most clearly when given space (as Chazal write on 57b, "nice living quarters help open a person's mind"). Mazikin crowd a person's thoughts and space, and in turn, they can take a person out of his element and take over his mind and psyche until he cannot function normally. However, Ben Yehoyada writes (end of ד"ה אלפא) that mazikin were only prevalent and numerous in earlier times when the "sitra achra" was stronger, but today the "sitra achra" is weaker and there are therefore fewer mazikin.

2. *Ideal places to daven* – The Gemara writes that it is best to daven in a shul and with a minyan. From the simple reading of the Gemara it seems that these are two separate important factors. Indeed, Shulchan Aruch (OC 90:9) writes that it is most ideal to daven with a minyan in a shul (see Mishnah Berurah 90:27), but if one must daven alone, then it is still better to daven in a shul than in one's home etc. However, the Tur (ibid.), as explained by Beis Yosef and Bach, understands that it is only ideal to daven in shul when one is davening with a minyan, but when one needs to daven alone there is no preference to davening in a shul. But this opinion seems difficult since we know that it is better to daven in a place with more kedusha, as is clear from Pesukim regarding davening in the Beis HaMikdash or Mishkan (i.e. Chana's prayer in beg. of Sefer Shemuel; Shlomo HaMelech's speech in Melachim 8:28-53 regarding greatness of prayer in Beis HaMikdash). Nonetheless, Tzlach adds that it is certainly better to daven in shul when the tzibur is still present, even if they have mostly finished their Tefilla. (See Halichos Shlomo ch. 5 note 6 that even when R. Shlomo Zalman Auerbach had ten men in his home, he would make everyone go to a shul to daven.)

3. *What are the various degrees of the Shechina's presence?* – We know that the Beis HaMikdash and the Mishkan have more of "Hashem's presence" than other places in the world. That is, when someone is in those holy places he can more deeply feel Hashem's governance over the world. A similar idea holds true in a shul: Hashem's presence in a shul is constant and "precedes" the minyan of people who gather to daven. But Hashem's presence is certainly stronger in the Beis HaMikdash, and the laws of displaying fear and honor are therefore stricter in the Beis HaMikdash than they are in a shul (see 62b). Similarly, the degree of the Shechina's presence when only one person is present is not as great as when two or three people gather. The more people toiling in the service of Hashem, the greater the honor given to Hashem, and hence the more one is able to feel the presence of the Shechina (see Meiri Avos 3:3). (Even though the distinction between one and two people toiling in Torah refers to two people learning *together* [see below], nonetheless, it is clear from R. Chananel's understanding of the Gemara on the bottom of 5b that even when two people are davening by themselves there is a greater presence of Hashem; see notes on 5b further.)

4. *What is the uniqueness of one person learning Torah alone vs. two people learning together?* – Maharal (Derech Chaim on Avos 3:2) explains that when two people learn together, their Torah is considered "Torah gemura" (complete Torah), whereas when a person learns by himself his Torah remains mostly in the world of "thought". For this reason, the Shechina is more keenly present when two people learn Torah together, for the Shechina is found wherever there is Torah. That is, the Torah is most "complete" when it is "lived", as opposed to just "studied". When two people learn and speak about Torah together, the Torah is taken from the minds of individuals and becomes part of the actions of life. It is possible that this is part of the meaning of the Gemara that Hashem "records" the Torah of two people learning together. On the other hand, there is also a uniqueness of one person learning alone. We have already seen (see notes on 3b) that Dovid would rise in the middle of the night to learn Torah alone, and his Torah at that time had the special depth of "rina shel Torah" that penetrated the soul. It seems that this depth is attained when one learns alone because the Torah remains in the world of one's thought which is loftier and holier than Torah which takes form through expression to others. A "thought" often comes from the deep recesses of one's psyche and soul, and although it is often unintelligible until given form and expression, it nonetheless contains a depth which is lost when it finally takes form. (See Michtav Me'Eliyahu vol. 1 bottom of pg. 221.) Therefore, the Gemara here refers to Torah learned by a single person as a "calling" of Hashem's name; a sort of Tefilla. Just as Tefilla is the service of the heart and connects to one's soul (see Maharal Nesiv HaYissurin ch. 1), so too Torah learned alone hits one's soul in a way that learning Torah with a partner does not. Similarly, the Mishnah in Avos (3:2) quotes the Pasuk "ישב בדד וידם" as referring to learning Torah alone. This Pasuk connotes a degree of "hisbodedus" (solitary rumination), for learning alone can indeed have that effect. Maharal (ibid.) further explains that when one learns Torah alone he "accepts the burden of Heaven", whereas learning with another person engenders a give-and-take which does not have this added aspect of pure "acceptance" of the Torah. He also adds that the beracha on Torah is actually recited more specifically for learning alone, not necessarily for verbalizing Torah with others. Even though only spoken Torah is considered "Torah gemura", the main mitzvah of learning Torah is toiling to understand it, and this is done more keenly when learning and thinking alone. See also 6b that the main reward for learning Torah comes from toiling to understand it.

(Nonetheless, the give-and-take with a partner often sharpens and helps clarify one's understanding and is therefore essential as well; see Maharsha here.)

5. *Is "din" (judgment) considered Torah?* – Einayim LaMishpat points to Shabbos 10a that two Amoraim involved themselves in "din" all day, and at the end of the day they were saddened by the fact that they were involved in judgment all day and did not get a chance to learn Torah. It seems clear that involvement in judgment is not considered "learning Torah". Yet, our Gemara seems to conclude that "din" is indeed considered Torah and not mere peacemaking. Perhaps the ostensible contradiction can be reconciled as follows: "din" does not carry with it the enjoyment and religious elevation of high level Torah study, but it is nonetheless considered "Torah" and invites the Shechina.

6. *Trying to perform a mitzvah is equivalent to performing it* – Our Gemara (and Gemara Kedushin 40a) teaches this idea based on a Pasuk in Malachi. Medrash Tehillim (on 62:13) records this same idea in reference to Dovid's desire to build the Beis HaMikdash; see there.

7. *What does the Gemara mean that Hashem "wears tefillin"?* – The commentaries note that there are deep esoteric meanings behind this statement, but they nonetheless explain this comment on a simple level as well. The upshot of the various commentaries (see Rashba's Chidushei Hahagados and Gra) is that just as our wearing of tefillin displays our connection to Hashem and that He and His Torah are on the forefront of our mind and body, so too Hashem (kaviyachol) has us on the center of His mind at all times. And just as tefillin beautify us with G-dliness, so too we "beautify" and honor Hashem with our holiness and actions. Tzlach adds that tefillin express the great love and connection between Hashem and Bnei Yisroel, and tefillin therefore frighten all of the nations of the world and the "opposing" angels from attacking Bnei Yisroel. But Rashba (Chidushim) quotes R. Hai Gaon who explains completely differently, that the point of the Gemara is not that Hashem wears tefillin each day, but that Hashem "wore" tefillin once in order to show Moshe how to perform the mitzvah of tefillin. But see Rashba and Tzlach who question this understanding. (R. Chananel stresses the fact that Hashem certainly does not have a body and that only the heart, not the eyes, can see this "picture" of Hashem.)

Short Notes on Berachos 6b

1. *Does making a livelihood trump attending Tefilla b'tzibur?* – The Gemara states that someone who does not go to shul due to a non-mitzvah purpose lacks proper bitachon (trust) in Hashem. The Maharsha and Gra explain that although a person is required to make a livelihood to support himself and his family, this obligation does not constitute a "mitzvah" in relation to Tefilla and therefore does not override the obligation to daven in shul. R. Moshe Feinstein (Igros Moshe OC vol. 2 #111) provides the guidelines as to when an action is considered proper "hishtadlus" (necessary human effort) and when extra human effort indicates lack of proper "bitachon" in Hashem. He explains that one must first determine and block of the requisite amount of time for one's "mitzvah obligations", and only then utilize the remainder of his time to make a livelihood. He explains that just as it is obvious that one may not work on Shabbos in order to sustain himself (unless he is literally in a state of immediate "pikuach nefesh") and that he must trust that Hashem will provide some other means by which he will find sustenance, so too one must daven properly each day (as well as give himself time to learn Torah in order to become a talmid chachom; see there) and "block off" this time from time spent on "hitshtadlus" to make a livelihood.

2. *Who comes to shul first: the Shechina or the minyan?* – The Gemara (6a) states that the Shechina presents itself in the shul even before the minyan arrives, whereas the Gemara here implies that it is improper for the Shechina to "arrive" before ten men are present. The Rashba (vol. 1 #50, cited in Gilyon HaShas here) first writes that we do not learn aggadic portions of the Gemara in the same style as halachic pieces and therefore do not need to be bothered by this question. That is, when learning aggada, one should try to understand the meaning of Chazal in each particular place and not be so concerned with reconciling details of various teachings. But he continues to offer an explanation that the Shechina arrives *with* the minyan, that the word "kodem" (usually translated as "before") can sometimes mean "concomitantly". The Meiri seems to explain slightly differently, that the Shechina arrives immediately before the z'man Tefilla, and the minyan should therefore be present when the "z'man Tefilla" arrives. (Sefer Daf al HaDaf quotes R. Soloveitchik that arriving at shul early (or at least on-time) expresses more than general "alacrity" in the performance of mitzvos, but it carries with it an extra aspect of "greeting the Shechina" with due respect.)

3. *Why is having a "set place" for Tefilla important, and what is considered a "set place"?* – Maharal (Nesiv HaAvoda ch. 4) explains that attaining true closeness with Hashem through Tefilla requires making this relationship "kavua" (set and permanent), as opposed to "mikreh" (happenstance). One must create a "zone" for himself through which he can enter the close relationship that he has with Hashem. The Shulchan Aruch (98:4) adds that davening in a specific place provides a structure similar to the structure of korbanos (just as much of Tefilla is patterned after korbanos). The Meiri adds a crucial practical point: praying in one's "set place" makes it much easier to concentrate on one's prayers (see also Rashba in Chidushei Hahagados). Having a set place for Tefilla also connects one's current Tefilla to all of his previous Tefillos. That is, one of the goals of Tefilla is to focus one's mind on Hashem and on one's true goals in life as he goes about his daily activities. When entering into Tefilla, one must try to "pick up where he left off" from the previous Tefilla; he had a certain train of thought to which he now reconnects as he continues to contemplate the map set for him to attain his purpose in life. (R. Meir Goldvicht compares the many Tefillos recited in a "makom kavua" to drops of water dripping slowly over numerous years; they combine over time to make a noticeable mark on the hard rock below them. See also Piskei Teshuvos 90 note 264.) Many commentators (Kehillas Yaakov by the Nesivos HaMishpat and Sfas Emes here) add that one's makom kavua is imbued with the kedusha (holiness) of all of his previous Tefillos that make his makom kavua somewhat of a "personal Beis Kenesses". (The Maharsha interestingly points out that there is also an advantage to davening in different places, for each place contains its own unique kedusha and spiritual energy, but nonetheless, the oneness created and expressed through having a single set place for Tefilla is still more ideal.) This idea is expressed most poignantly through the opinion of Rabbenu Yonah (here) that it is only necessary to create a makom kavua when davening in one's home where someone needs to create a "mini Beis Tefilla" for himself, but it is not necessary to have a makom kavua in shul since the entire shul is already a holy place of Tefilla. Nevertheless the consensus of the Poskim (OC 90:19; see also Einayim LaMishpat) is that one should have a makom kavua for himself in shul as well. Halichos Shlomo (Tefilla ch. 5 note 2) adds, however, that it is considered a makom kavua even if someone has one shul for Shacharis, another for Mincha, another for Maariv and Shabbos etc. But it seems (see language of Tur and Shulchan Aruch ibid.) that it is not enough to have a specific place in each shul when one happens to find himself in that shul, but rather, one should have a specific shul (and place in that shul) for each specific Tefilla. Indeed, the Kol Bo (towards end of #11 ד"ה חייב) understands that this is the very meaning of our Gemara: one needs to establish a specific shul for himself. This affords Tefilla with a sense of "keviyus" (permanence and prominence), as described. Regarding the importance of having a makom kavua vs. other ideals, Halichos Shlomo (ibid. note 4) writes that one should daven in his regular minyan even if he will need to skip Pesukei D'Zimra in order to catch up to the congregation. (But it is obvious that one should not argue with a guest etc. in order to daven in his personal seat; see Piskei Teshuvos 90 note 270.) Mishnah Berurah writes that the entire area of 4x4 amos around him is considered part of his makom kavua. Ben Yehoyada adds another type of "makom

kavua", namely that one should establish a "set place in his heart" for Tefilla. Even when one cannot go to his physical makom kavua, he should nonetheless find that emotional chord that he utilizes when in his physical spot. The Gemara here speaks very highly of someone who davens in a makom kavua. R. Yonah explains that such a person clearly takes Tefilla very seriously and is also most probably a humble person (for Tefilla requires humility; see also Einayim LaMishpat) which will lead him to attain the heightened level of "chasid".

4. *Walking/running to and in shul* – Shulchan Aruch (90:12) rules that it is a mitzvah to run (not just walk) to shul and when performing any mitzva in order to show love for the mitzvah (see Levush) and to stimulate one's desire for the mitzvah (see R. Yonah). Tzitz Eliezer (vol. 12 #17, based on Tzlach and Rambam) qualifies that it is only a *mitzvah* to run to shul on weekdays, but on Shabbos it is merely *permitted*, and one should only run if he would otherwise be late. Poskim debate if the mitzvah is to run the entire way from one's home or only when close to shul when it is clear that he is doing a mitzvah (see Elya Raba 90:13; MB 90:40 with Piskei Teshuvos). Tzitz Eliezer (ibid.) writes that it is proper to walk/run to shul as opposed to drive because this shows extra care and exertion for the mitzvah. (See also Sefer Magadim Chadashim on Chagiga 3a pg. 26-28 for more on the uniqueness of using one's feet to perform this mitzvah.) Nevertheless, when one arrives at shul he may not run; he must enter with awe and fear (see Magen Avraham 90:24 based on Shvilei Emunah Nesiv 7 ד"ה אלה and note on Magen Avraham in Friedman ed. of Shulchan Aruch). From the wording of the Poskim it seems that it is *always* forbidden to run in shul. But see Tamid end of ch. 5 and Yoma 22a with Tos. HaRosh that the Kohanim ran in the Mikdash for mitzvah purposes. Yet it is possible that they did not actual "run", but walked very quickly, as in fact is clear according to one opinion in Tos. HaRosh there. Indeed, the Mishnah Berurah (141:25) states that one may not "run" but should walk with alacrity.

5. *Running on Shabbos* – The wording of the Gemara implies that "non-Shabbosdig" action can be called "chillul (profaning) Shabbos".

6. *Sometimes "effort" is most important* – The Gemara states that the main reward for going to a crowded shiur is for running there and for sitting in the crowded area (see our notes on 17b for further description of the "kallah" event). Clearly the effort and desire to perform mitzvos is sometimes more important than the mitzvah itself. (See also Horayos 10b that Lot's daughters were praised for their positive intentions even though in reality they were not performing a positive act at all; quite the contrary – they were sinning! Nonetheless, their intentions matter most. See also Michtav Me'Eliyahu vol. 5 pg. 174; Sefer HaIkarim 3:29.)

7. *What is the proper response to death?* – The Rishonim explain (see Einayim LaMishpat) that the most prevalent conduct of both a mourner and the visitors should be silence (as the Pasuk states when Aharon heard of the tragic death of his sons). Besides other things, this silence allows for all people involved to contemplate the situation and let it settle upon their hearts.

8. *What is the goal of a fast day?* – Meiri stresses that the main point of a fast day is to do teshuva and to put the "fasting" into action, such as by giving charity (see also Rambam hil. Taanis 5:1). Similarly, Rashi explains that we must remember that the destitute do not have food to eat after the fast, and we must make sure to provide for them. But nonetheless, the fasting itself is also crucial. Sefer Daf al HaDaf here quotes early sources that the obligation to fast cannot be fulfilled simply by giving charity, because fasting works through affecting one's body which is most keenly felt by the individual. Yet, our Gemara is stressing that fasting is only done properly when put immediately into action through good deeds.

9. *Goal of a eulogy* – It is clear from the Gemara that a eulogy is not just meant to give honor to the deceased. Rather, it is meant to deeply affect the people present and bring them to teshuva etc.

10. *What is the ideal way to bring joy to a bride and groom?* – The Gemara states that the main way to bring joy to a bride and groom is through "words". Commentators point to Gemara Kesubos (bottom of 16b/17a) where Beis Hillel and Beis Shamai disagree as to how exactly we praise each bride for her beauty. It seems from that Gemara as well that a crucial aspect of dancing is praising the bride with words (see Rashi there ד"ה כיצד מרקדים). Maseches Semachos (ch. 11) also describes participation in a wedding ceremony as "מקלסין", praising. It seems that the most essential aspect of gladdening the bride and groom is not merely giving them joy, but making them feel that this marriage is a source of great honor for them and that they are lucky to have merited such a mate. Yet, Birkas Avraham (Kesubos 16b) notes that the main praise mentioned is the praising of the bride to endear her to the groom and not vise versa. He explains (based on Kedushin 41a) that women are more prone to be happy with marriage than are men, and therefore men need to be gladdened more than do women. (For a seemingly different understanding of our Gemara, see Maharsha here who points to Nedarim bottom of 50b/51a where Bar Kapara would use his words, specifically of Torah, to make Rebbe laugh at his son's wedding.)

11. *Laws pertaining to davening in the lobby of a shul* – The Gemara states that one is not permitted to daven outside of a shul in a different direction than the tzibur prays inside the shul. The Rishonim (see Rashi and story recorded in the Gemara here) explain that doing so appears as refusal to daven to the same G-d as the tzibur (Heaven forbid) and also reflects a lack of honor for the shul (see Teshuvos Rambam quoted in Beis Yosef 90:7). (It should be noted that someone who davens in the shul is also supposed to take care to daven in the same direction as the rest of the tzibur, see MB 94:10, but davening *outside* of the shul in a different direction may be even more problematic because it differentiates him completely from the tzibur; see R. Yonah here. This distinction may show itself in a case where the tzibur does not face east when davening: when davening in the shul, there are Poskim (see Be'er Heiteiv 94:3) who write that an individual can face east in such a situation even though the tzibur does not face that direction, but when davening outside the shul doing so may be more problematic. But this point requires more research.) The Rishonim dispute what one should do when one finds himself needing to daven outside in the front of the shul: some say to face the same direction as the tzibur, even though his back will be turned to the tzibur, while others say that he should face the tzibur even though he would be davening in the opposite direction from the tzibur. In order to avoid this dispute, the Shulchan Aruch (90:7) writes that it is best not to daven outside in the front of the shul. But it is permitted to daven (when necessary) outside in the back of the shul and face the same direction as the tzibur. The Shulchan Aruch (ibid.; see also Piskei Teshuvos) further records the Rambam that this prohibition only applies when davening in the courtyard or lobby of the shul, but if one davens in an adjacent room or building, or courtyard that belongs to another building, this prohibition does not apply, for in such situations facing another direction does not appear as a disregard for the tzibur or the shul.

12. *Is Tefilla Heavenly or worldly?* – The Gemara here describes Tefilla as "standing in the heights of the world" (i.e. in the Heavens), but the Gemara in Shabbos (10a) describes Tefilla as "chayei sha'ah" (this worldly and transient). But there is no contradiction: on one hand Tefilla operates by affecting the Heavenly spheres (Rashi here), but on the other hand Tefilla describes worldly needs (Rashi in Shabbos). Whereas Torah preceded the world and is the very blueprint of the world (and is therefore essentially loftier than this world), Tefilla is man's way to connect the worldly needs (both physical and lofty) to the Heavenly spheres.

13. *What tragedy happens to a person who is forced to become dependent upon others?* – The Gemara writes that when a person is dependent upon others he "changes to multiple colors" and is subject to opposite forces of "fire and water". That is, such a person is conflicted and pulled in different directions because he cannot live according to his own personality but must appease others in order to sustain himself.

14. *What are the different characteristics of the various Tefillos of the day?* – Rashba in Chidushei Hahagados explains (see also Meiri) that the various Tefillos of the day were enacted at specific times to express many unique aspects of Hashem's creations and our experiences in the world during various points of each day and in our lives as a whole. He explains that Shacharis represents "rising" (aliyah); Mincha "standing" (amida); Maariv "descending" (yerida). Every person's day and life as a whole consists of these three experiences, and we need to recognize Hashem during each one of them. This is in stark contrast to the followers of "Ba'al" who erroneously focused their prayers towards the sun and prayed only when the sun was strongest. To blatantly challenge this error, Eliyahu prayed during Mincha when the sun is the weakest and thus showed that we must recognize Hashem's sovereignty over all of the various experiences and creations in His world.

15. *Connection between gladdening a bride and groom and Har Sinai* – Maharsha explains that Har Sinai was our "wedding" with Hashem. The close connection that we enjoy with Hashem and His Torah began at Har Sinai, and this connection is fostered in every new household in Klal Yisroel, beginning at every wedding. (See our notes on 17b for further sources for this idea.)

Short Notes on Berachos 7a

1. *What do Chazal mean that "Hashem davens"?* – Rashba (Chidushei Hahagados) first quotes R. Hai Gaon who explains that Hashem does not really daven; rather, He shows people how to daven (see parallel idea in notes on bottom of 6a regarding Hashem wearing tefillin). The Rashba himself writes differently, explaining that Hashem wants the best for Bnei Yisroel, and He therefore wants us to perform his mitzvos so that He can reward us as opposed to punishing us. This is what Hashem means when saying that He wants His "mercy to outweigh His anger": He wants us to act in a way that warrants Him to act with mercy and not anger. This is also the meaning of the Beis HaMikdash being Hashem's place of Tefilla: when we daven it is as if He (kaviyachol) is davening, for our desires are His desires. This is also why He wants us to bless Him etc. (See Nefesh HaChaim 2:2-4 further.)

2. *What do Chazal mean that Hashem "gets angry", and why does this occur for a split second each day?* – Ben Yehoyada notes that there are numerous Pesukim that describe Hashem as being angry. Nonetheless, the Gemara here had to search for a Pasuk because the anger referred to here is unique. Anger from Hashem means that He "removes" Himself from the world to a degree (kaviyachol) and "holds back" some spiritual energy ("shefah"). Usually Hashem acts in this manner through His attribute of "Gevura" (strength, especially in judgment), but He does not "pull back" *completely* as He continues to sustain the world through His attribute of "Chesed" (kindness). The Gemara here refers to times of "extreme anger" when Hashem decides to hold back even the attribute of chesed. (Hashem afforded Bilaam with a heightened level of near-prophecy with a predilection towards evil, and Bilaam therefore knew how to utilize this moment of "anger".) The world cannot continue to exist if Hashem does this for an extended period of time, and that is why this only occurs for a split second. (Ben Yehoyada adds that besides for the "slight moment" of Hashem's *extreme* anger, that entire "hour" is a time of *heightened* anger.) Building off of the Ben Yehoyada's framework, it can possibly be added that Hashem's "holding back" from the world is a part of the regular course of His governance over the world, and it will remain this way until the time when the world attains its completeness. It is logical that the reason that the world did not yet reach its perfection is due to the sins of mankind, as the Gemara states here that Hashem is angered when the kings rise in the morning with the notion that something other than Hashem is in control of the world.

3. *Are we allowed to daven for evil people to perish?* – Tosafos (here and Avoda Zara 4b) explain that even if we are permitted to *kill* a heretic, we may not *curse* him in order to make the Heavens kill him. See notes on 10a that Hashem is not "happy" when people die (even evil people), and we therefore may not "force" Hashem to do this. If Hashem decides that the person should die, He will either deliver the person into our hands for us to kill him, or He will make sure that the heretic dies in some other fashion. But to "force" Hashem to do this is improper. Some commentators (including Maharal in Be'er HaGolah #7 pg. 149-150) write that we should also not *daven* for heretics to die just as we do not curse them. But many others (Abudraham printed in ד' גליון א' שנה ט"תשמ תמוז, pg. 18; R. Yehuda ben Yakar) explain Bircas HaMinim in our daily Shemoneh Esrei as in fact a prayer for just that. They explain (as does Raavya here #16) that only *cursing* is wrong since it "forces" Hashem, but *davening* (which is not as "strong" as a full-fledged curse) is indeed proper. Nonetheless, there are some circumstances when it seems that most everyone agrees that we are permitted to daven for evildoers to die; see notes on 10a. See also the Hebrew essay printed in the back of this kuntrus for an extensive discussion of the topic.

4. *Are children punished for the sins of their father?* – Rambam (hil. Teshuva 6:1) writes that young children are similar to the property of their father and can therefore sometimes be punished for his sins just as Hashem sometimes takes away other property from a person as punishment for sin (see notes on side of Frankel ed. of Rambam for sources). (Mishneh Kesef on Rambam writes that this idea is seen in Gemara earlier beg. of 5b.) Hence according to the Rambam, our Gemara must be referring to adult children who are not punished for the sins of their father unless they continue in their father's ways. But if they indeed continue the evil of their father, the commentators discuss if they receive some actual punishment for their father's sins (see Abarbanel and Chizkuni Shemos 34:7 that Hashem shows mercy on the father and places some punishment on the children that would otherwise be placed on the father) or if they do not actually receive punishment for their father's sins, but Hashem does not withhold judgment against them for very long since this sin is already generational and therefore deserving of immediate retribution (see Seforno Shemos 34:7 and Meiri Sanhedrin end of 27b). Why do children suffer because of the sins of their father? And even more difficult, some commentators point to circumstances where the children suffer due to their father's sins even if the children do not sin at all: a) Ramban (Shemos end of 20:5) posits that children endure punishment for their father's sin of avoda zara, seemingly even if the children did not sin. b) Sefer Chasidim (#164) seems to understand (although his opinion seems to contradict our Gemara) that four generations of offspring can be punished for each sin of the father even if the children are tzadikim; if the father sins numerous times he can affect tens or even hundreds of generations! Sefer Chasidim (ibid.) explains this phenomenon based on Chazal who write that Hashem will protect a completely righteous person even before he enters the world so that he will not have impurity in his lineage. If Hashem

does not protect a child in this fashion it indicates that the child himself is not 100% righteous; in a sense, he had a part in his father's sins since he could have prevented them. Conversely, the actions of the father can also affect the child: mitzvos add purity into the children whereas sin injects impurity into the offspring. This impurity requires "cleansing" through punishment. (See there further for additional approaches.) We can add (see also end of the Ramban ibid.) that since part of a child's purpose in life is to continue the fulfillment of his parents' life-purpose (see Michtav Me'Eliyahu vol. 2 pg. 217 that this is the depth behind the law that a child inherits his parents' property and also explains why children often share physical features and personalities with their parents), he therefore must sometimes bear the consequences of his father's sins in order to have the chance to "fix" them. But if a child does not follow his father's evil, he may not need to endure the punishment and challenges of his father since he has clearly already overcome the main obstacles to which his father fell trap. (This idea may also explain the ability that a child has to raise the spiritual level of his father even after his father's death. See R. Reuven Margaliyos's discussion of this concept in the back of his addition to Sefer Chasidim pg. 591. See also Tevuos Shor and HaKesav V'Hakabbala quoted in Shaarei Aharon Parashas Ki Sisa 34:7.) Based on some of the above ideas, commentators quote the Arizal (and others; see Margaliyos HaYam Sanhedrin 27b #24) that children are only affected by the impurity of the father's sins that occur *before* the birth of the child, but once the child is born he is not as deeply affected by the actions of the father. (For a halachic ramification of these ideas, see Noda B'Yehuda YD #69 that someone may renege on a shidduch if a family member of the other party turns evil, for evil in the family has ramifications on all offspring.) It is important to note that Gemara Makkos (24a) records that Yechezkel davened that children should no longer be punished for the sins of their fathers (see Maharsha there); further research is required to determine how this affects all of the aforementioned commentators who assume that this rule still applies. It should also be noted that this concept may apply most keenly regarding a father as opposed to a mother just as laws of inheritance are based on the father's family (see Sefer Daf al HaDaf here).

5. *Why do good things happen to bad people and vice versa?* – Our Gemara records that Moshe himself was bothered by this question, and we know that many other greats were bothered by this problem as well (see much of Sefer Iyov; Yirmiyahu 12:1; Chabakuk 1:2-4 and 1:13). The Gemara here offers an answer but also quotes the opinion of R. Meir that Hashem did not reveal the answer to this question. The commentators further discuss this question at length (see Artscroll Gemara here note 50 for a list of sources). It seems that our basic outlook on the issue must be that we cannot understand the ways of Hashem; only He understands His calculations because He sees a broad picture of the world, and we are not privy to this information (see Michtav Me'Eliyahu vol. 1 pg. 19). It is also important to note that when Moshe and the other great prophets asked this question, they were not *challenging* Hashem (as is clear in Yirmiyahu ibid.). Rather, they were expressing how very much it bothered them to see good people in pain while evil people prosper. This phenomenon itself is an expression of that fact that we are still in an imperfect world; this will not be the case in the End of Days. These tzadikim were not merely philosophizing or even complaining; rather, their argument was said as a form of prayer, entreating Hashem to turn His kindness towards the tzadikim (similar to the "argument" of Avraham regarding Sedom). Similarly, R. Volbe (Alei Shur vol. 2 pg. 145) points out that when we learn "Jewish Thought", we are not meant to merely philosophize. Rather, we discuss philosophical topics with the goal of getting closer to Hashem through understanding His ways (just like we try to understand the rest of the Torah), by utilizing these ideas in our service of Hashem, and in order to bring ourselves to teshuva or prayer etc. According to this understanding, we can add that these very prophets knew the "answer" (or the non-answer) to this question; they were not "asking" but "pleading". Iyov, on the other hand, may have "challenged" Hashem and was therefore punished. Michtav Me'Eliyahu (vol. 1 pg. 19-23) adds that for most people, the entire question only comes about because of a misconstrued outlook of this world. Once someone comprehends that this world is simply a preparation for the next world, he will understand that it is certainly worth much toil and hardship in order to reap greater benefits in the next world. Everyone is afforded with different tasks in this world in order to perfect himself to the point that he can enjoy his specific place in the World to Come. Hashem gives each individual varying obstacles that best suit that specific person with the hope that he will overcome his challenges and attain his particular completeness ("shleimus"). (See there further.) This explanation may be part of the meaning behind the distinction in our Gemara between a "complete tzadik" and an "incomplete tzadik": Hashem brings hardships upon an "incomplete tzadik" in order to perfect him. (When viewed in this light, this topic is related to the topic of "yissurin shel ahavah"; see our notes 5a.)

6. *Necessity to prepare oneself before plumbing spiritual depths* – The Gemara records a disagreement whether Moshe's reticence to look towards Hashem's presence in the burning bush was proper or improper. It is possible to explain that both are true: on one hand, Moshe acted properly by showing that only someone who is completely prepared and worthy can engage in such deep spiritual experiences; but on the other hand, it would not have been incorrect in such a situation to act a little bold in order to capitalize on this unique opportunity.

7. *What does the "knot of Hashem's tefillin" represent?* – Rashba (Chidushei Hahagados) explains that a person's tefillin are situated at the source of one's eyes and then surround his entire head and join in the back. They represent that Hashem's "eye" is constantly on the world as He controls everything and as He joins all of His creations together to carry out His plan. Hashem explained to Moshe ("by showing him the knot of the tefillin") that all creations indeed work together to carry out His will. But Hashem was not willing to show Moshe the "shoresh", the source, of His governance over the world. This is represented in the Pasuk that Hashem did not show Moshe His "face", or more precisely, the box of the tefillin in the front of His head (kaviyachol). Man is not able to comprehend *how* exactly Hashem sustains and governs the entire world; the most that we can understand is *that* He indeed governs everything harmoniously.

8. *Does Hashem ever rescind an auspicious prophecy?* – See our notes on bottom of 4a.

Short Notes on Berachos 7b

1. *What was unique about Avraham?* – Rashba (Chidushei Hahagados) explains that there were definitely "tzadikim gemurim" (completely righteous people) that lived before Avraham; namely, Adam, Sheis, Mesushelach, Chanoch, Noach, and Shem (and Ever). But Avraham was unique in his publicizing Hashem's sovereignty over the world. According to "mazal" (his lot in life with which he was born), Avraham was not destined to have any children, and all of the astrologers at the time (who were able to read a person's mazal) knew that. But through righteous actions a person is able to overcome his mazal, and Avraham did just that. When Hashem overrode Avraham's mazal due to his righteousness, everyone saw that Hashem is the true Master ("Adon") of the world, not "mazalos". And since Avraham constantly publicized this fact, he is credited with being the first to express Hashem as the "Adon" (master) over the world. And therefore when Daniel pleaded for the Beis HaMikdash which displays Hashem's mastery, he invoked the merit of Avraham, hoping that Hashem would clearly reveal His mastery once again.

2. *In what way was Leah the first person to ever thank Hashem?* – Rashba (Chidushei Hahagados) explains that Leah was the first person to ever receive kindness from Hashem that was originally destined to be afforded to someone else. When Leah had her fourth child she understood that she was given more than her allotted portion of the Shevatim, a display of extra "chesed" from Hashem beyond His constant bestowment of goodness. She therefore thanked Hashem in a manner above and beyond all previous generations. Rashba adds that Leah also merited that her descendants represent grand thanksgiving to Hashem: Dovid (through authoring Tehillim) brought many forms of beautiful thanks and praise to Hashem for all eternity, and the kingdom of Dovid (through Shlomo and others, and eventually through Mashiach) brings all nations of the world to recognize Hashem and give thanks to Him.

3. *Were Leah and Rus prophetesses?* – Gemara Megilla (14a) records that there were 7 prophetesses in our history (Sarah, Miriam, Devorah, Chana, Avigail, Chuldah, Esther). Maharsha here therefore explains that Leah (and Rus) did not experience prophecy when naming their children, but Hashem put these names into their mouths without them understanding the full hidden meaning behind their own actions. But Sfas Emes here disagrees with the Maharsha, writing that there is no reason to assume that Leah was unaware of her son's future, for numerous Midrashim (Bereishis Raba 67 and 72; see Rashi on Vayeitzei 29:34; Yerushalmi Berachos 9:5) write explicitly that our foremothers were prophetesses. He therefore explains that the aforementioned Gemara Megilla includes only the prophetesses that were sent to Bnei Yisroel to prophesize, but others certainly received prophecy for their own knowledge etc. (See notes on 13a end of Perek 1.) Other commentaries (on Rashi ibid.) explain that the Gemara records only the 7 whose prophecies were most explicit in the Pesukim.

4. *How does one's name affect his life's course?* – The Gemara explains (using Reuven and Rus as examples) that a person's name causes various consequences in one's life or progeny. Just as a person is given certain innate capabilities for him to utilize in life in order to fulfill his life's purpose, so too, a person's name gives him "kochos" (capabilities) for him to actualize. As mentioned above, a person's name can sometimes include a degree of ruach hakodesh (Divine spirit) implanted into the mind of the parent, either knowingly or unknowingly. There are also multiple meanings expressed in one name, some according to the "simple meaning" and others hinted to through "derash" (see Maharatz Chayes here).

5. *When should one cry due to hardship and when is it proper to accept the hardships happily?* – M'lo HaRo'im (notes in back of Gemara) asks why the Gemara states that it would have been more logical for Dovid to recite a "kina" (lamentation) when being chased as opposed to a "mizmor" (song of praise to Hashem); after all, is it not more proper to praise Hashem even for hardship? He answers that someone only accepts hardships with joy once he has reached the point where they cannot be reversed (without an open miracle, for we do not usually daven for open miracles; see Shome'ah Tefilla ch. 35 for sources), but when it is still possible to better the situation, the proper response is to cry, lament, and fast. It is possible to add, however, that it is possible to respond concurrently with both joy and lamentation. One happily accepts the yissurin as a challenge to better himself (see notes on 5a) as he concomitantly feels the pain of the hardships and repents and davens for them to end. In a sense, a person can recite a "kina" with inner peace and even joy (see Rambam hil. Berachos 10:3 along with hil. Aveilus 13:11-12).

6. *How did Dovid view his son's rebellion against him?* – The Gemara notes that Dovid defined this experience in a positive light ("mizmor"). On a simple level, Dovid saw that Hashem had mercy on him, for other insurgents would have been much more difficult and callous. R. Ephraim Wachsman adds (see also Gemara on 10a) that Dovid was blissful because he realized, through witnessing this wild occurrence (that his own son rebelled against him), that Hashem is most certainly behind this unnatural event. And just as Hashem is behind this event, so too, He governs all happenings and provides special attention to those involved in Jewish leadership and world history. In this way, this event provides assurance that the redemption (and war of Gog U'Magog; see 10a) will eventually occur, even if the possibility of redemption seems outlandish. Hence, Dovid's overall outlook on this event was characterized by "song",

even though on a personal, immediate level, the tragedy of a son turning astray was even more difficult than the worst of wars, which Dovid makes note of in this very Mizmor.

7. *Is one permitted to antagonize evildoers?* – In our current imperfect world (see notes on "tzadik v'ra lo" on 7a), Hashem often allows evil people to prosper, either as punishment towards their enemies who sinned or in order to punish these evildoers even more harshly in the World to Come. R. Hutner (Pachad Yitzhak Purim 9:2) explains that the ostensible success of evildoers is truthfully not success at all; quite the opposite, Hashem mocks them by allowing them to prosper in this ephemeral world only to punish them harshly in the world of eternity. (See also Sefer Matnas Chaim on Moadim, essay on Purim "עת לשחוק" who further develops this idea.) But nonetheless, since the evildoers' "success" is divinely ordained and part of Hashem's larger plan, it is often improper to directly fight and disparage the evil, and doing so will not help. Indeed, the Gemara (Sotah 41b) writes that it is sometimes even permitted to "flatter" evildoers in order to save one's life etc. through political maneuvering and the like, just as Yaakov "flattered" Eisav with gifts and praise (see Gemara and Maharsha there). A large degree of our battle against evil is to perfect ourselves and cry out to Heaven for assistance until Hashem deems it proper to put an end to the evil Himself, or until He affords us with a situation where we can clearly "beat" the evildoer as opposed to merely taunting him which may just encourage him to perform further evils. But the Gemara distinguishes between various situations: if the form of evil is "towards Heaven" or "against other people" (monetary issues etc.); if it appears that the evildoer is currently enjoying extra divine "assistance" or if it appears that he can truly be conquered; if those battling against the evil are completely righteous or not. (The conclusion of our Gemara seems to slightly contradict the conclusion of Gemara Megilla 6b and Yalkut Shimoni Tehillim #649. There are also some questions regarding the concluding statement of our Gemara: see explanation of Maharshal in Chochmas Shlomo here; and see Meromei Sadeh who writes that there is an editor's mistake. Practically, Ravya here warns even a complete tzadik against antagonizing evildoers whereas Meiri advises the Rav of a community to not fear evildoers. It would seem that it all depends on each individual situation.) Regarding the distinction between a "complete tzadik" and an "incomplete tzadik", see Gra and Meromei Sadeh here (as well as Pachad Yitzchak ibid.) that a "complete tzadik" can often function outside of the natural course of the world. As opposed to most people, a complete tzadik clearly sees Hashem "mocking" the evildoer through his worldly "success" and does not fear the evildoer at all, and he therefore has the ability to function according to this "clearer" viewpoint and to antagonize the evildoer as well. Indeed, Mordechai HaTzadik refused to bow to Haman whereas the rest of the Jewish people were naturally afraid, and it was precisely Mordechai's outlook which brought about the eventual open mockery of Haman and the entire story of Purim (see Michtav Me'Eliyahu vol. 2 pg. 130). But in many situations even completely righteous people must be afraid that some sin may prevent them from triumphing over evil, as Yaakov was afraid "shema yigrom hacheit" (see above bottom of 4a; Sotah 41b). Nonetheless, this outward bowing to evildoers is a less-than-ideal necessity to utilize natural means to survive amongst evil. Therefore, as we follow Yaakov's example throughout our history (especially in Galus), we also suffer consequences for acting in such a manner (see Ramban Vayishlach 32:4; Bereishis Raba 75:11 and 75:5; Tanchuma there; and "מתורתו של הגאון רבי אריה ליב" Maamarim #2). (See also English essay printed in the back of this kuntrus for more elaboration of this topic.)

8. *What is the significance of setting aside a place to learn Torah?* – Our text of the Gemara (along with Ravya's text) reads "kove'ah makom l'Tefillaso" and refers to davening (which was discussed on 6b; see there). But the Rif (and She'iltos #19) has the text "kove'ah makom l'Toraso". Y'feh Einayim (in the back of the Gemara) notes that the Medrash (Yalkut) also has this text. Based on the idea of the Maharal (quoted in notes 6b) regarding the term "kove'ah", the point of our Gemara would seem to be that besides for the need to "kove'ah *ittim* l'Torah" (set aside a specific *time* to learn Torah), one should also set aside a specific *place* to learn, for this adds a degree of importance and permanence to his Torah study (see also Meiri here). Indeed, Sefer Daf al HaDaf quotes from Kav HaYashar that one should designate a specific part of his house for his sefarim and to learn Torah, and by doing so he affords that area with a degree of kedusha of a real Beis Medrash where the Shechina resides. Rabbenu Yonah (here; codified in Rama OC #155) explains differently, that the Gemara refers to a real Beis Medrash and directs every individual to spend some amount of set time in the city's Beis Medrash every day. The Beis Medrash has a particular kedusha above and beyond other places, for Hashem "resides" in the "4 amos of Halacha".

9. *What are the parameters of the obligation to "serve the Torah" and why is it greater than learning the Torah itself?* – Maharatz Chayes explains that "serving" a talmid chachom is a form of study: besides for learning with one's ears, one needs to also observe a talmid chachom's actions and learn from his actions. He quotes the Gra as stating that this form of study becomes more deeply imbedded in the student's heart. "Serving a talmid chachom" can also refer to conversing with him or observing him apply the Torah to various situations. Indeed, Ravya, Meiri, and Maharsha here explain that "serving" a talmid chachom teaches the student "halacha l'maaseh" (how to practically apply the Torah's teachings). "Shimush Chachomim" is listed as one of the things necessary to "acquire the Torah" (Avos 6:6). Medrash Shemuel (there) explains that a student needs to establish himself in a permanent form ("keva") with his Rebbe, and

by doing so he will learn constantly from his Rebbe's teachings, informal conversation, and actions. According to all of these commentaries, "shimush" does not refer to *serving* a Rebbe literally, but to learning from being in his presence. Similarly, Rashi in numerous places (Berachos 47b and 61a, Chagiga 10a, Sotah 22a; also clear from Gemara Eruvin 13a) explains this term as referring to learning from talmidei chachomim how to properly answer ostensible contradictions in Mishnayos etc. Accordingly, learning Gemara is a form of "shimush talmidei chachomim" (see Rashi Chullin end of 44b; Sotah ibid.; Rashi Bava Metzia 33a/b). Nonetheless, the source quoted in our Gemara indicates the importance of serving one's Rebbe literally (pouring him water etc.) as well. Indeed, see Rambam (hil. Talmud Torah 5:8) that a student must perform for a Rebbe all tasks that a servant performs for a master. Sefer Chareidim (16:50) connects that halacha to our Gemara and adds that this idea is hinted to in the mitzvah (Shemos 23:25) "ועבדתם את ה' אלקיכם", explaining that the word "את" adds talmidei chachomim, that one needs to "serve" them with his "hands and body". (See Nachalas Shimon Melachim 2 vol. 1 21:17 for more sources in Tanach and Chazal.) Medrash Shemuel (ibid.) connects these two ideas and explains that through serving one's Rebbe, the student puts himself in close proximity to the Rebbe and can learn from all of his ways. But from the above sources there seems to be an even deeper idea. Shaarei Yosher (intro. ד"ה ולכן) quotes his brother-in-law who explains that there are many difficult ideas and deep concepts that require a lot of thought in order to understand, and only someone who believes in the greatness of his Rebbe and nullifies himself to his Rebbe will have the patience and wherewithal to work tirelessly to understand his Rebbe and the Torah. Similarly, Chovos HaLevavos (Shaar Hacheniya ch. 2) explains that the student must make himself "lower" than the Rebbe in order to learn properly. Maharal (Avos ibid.) also stresses that a student only "becomes close" to his Rebbe through "serving him" as opposed to merely learning from him, and that closeness will raise the student closer to the level of the Rebbe. Hence serving talmidei chachomim through conversation, observation, and literal "service" raises a student from someone who simply culled a lot of knowledge to someone who knows how to truly understand and utilize the wisdom of the Torah. Indeed, the Gemara states (Sanhedrin 88b; Sotah end of 47b; see Rashi Bava Metzia ibid.) that the decrease of wisdom and therefore the plethora of disagreement found in the Gemara between the students of Shamai and Hillel was due to the fact that "לא שמשו כל צרכן" (they did not "serve" their teachers completely). Regarding the elevated halachic status of "serving" talmidei chachomim, Gilyon HaShas cites Tosafos (Kesubos 17a) that burying the deceased trumps only "studying" Torah, but "serving" talmidei chachomim trumps even burying the deceased, seemingly because the opportunity to serve talmidei chachomim is considerably great and not readily available. (For more on the importance of learning from a Rebbe as opposed to simply reading sefarim, see Igros Moshe OC vol. 4 #39 and Mishneh Halachos vol. 14 #163.)

10. *Is it better for a minyan to daven in shul or to daven in an individual's home if he otherwise would not be able to join the minyan?* – Einayim LaMishpat proves from our Gemara (end of 7b) that the minyan should indeed convene in the private home in such a situation.

1. *Is davening with the tzibur an obligation?* – Davening with a minyan is certainly a very important mitzvah and also an extremely wise thing to do because it is much harder for one's prayers to be answered when davening privately. Moreover, the Gemara coins someone who does not daven with the tzibur as a "bad neighbor"; to a large degree, he removes himself from the community. Poskim further point out that besides for the mitzvah of davening with the tzibur, one also gets the opportunity to perform the additional mitzvos of answering kedusha, kaddish, and barchu (which the Tashbetz vol. 2 #163 says is a mitzvah mid'Oraysa, but see Piskei Teshuvos siman 90 note 80). Nonetheless, Poskim debate if there is an actual *obligation* to daven with a minyan or if it remains a great *mitzvah* but not an obligation. From the wording of the Gemara (here and 6a) it is clear that davening with a minyan is extremely important, but there is no indication of it being an obligation. The wording of the Shulchan Aruch as well (90:9) lends to the understanding that a man should "try hard" to go to minyan, but not that it is a complete obligation. Indeed, Maharil (Minhagim, Eruvei Chatzeros #7) writes explicitly that it is not an obligation since one can concentrate (if he puts his mind to it) even when davening by himself. So too, Emek Beracha (Birchos Keriyas Shema #1, pg. 7) quotes a number of Poskim that write that it is not an obligation, and he adds that it appears this way from the wording of the Rambam as well. See Piskei Teshuvos (ibid. note 85) for other Acharonim who opined this way (Krach Shel Romi #6; Chavas Yair #115; Be'er Hetev 90:12 etc.). On the other hand, Igros Moshe (OC vol. 2 #27) explains that it is in fact a real obligation, pointing to the language of the Shulchan Aruch (90:16) who uses the term "tzarich" (*needs* to). (But this is also the language of the Rambam hil. Tefilla 8:1, and yet the Emek Beracha ibid. understood that the Rambam held it was not obligatory. Clearly he understood that the term "tzarich" does not necessarily indicate an obligation. Conversely, Igros Moshe explains that the wording of the Shulchan Aruch 90:9 ibid. does not necessarily mean that it is not an obligation; see also Piskei Teshuvos ibid. notes 83 and 84.) Other Poskim rule this way as well (Chasam Sofer vol. 6 #76 [86] ד"ה בנ"ץ; Toras Chaim OC 90:14; however, the Rishonim listed in Piskei Teshuvos ibid. note 79 do not seem to indicate one way or the other regarding this question). But in truth, Igros Moshe himself (vol. 1 #31 ד"ה והנה לכאורה) explains that this issue may be a matter of debate amongst the Rishonim. Nonetheless, Minchas Yitzchak (vol. 7 #6), after quoting Poskim on both sides of the issue, writes that the conclusion of "the expert Poskim" is that it is a real obligation. (He also writes that it is more of an obligation than listening to Keriyas HaTorah; but see his final paragraph further.) However, Igros Moshe concedes (vol. 2 ibid.) that since someone is in fact able to daven the main parts of davening even without a minyan, Chazal allowed various leniencies in regards to the obligation to attend a minyan, not requiring someone to go too much out of his way to fulfill this mitzvah (see story bottom of 7b; see also Piskei Teshuvos 90:9 for elaboration). The Poskim discuss many possible implications of the aforementioned debate: How much money does someone need to lose/not profit in order to attend minyan? Can someone vacation in a place in which he will not have a minyan? Can someone violate a Rabbinic prohibition if necessary to gather a minyan? How much weight is given to this mitzvah when it stands in the way of performing other mitzvos or learning Torah? To be sure, everyone agrees that there are instances in which a person can violate a mitzvah in the Torah in order to gather a minyan, as explicit on 47b that R. Eliezer freed his slave (which is generally prohibited) in order to have a tenth man for a minyan. But Chavas Yair (ibid.) notes that R. Eliezer only did as such in order that the *tzibur* would have a minyan; we cannot conclude from there that an *individual* may violate a prohibition in order to attend an existing minyan. (See Rivash #518 and Shulchan Aruch 55:22 and MB 55:73 that there is a much stronger obligation to assure that there is a minyan in the community so that Tefilla b'tzibur and kaddish and kedusha are recited in the community at large.) He also writes that it is possible that a rabbinic *prohibition* is stricter than a *positive mitzvah* of the Torah. Regarding someone who says that he has more kavana (intent) when davening privately than when davening in shul with a minyan, Igros Moshe writes (OC vol. 3 #7) that he should nonetheless daven in shul. But the Chazon Ish (גנזים ושו"ת חזו"א vol. 1 pg. 50 Tefilla #30) writes that such an individual should choose one Tefilla a week to daven by himself with extra intense kavana. Regarding someone who cannot attend the minyan in shul, the Gemara writes that he should nonetheless daven at the same *time* as the tzibur, for this too is a form of placing oneself as part of the tzibur, and Hashem attends more closely to the tzibur at large. (There may have been some Rishonim who did not have the line in the Gemara that instructs davening at the same time as the tzibur; see Rosh with Maadanei Yom Tov #6 and Einayim LaMishpat. But nonetheless this law is codified in Shulchan Aruch 90:9.)

2. *Creating "Eretz Yisroel" and "redemption" in Chutz La'aretz and "exile"* – Based on Megilla 29a that states that all shuls outside of Eretz Yisroel will eventually be replanted in Eretz Yisroel, Maharsha (here) explains that when someone is present in a shul it is as if he is situated in Eretz Yisroel. He writes that it is for this reason that when someone refrains from attending the communal prayer in shul, he essentially puts himself into exile. But someone who spends time in shul affords himself with long life which Hashem reserves for those who reside in Eretz Yisroel. Similarly, a shul is considered a "Mikdash Me'at" (a mini Beis HaMikdash). So when someone attends a shul he is essentially free from galus (exile) altogether: he is in a distinct spiritual zone; he *has* the Beis HaMikdash! (Interestingly, Rivash vol. 2 beg. of #518 implies that shuls had a status of Mikdash Me'at only once we were cast into

exile.) It is possible to add that just as davening in a shul is tantamount to being present in Eretz Yisroel, so too, the holiness of a shul adds to a person's wisdom and general spiritual psyche just as Eretz Yisroel is "machkim" (makes people wise). Ritva and Rabbenu Yonah explain further that when the Beis HaMikdash was in existence, we merited to have Hashem's presence felt in the world at all times, but after the destruction of the Mikdash, we can nonetheless merit His presence in such a manner when we involve ourselves in Torah, Tefilla, and Chesed. When performing these mitzvos, it is as if the Beis HaMikdash exists even today.

3. *Entering "two openings" into a Beis haknesses* – Shulchan Aruch (90:20) codifies three explanations offered by the Rishonim: don't stand right next to the doorway because it looks like you want to leave (unless your official seat is there); don't keep the door open to the reshus harabim (busy public domain) so as not to hinder your concentration; wait the amount of time it takes to walk "two openings" in order to enable concentration before davening.

4. *What should one pray for with extra emphasis?* – The Gemara offers various things for which a chasid should pray to be available for him at time of need: a good wife, the Torah, an easy death, a proper burial, and a bathroom. The Gemara concludes that the most prudent of all is to daven to always have a bathroom handy. A bathroom, as simple and menial as it may sound, can impact one's entire existence. It enables a person to be at ease and focus on the important things in his life. The other things mentioned in the Gemara similarly affect one's daily outlook. A wife can either be a source of joy and peace or she can be a source of the exact opposite: strife and discomfort (Heaven forbid). To daven for the Torah to be available is like davening for life itself, as opposed to davening for a bathroom which *sets the scene* for a productive life. Reminding oneself constantly of the hope for an easy death and a proper burial keeps one's end on his mind and thus keeps him in constant check.

5. *In what way does Hashem "reside in the 4 amos of halacha" nowadays as opposed to during the era of the Beis HaMikdash?* – Rabbenu Yonah and Maharsha explain that although the Shechina resides in a shul and in a beis medrash used for learning *any* part of Torah, there is a uniqueness to a beis medrash in which talmidei chachomim learn Gemara through which they conclude with an understanding of the correct halacha. Just as the Sanhedrin convened in a room in the Beis HaMikdash and provided halacha for all of Bnei Yisroel (see Maharsha), and just as the Beis HaMikdash was a place of permanent Torah study (see R. Yonah), so too, a beis medrash in which talmidei chachomim learn Gemara and halacha contains a unique level of kedusha. It could also be added that during the era of the Beis HaMikdash, we were able to relate to Hashem extremely deeply through the spiritual experiences of avoda and Tefilla that occurred in the Beis HaMikdash, but during Galus the keenest way to relate to Hashem is through the depths of understanding the halacha. Einayim LaMishpat points to the Gemara 32b that states that since the destruction of the Beis HaMikdash the "gates to Heaven" have been locked, so our path to Heaven is more heavily through halacha than prayer. (This may also explain why Neviim in Tanach often censure Bnei Yisroel regarding general love and fear of Hashem as opposed to specific details of halacha, for during the era of the Beis HaMikdash we felt an extreme closeness to Hashem not only through the details of halacha but also through emotional and spiritual experiences in the Beis HaMikdash and the like. So if the Navi perceived that we were deficient in this emotional experience it was indicative that our overall service of Hashem was greatly lacking. In today's world that close emotional bond is very weak, and we therefore focus most intently on the intellectually rigorous halacha to forge a bond and to provide a detailed account, step-by-step of how to do so. This idea also relates to the Netziv's introduction to his commentary on the She'iltos where he explains that the Kohanim during the era of the Beis HaMikdash received Divine inspiration to help instruct each individual according to his unique situation. After the destruction of the Beis HaMikdash, we lost this Divine inspiration and only have the more general tenets of halacha to guide us.) The Rambam (intro. to Perush HaMishnah ד"ה ונשאר) explains that "Hashem residing in the 4 amos of halacha" refers to the fact that the world was created for man who studies the depths of Hashem's mandates and lives based on those commandments. Einayim LaMishpat writes that it is possible that the Rambam's text did not distinguish between before and after the destruction of the Beis HaMikdash.

6. *Why is it better to daven in a place where one learns Torah and what are the parameters of this halacha?* – According to some Poskim, the Gemara is simply distinguishing between the heightened kedusha of a Beis Medrash and the somewhat lesser kedusha of a shul, noting that it is better to daven in the holier place (see language of Shulchan Aruch 90:18 and Igros Moshe OC vol. 1 #31 ד"ה הנה, והנה מלשון who explains this way based on the language of R. Yonah here). Others explain (see Rishonim quoted initially in Tur 90:18 and Tzlach here) that there is a preference to daven in the place where one personally learns Torah. It seems that his studying Torah creates a unique bond between him and Hashem in that place, and he tries to build off of that relationship and holiness (both psychologically and spiritually) when he davens. A third group of Poskim focus heavily on the concern for the talmid chachom's time: a great talmid chachom who spends all of his time learning and never wastes time may daven in the place that he learns so that he does not need to spend time traveling to shul and hence detract from his learning hours (see R. Yonah's addition here to the opinion of the Rambam, and see Rama 90:18 and the explanation of Igros Moshe ibid.). The

Rishonim also debate if it is better to daven in the place where one learns even if one would need to daven alone, or if davening with a minyan is more ideal. The Rosh (quoted by Tur and Rama ibid.) writes that even a great talmid chachom (who does not waste any time) should not make a habit of davening privately, for the rest of the community will perceive his actions as proof that davening in shul is unimportant and many people will end up taking davening lightly. (Similarly, the Rama remarks that a talmid chachom who is davening with a minyan should not learn Torah in shul while they recite extra prayers, for his actions will cause the rest of the congregation to take those prayers lightly.)

7. *May one leave the shul or talk before and after Torah reading and between aliyos?* – The Gemara and Poskim (see Shulchan Aruch 146:1) state that it is a disgrace to the Torah to leave the shul during Torah reading. Rabbenu Yonah states (see Einayim LaMishpat #7) that shaming the Torah in such a fashion is an issur mid'Oraysa (Torah prohibition). It should follow that the prohibition against talking during Torah reading represents a similar disgrace of the Torah, especially when speaking about subjects other than Torah. Indeed, Beiur Halacha (146:2 ד"ה והנכון) writes that talking during Torah reading is often an utter disgrace of the Torah, stating that this transgression is "too great to bear" and that is certainly worse than even abandoning shul altogether. He adds that such action also contains a possible public chilul Hashem (profaning Hashem's name) along with other transgressions (see there further). But we have seen (according to various Poskim) certain leniencies pertaining to talking in shul vs. leaving shul: a) Numerous Rishonim understand that one is allowed to learn Torah quietly during the Torah reading (as long as a number of conditions are fulfilled; see below), whereas we do not find permission to abandon the shul altogether. Leaving the shul is perceived as abandoning and thus dishonoring the Torah, whereas learning Torah quietly is simply another form of partaking in the word of G-d. b) Shulchan Aruch (146:1-2; see also Beiur Halacha beg. of 146) writes that one may not leave shul once the Sefer Torah has been *opened*, but talking in shul is only prohibited during the *reading* itself. Leaving while the Torah is open constitutes an abandonment of the Torah which will be read imminently, but talking before the Torah has been read is not perceived in such a light, for the individual is merely waiting for the Torah reading to begin. (Bach explains that leaving the shul between aliyos is not problematic since the Torah is not open, and it is therefore not perceived as abandoning the Torah. But Shulchan Aruch prohibits *speaking* between aliyos because his conversation can easily lead to speaking during the reading itself, as he explains in Beis Yosef.) Others disagree, however, with this distinction of the Shulchan Aruch: Rambam (hil. Tefilla 12:9) writes that both talking and leaving are only prohibited during the reading itself; Mishnah Berurah (146:4) quotes Magen Avraham and Gra that both are prohibited from the time that the Torah is opened; Einayim LaMishpat quotes Meiri with the opposite distinction of the Shulchan Aruch, ruling that speaking is prohibited immediately once the Torah is opened, but leaving the shul is only prohibited once the Torah is being read. Regarding talking between aliyos, Einayim LaMishpat explains differently than the Beis Yosef (ibid.), writing that speaking between aliyos is prohibited because it itself is considered a disgrace to the Torah, not simply because it will lead to speaking during Torah reading. But the Bach (146:4) disagrees with R. Yonah and the Shulchan Aruch altogether and writes that it is *permitted* to speak between aliyos. Yet it seems that even he only allows speaking words of Torah, as noted by Mishnah Berurah (146:6). R. Chaim Kanievsky Shlit"a (quoted in Dirshu ed. of MB 146 note 6) rules that it is permitted to wish someone "mazal tov" between aliyos since that it considered a mitzvah need. Some Poskim add that this prohibition was possibly never said regarding congregations that take lengthy breaks between aliyos for various tefillos; see Aruch HaShulchan (146:3) and Be'er Hetev (146:3). Pri Chadash (146:2) writes that it is permitted to speak even about non-Torah topics between aliyos. Piskei Teshuvos (146:3) quotes these sources as a "limud zechus" for many people who are not careful about this halacha.

8. *Is someone permitted to engage in other activities during Torah Reading?* – Besides for the *prohibition* of disgracing the Torah, it is also a *mitzvah* to pay attention to the Torah Reading. (See Rambam end of hil. Chagiga who beautifully describes how one should listen to the Torah Reading and how it can enhance one's fear of Heaven. Most Poskim hold that Torah Reading is a Rabbinic mitzvah, although some opine that it is a Torah commandment; see Ritva Megilla 17b and Piskei Teshuvos 90 note 80 and 125:1.) Nonetheless, the Gemara (here) states that it is permitted to learn Torah privately instead of following the public Torah Reading. Tosafos point to Gemara Sotah that ostensibly contradicts this leniency. The Rishonim answer the contradiction in numerous ways, differentiating between speaking aloud and quietly, between someone who learns constantly and other people, etc. (See Einayim LaMishpat for nine approaches; many are cited in Beis Yosef and Shulchan Aruch 146:2.) Practically, the Shulchan Aruch (end of 146:2) writes that it is most proper to pay attention to the Torah reading. (But see Shulchan Aruch 285:5 who writes that it is permitted to learn "shnayim mikra" during Torah reading; see MB and Beiur Halacha there.) Yet the Beiur Halacha on Shulchan Aruch 146 (ד"ה ויש מתירים) is exceedingly bothered by this entire discussion, for he understands that each individual has an obligation to listen to the entire Torah Reading, which is not possible while learning something else. (He quotes Shibolei HaLeket, cited in Beis Yosef, as an explicit source.) The Poskim discuss this question at length, whether listening to Torah Reading is incumbent upon each individual ("chovas ha'yachid") or only upon the congregation at large ("chovas ha'tzibur"); see notes (#8-11) in Dirshu ed. to MB as well as many others. (There is a

strong proof that it is *not* incumbent upon every individual from Gemara Megilla 21b; see question posed by Birchas Avraham there note 5.)

Short Notes on Berachos 8b

1. *What is the reason for the mitzvah to learn "שנים מקרא ואחד תרגום" and what are some parameters of this mitzvah? –* Einayim LaMishpat (8a) quotes various explanations: a) Some commentators understand (see intro. to Sefer HaChinuch) that this mitzvah is intended to ensure that each person knows the Torah. Just as Bnei Yisroel originally (when first receiving the Torah) learned the Torah 3 or 4 times (see there), we should also learn the Torah 3 or 4 times (2 mikra, 1 targum, 1 Keriyas HaTorah) each year. b) Other Rishonim understand that the main reason for this mitzvah is to prepare everyone for reading the Torah in shul. According to this opinion it would seemingly be proper to recite שנים מקרא with the correct pronunciation and tune ("trup"). Yet this opinion may hold that the obligation of שנים מקרא is no longer relevant given today's custom that a previously chosen individual reads the Torah for everyone. c) The Raavan understands that this mitzvah applies only to someone who is unable to attend the Torah Reading in shul, and he therefore must rectify the situation to the best of his ability by learning the Parasha on his own. d) It is possible to add another reason (not mentioned in Einayim LaMishpat) based on the Zohar (Teruma 132b, quoted in Maseches Shel Tefilla on U'va L'tzion pg. 125) that implies that the reason that we translate the Torah into Targum is in order to "lower" spiritual energy from the lofty world of the Written Torah into our human language which man can more easily inculcate into his essence. Some specifics of the mitzvah: a) During the time of some Rishonim there was a custom that the entire congregation would pause before the official Torah reading to learn שנים מקרא ואחד תרגום on their own or together. (They would literally learn the Torah "עם הצבור", as the wording of the Gemara implies.) b) From the wording of the Gemara it would appear that this mitzvah is not fully obligatory (see Tur as well). But Rambam (hil. Tefilla 13:25) and Shulchan Aruch (285:1) write clearly that this is a full-fledged obligation. c) Poskim further discuss numerous details regarding this mitzvah: should one recite each Pasuk with its Targum or all Pesukim together and then all of the Targum at the end? Is it ideal to recite Targum, Rashi, or another language that you understand (see Tosafos)? When is the ideal time to learn שנים מקרא, and what does someone do if he did not learn it before the proper time? See Einayim LaMishpat and the Poskim on Shulchan Aruch. I was told in the name of a couple leading modern-day Poskim that since many people are lax in this mitzvah altoegher, one can follow the lenient opinions on these issues (i.e. translating the Pesukim into English etc.) in order to ensure that he performs the mitzvah on at least some level, even if not in the most ideal form.

2. *Why is there a mitzvah to eat on Erev Yom Kippur and what are the parameters of this mitzvah? –* Einayim LaMishpat quotes numerous reasons according to various Rishonim for this obligation: a) Many Rishonim explain that we eat on Erev Yom Kippur in order to prepare for Yom Kippur; this mitzvah is an example of the idea that preparing to do a mitzvah is itself a mitzvah (see Meiri). The Rishonim explain this "preparation" in various ways: i) Some write that we eat in order to be healthy for the fast on Yom Kippur. ii) Others write the exact opposite, that eating on Erev Yom Kippur whets our appetite, making fasting on Yom Kippur more difficult and therefore a greater mitzvah with more "inuy" (affliction). iii) Yet others explain that eating on Erev Yom Kippur forces us to clearly *stop* eating and thus highlights that our refraining from eating on Yom Kippur is because of the mitzvah to fast. iv) R. Nebenzahl (Sichos L'Yom Kippur pg. 189-196, cited by R. Beinish Ginsburg) cites Midrashic sources to explain that Avraham "fattened" Yitzchak before bringing him as a korban on Yom Kippur; we too "fatten" ourselves in commemoration (and to figuratively act as "korbanos" ourselves, renewing our complete commitment to Hashem on Yom Kippur). b) Other Rishonim explain the mitzvah entirely differently, writing that the eating is not mere preparation or meant simply to highlight the fasting on Yom Kippur; rather, eating itself is a mitzvah. This idea can be explained in a couple different ways: i) Many explain that we need to have a "Yom Kippur meal" just like we have on all holidays, and since we cannot eat on Yom Kippur itself, we therefore eat this meal the day before. This meal displays our joy for the mitzvah of Yom Kippur and the holiness of the day. Yom Kippur is not a dark day that we try to minimize, but a great day (see Gemara Taanis 30b), and we anticipate its state of "inuy". ii) Other commentators explain that eating on Erev Yom Kippur is "inuy" (affliction) for the *soul* of a person, since the soul dislikes physical pleasures and "suffers" when the person eats. Hence, through eating on Erev Yom Kippur and then fasting on Yom Kippur, one "afflicts" both his soul and his body, and he can thus attain full atonement. Einayim LaMishpat raises numerous possible ramifications of this disagreement: Does someone who is sick and not allowed to fast on Yom Kippur nonetheless have a mitzvah to eat on Erev Yom Kippur? Are children who do not fast obligated to eat on Erev Yom Kippur? Is this mitzvah part of Yom Kippur itself and women are therefore obligated, or is this a separate time-bound mitzvah and women are exempt? (See Einayim LaMishpat and the Dirshu ed. of the Mishnah Berurah (beg. of siman 604) for further sources and possible ramifications of this disagreement.) Einayim LaMishpat also discusses whether this mitzvah is Rabbinic or sourced in the Torah itself. See also the Dirshu MB (ibid. note 2) who quotes some Poskim who had the practice to eat light fruit etc. *all day* and some who say that it is proper to have two complete meals with bread. Einayim LaMishpat, however, quotes some Rishonim who seem to assume that even a small amount of food is enough. (The various opinions may correspond to the aforementioned reasons for the mitzvah itself.) Nonetheless, from our Gemara it seems clear that eating on Erev Yom Kippur takes a significant amount time (and prevents someone from learning Torah for a lengthy period of time), and thus a semi-lengthy holiday-style meal would seem most fitting.

What emerges from our Gemara according to many opinions is that Yom Kippur is a two-day event: one of physical affliction and one of physical indulgence and joy. R. Nebenzahl (ibid.) further comments that eating and fasting together illustrates our complete service for the sake of Heaven in all facets of life. (Some commentators point out that Yom Kippur is similar to Purim in this regard, "Yom Ki-Purim", including a "fast" (Taanis Esther) and a day of physical joy (Purim day itself).) Interestingly, there is yet another halacha that commands us to celebrate Yom Kippur on part of the 9th of Tishrei: the main source for "adding" to holidays is written in regards to Yom Kippur ("Tosefes Yom Kippur"); see Yoma 81b. Thus the 9th of Tishrei paradoxically includes both a command to eat and a command to fast, for both eating and fasting are integral aspects of the Yom Kippur experience, as described.

3. *Why do we give honor to a talmid chachom who forgot his wisdom?* – Maharal (Nesiv HaTorah beg. ch. 12) explains that our deep respect for a talmid chachom does not emanate simply from his vast Torah knowledge, but from the fact that his wisdom has raised him to an exceedingly high level of G-dliness ("closeness to Hashem"). This G-dliness remains even after he forgets his Torah due to physical illness etc. Moreover, since his elevated level of G-dliness remains with him, his knowledge will eventually return to him in the Afterlife when bodily impediments do not exist. Einayim LaMishpat notes that Rambam and many Poskim do not mention this halacha. He raises the possibility that they understood this halacha as a "middas chassidus" (above the letter of the law). But perhaps the opposite is true: they understood that the Gemara is simply stating the obvious (we honor a talmid chachom due to his spiritual greatness, not simply because of his knowledge), and it is implicit in all already codified halachos.

4. *Is it ideal to marry a convert?* – The Gemara seems to indicate that it is less than ideal to marry a convert. (See also Rashi's language in Horios 13a ד"ה הכל.) Hagahos Yaavetz explains (see also Rashbam Pesachim 112b ד"ה לא תינסוב) that a convert and his progeny possess some impurity from before the conversion. See also Sefer Mishbatzos Zahav on Rus (pg. 44 and 89) and our notes on 19a for more sources that indicate as such. On the other hand, some of the greatest people of our history were or came from converts, such as Yisro, Dovid HaMelech, Rabbi Akiva, Onkelos etc. There is also an extra mitzvah to care for converts, and marrying them with this intention would therefore be a great mitzvah. Each individual case needs to be carefully considered on its own; the Gemara here offers one important side of the discussion. (See Hebrew essay printed in the back this kuntrus for further elaboration.) It should further be noted that some commentators explain that our Gemara refers only to the prohibition of a Kohen marrying a convert. See further in Sefer Daf al HaDaf and Einayim LaMishpat.

5. *Is one permitted to speak positively about evil people?* – The Gemara records Tanaim making positive statements about the Medians and Persians. Sdeh Tzofim quotes R. Chaim Palagi who questions why this is permitted as it seems to be a transgression of "lo sechanem", that one may not praise evil non-Jews. He answers that it is permitted to praise their character traits in a way that will teach and encourage us to follow those same positive traits. Sefer Daf al HaDaf explains similarly based on Yerushalmi Avoda Zara (1:9) that one is allowed to praise Hashem for creating a beautiful gentile, for this is not a praise of the person but of the Owner. So too here, the praise is directed towards the character traits, not the people. (For further discussion and parameters, see Tzitz Eliezer vol. 15 #47; Ateres Paz Even HaEzer vol. 1 #5; Ohalei Yaakov Devarim pg. 156.) Perhaps we can add that it is for this reason that the Gemara made a point to immediately follow the praise with a statement that the Persians are destined for Gehenom; clearly the "praise" was not intended for us to become close to the Persians, but to simply learn from some of their characteristics. (But see Megadim Chadashim here who quotes Midrashim that may indicate that this second statement disagrees with the first. But many commentators here do not understand as such. See also M'lo Haro'im in the back of the Gemara here who writes that there is even a positive aspect to the fact they are destined for Gehenom so that they can get spiritually cleansed, as opposed to going to a place with no hope at all. The Persians merited this spiritual cleansing because they allowed us to build the 2nd Beis HaMikdash.)

6. *Were the Persians modest or immodest?* – Our Gemara states that the Persians are modest in the way that they "eat, attend the bathroom, and have marital relations". Yet Gemara Megilla (11a; 12b) remarks that they "eat and drink like bears" and openly discuss and flaunt private marital matters. It can be explained that the Persians were indeed lustful, always seeking food and women to fulfill their every desire, but they nevertheless conducted themselves in an outwardly refined manner, eating with dignity and covering themselves in the bathroom and with their wives. (R. Chaim Kanievsky, commenting on our Gemara, briefly makes a similar point; see Asichah pg. 161.) Radak (Yeshaya 66:17) likewise writes that the Persians constantly wash themselves and give off a veneer of purity, but internally they are morally decrepit and licentious. (See also Maharal (Or Chadash pgs. 314-316; 423-427; note 1089 in Mechon Yerushalayim ed.) who further describes the Persians' and Achashverosh's modesty and concomitant immodesty.) It is interesting to note that we see a similar dichotomy regarding the descendants of Yishmael. On one hand they exemplify the trait of modesty (see Peleh Yo'etz entry "מחשבה", ד"ה ועל אחת; R. Avigdor Miller in Or Olam vol. 5 pg. 74; Levusha Shel Torah pg. 290; Matzmiach Yeshuah pg. 45-50), yet they are also considered terribly promiscuous, as described in Kedushin 49b (see further sources in Aromimcha Elokai HaMelech vol. 2 pg. 152 note 61; R. Tzadok

HaKohen quoted in Aspaklaria entry "Yishmael"). It can be explained that Chazal define a person's essence based on his deepest desires; even though Yishmael's descendants act with extreme *external* modesty, their essence is defined by their drive for wanton lusts that they believe await them after death (see Kuzari 1:5) and by their concealed immoral acts. (Conversely, many of the aforementioned sources define Esav's descendants as bloodthirsty, but not as lustful as Yishmael's descendants. Apparently, Esav's immoral acts are performed in a more perfunctory fashion and do not constitute their most fundamental drive.)

7. *"Walls have ears"* – Mahartz Chayes asks why Rashi quotes this phrase as merely "said by people" and did not quote the Medrash Raba that records this phrase. See also Sdeh Tzofim (end of the amud) who quotes a number of Midrashim with this phrase.

Short Notes on Berachos 9a

1. *What is the status of the time between alos hashachar and sunrise, and can the evening or morning Shema be recited during that time?* – The period of time between alos hashachar and sunrise contains aspects of both night and day, and there are therefore varying opinions in the Gemara and Poskim as to which feature is superior to define that phase. The Mishnah in Megilla (20a) states that, in general, mitzvos which are to be performed during the day may be performed from alos hashachar but should ideally be performed only after sunrise. Rashi (there) explains that it is considered "day" from alos hashachar, but because it still appears as night the Rabbis instituted that one should ideally perform the mitzvos from sunrise onward. Yet there are sources that prove that the obligation to wait until sunrise is not merely due to "appearance" but because it is essentially not considered "completely day" until sunrise. For example, according to Beis Hillel (Pesachim 55a), one is permitted to work the entire night until sunrise of the 14th of Nissan (even in places where work is forbidden on Erev Pesach). The Meiri explains that since this prohibition is not very strict, the Rabbis were lenient and allowed work until it is "completely day" (יום גמור). Similarly, R. Yonah (here) and Levush (#652) write that the "essence of day" (עיקר יום) only begins at sunrise. Indeed, Reshimos Shiurim here explains the aforementioned Mishnah in Megilla (according to Rabbenu Tam in Tos. in Yoma end of 37b) as saying that sunrise is the ideal time for day mitzvos according to Torah law, not merely m'derabanan. Tosafos (here and bottom of 8b) seem to understand that the two Beraisos quoted in our Gemara debate this very issue: whether this period is essentially night or day concerning mitzvos that need to be done during the day. Even though the Mishnah in Megilla (ibid.) clearly states that it is essentially day (Rashba 8b indeed raises this difficulty), Tosafos may understand that the Beraisa here disagrees with that Mishnah. (But see Reshimos Shiurim for an alternative approach to Tos.) Since this period contains aspects of both day and night, there is therefore a debate in our Gemara regarding the recital of Shema during this time. Some Rishonim understand (see Baal HaMor and Raavya) that the two Beraisos quoted in our Gemara disagree with one another about this point, and there are opinions that even though "day" begins at alos hashachar concerning other mitzvos, Keriyas Shema is different since it depends on the time when people sleep, which may extend until sunrise. Other Rishonim (Rif, Rambam, Shulchan Aruch 58:3-5, 235:4) explain that we accept *both* Beraisos, and this time between alos hashachar and sunrise can serve, when under duress ("אונס"; see some guidelines in Einayim LaMishpat ד"ה ובאו בניו), as either night or day for Keriyas Shema. But the Rosh (codified in Shulchan Aruch ibid.) qualifies this ruling and writes that on a day that someone utilizes this period as "night", he may no longer utilize it as "day" as well. Tosafos, however, seemingly disagree. The Rashba (quoted in the end of the Magen Avraham 58:6) points out that even though some people sleep a few hours past sunrise (and the daytime Shema can therefore be recited until the 3rd hour; see 9b), nonetheless, one cannot read the nighttime Shema after sunrise since that is "completely day". That is, even though the obligation of Shema mainly follows the times of sleeping/arising, nonetheless, it is also patterned after the night/day schedule. (See also notes on 2b regarding this issue.)

2. *Can one say the beracha of Hashkivenu or daven Maariv after alos hashachar?* – The Gemara states that one does not say "Hashkivenu" at this time. Most Rishonim understand (and Shulchan Aruch 235:4 codifies as such) that one should recite the rest of the berachos (two before Shema and one after), and only leave out Hashkivenu. The Mishnah Berurah explains that even though some people are sleeping during this time (and therefore one can recite the nighttime Shema when under duress), it is not a time when people *go* to sleep, and therefore Hashkivenu cannot be recited. There are a few minority opinions in the Rishonim on this issue: a) Rashi holds that Hashkivenu cannot be recited even slightly *before* alos hashachar since that is also not a time when people go to sleep. b) Tur quotes an opinion that the beracha of Hashkivenu *can* be said as long as the initial phrase "Hashkivenu" is skipped. c) Meiri quotes an opinion that even the *first* beracha ("Maariv Aravim") is not said. Nonetheless, the Shulchan Aruch and Poskim do not codify these opinions. Concerning Maariv, the Mishnah Berurah (235:34) writes that it may not be said. This ruling is rather sensible since after alos hashachar it is considered daytime for most mitzvos, the previous day's offerings can no longer be offered, and they begin the service of the morning korban Tamid. See Sefer Birur Halacha (on siman 235) who adds numerous proofs for this opinion. Nonetheless, the Aruch HaShulchan (end of 235) writes that one *may* daven Maariv, and Einayim LaMishpat adds a few sources for this opinion (but based on Kapach ed. it is clear that the Rambam's Perush HaMishnayos should not be used as a source for this). This opinion can be explained based on the idea found in the Rambam (hil. Tefilla 3:7) that the Rabbis were less exacting regarding the precise time for Maariv. Einayim LaMishpat adds that it is possible that they patterned Maariv to a degree after Shema, at least when under duress.

3. *What is the disagreement between the Chachomim and Rabban Gamliel regarding the timing for Keriyas Shema and how does the halacha conclude?* – The Gemara states (here and top of 4b) that the Chachomim and R. Gamliel agree that according to Torah law Shema can be recited all night; they disagree only on a Rabbinic level. The Rosh explains that the Chachomim held that the Rabbis enacted a law that one must recite Shema before midnight (lest he forget or fall asleep and not recite it at all), but according to R. Gamliel such an enactment was never made. The Rosh

understands that we indeed rule in accordance with the opinion of R. Gamliel, and one is not required to recite Shema before midnight. (Tosafos Anshei Shem on the Mishnah (ד"ה עד שיעלה) explains that the story quoted in the Mishnah and Gemara here discusses the period of time prior to the point when the Rabbis decided the halacha in accordance with R. Gamliel. Therefore, R. Gamliel responded to his sons according to the Chachomim's opinion.) Other Rishonim explain that even R. Gamliel agreed that Shema should ideally be read before midnight, and R. Gamliel and the Chachomim only disagree in a case when one did not do so, whether or not the Rabbis *uprooted* the mitzvah after midnight so that people will be careful to recite Shema early. According to this understanding of the Chachomim, one does not fulfill the mitzvah by reciting the Shema after midnight and the berachos should not be said at that point. (See R. Yonah 1a on Rif. This is an example of "עוקר דבר מן התורה בשב ואל תעשה", similar to the Rabbinic enactment against blowing the Shofar on Rosh Hashona when it coincides with Shabbos. Regarding the general question whether or not the Chachomim have the ability to make it as if a mitzvah was not performed, see debate surrounding Tosafos Succah 3a and Rishonim and Acharonim quoted in Kobetz Beis Aharon V'Yisroel vol. 123 pg. 152. It should also be noted that R. Yonah himself points out that one could make an argument that even if the mitzvah of Keriyas Shema does not apply after midnight, one may still recite the berachos of Keriyas Shema at that point, for the berachos of Keriyas Shema may be an independent Tefilla and patterned after Maariv just as Birchos Keriyas Shema in the morning can be recited even after the final time for Keriyas Shema; see notes on 10b. Yet, he explains that this opinion holds that the Chachomim were stricter regarding the timing for Birchos Keriyas Shema at night in order to ensure their recital.) According to these Rishonim (and Shulchan Aruch 235:3), the halacha (in accordance with R. Gamliel's opinion) dictates that one should read Shema before midnight, and waiting until after midnight is not ideal. (To explain the conversation in our Gemara, Pnei Yehoshua writes that R. Gamliel was telling his sons that the Chachomim agree with him regarding the Biblical obligation, and since they were only arguing on the Rabbinic level, his sons were therefore allowed to follow his minority opinion.) Some other Acharonim arrive at this same halachic conclusion but based on different reasoning; see further in Einayim LaMishpat 2a (ד"ה וחכמים אומרים) and Tosafos Yom Tov on our Mishnah (ד"ה עד שיעלה).

4. *Why did the children of Rabban Gamliel not pasken the halacha in accordance with their father?* – It is clear from our Gemara that R. Gamliel's children wanted to follow the majority opinion against the opinion of their father. At first glance this is baffling since the Poskim write (see Teshuvos HaRashba vol. 1 #253 and many others) that one is supposed to follow his Rebbe or the Rav of his town even against the majority opinion (unless they all sit in a Beis Din together and overrule him or the Sanhedrin rules against him; see notes on 11a). Pri Chadash (OC 496:11) explains that even though R. Gamliel was the Rav (R. Gamliel was the "nasi" and resided in Yavneh along with most other leading Rabbis at the time), nonetheless, even the Rav of the town should capitulate when disagreed upon by the majority of his peers. It could also be explained that R. Gamliel himself only held of his opinion in theory but not in practice (see Tosafos Anshei Shem ibid.), for in practice he was reticent to disagree with the Chachomim on the issue. (Based on the Pnei Yehoshua ibid., it seems that R. Gamliel had the *right* to rule according to his own opinion, but he did not want to do so regarding Torah law, and he therefore only ruled according to his own understanding on matters of Rabbinic law.)

5. *Do the mitzvos of Pesach night apply all night or only until midnight?* – Our Gemara records a dispute amongst Tanaim regarding this matter pertaining to korban pesach, and Gemara Pesachim 120b states that this same disagreement applies to the mitzvah of eating matzah as well. Einayim LaMishpat quotes a lengthy disagreement amongst the Rishonim and Poskim how the halacha concludes: some say that we may eat all night; some say only until chatzos; and some say that according to the Torah we may eat all night but the Rabbis enacted that we eat before chatzos so that we do not become remiss in this mitzvah. Some Poskim make a distinction between the mitzvah of eating korban pesach (which carries with it the punishment of kares for someone who is negligent in fulfilling it) for which the Rabbis required its fulfillment by midnight, and the mitzvah of eating matzah which is not as strict. Practically, Mishnah Berurah (477:6; Beiur Halacha there) codifies that a person must be very careful to eat a kazayis of matzah before chatzos, since this is a "safek d'Oraysa" (it is not clear what the halacha is, and this is a Torah law about which we must be extra strict). He writes that someone should also be careful to eat maror before chatzos, even though maror today is only a Rabbinic mitzvah. (But Binyan Shlomo by R. Shlomo Cohen, vol. 1 #29, explains that there is more room to be lenient regarding this mitzvah since it is Rabbinic today. See also wording of Tosafos Megilla top of 21a.) If someone did not perform these mitzvos before midnight, the Mishnah Berurah writes that he should eat matzah and maror after chatzos but not recite the "birchas hamitzvah" (special beracha made before performing a mitzvah) since it is not clear that he can in fact fulfill these mitzvos at this point in time. Einayim LaMishpat (end of 9a), however, quotes some Acharonim who write that a person indeed makes a birchas hamitzvah even after chatzos, either because the halacha is in accordance with those who say that the mitzvah applies all night, or because one is nonetheless required to perform the mitzvah, albeit "m'safek" (due to doubt). Regarding eating the afikoman which is eaten as a remembrance for the korban pesach, the Shulchan Aruch (477:1) writes that it should ideally be eaten before midnight just as the korban pesach was eaten at that time. But numerous people are not careful to do so, and many Poskim

defend their actions for various reasons (see Piskei Teshuvos 477:1; Haggada of Minchas Asher pg. 320; Mo'adaim U'zmanim vol. 7 #188). The Avnei Nezer (#381) famously offered a novel idea, explaining that a person can eat the afikoman twice, once immediately before midnight and again when he finishes his meal, and he can make the following condition: if the halacha requires one to eat it before midnight, then he is doing so, and if the halacha allows it to be eaten after midnight then the second afikoman should be considered the true afikoman. Some Poskim question his condition and offer varying, yet similar, ideas how one can cover all his bases (see Minchas Yitzchak 9:47-48 and Piskei Teshuvos ibid.). (One must recall that there is more room to be lenient with the timing for afikoman since it is only Rabbinic in nature. It is also possible that the Rabbis (according to R. Akiva) never decreed that it be eaten early as they enacted for the Torah commandment of matzah. See, however, Rashi and Rashbam Pesachim 119b and wording of Tosafos Megilla 21a that even afikoman is somewhat of a Torah law; see explanation of Minchas Asher ibid. pg. 249 and note of Shaar HaTziyun 477:4.) It should be noted, however, that from the fact that the Rishonim and Shulchan Aruch did not offer such a novel idea, it appears that they did not necessarily agree to the logic of the Avnei Nezer. The Avnei Nezer needs to assume that the prohibition of eating after partaking in the afikoman only applies during the time when the mitzvah of afikoman can be performed, and therefore it is permitted to eat after midnight according to those who opine that the afikoman needs to be eaten before midnight (and this allows for one to continue his meal and later fulfill the mitzvah again according to the other opinion). But Minchas Asher (ibid. pg. 320) and Divrei Shira (R. Eliyahu Levine on Pesach pg. 105) write that the prohibition against eating after afikoman extends even after the time of the mitzvah, for eating anything else after the meal detracts from the encompassing nature of the matzah as the defining element of the meal. This point is somewhat related to another important question: do any mitzvos of the night apply after midnight even according to the opinion that korban pesach and matzvah do not? Indeed, the Rishonim and Poskim debate (see Einayim LaMishpat; Rama 477:1 with MB and note 11 in Dirshu ed. of MB) if there is a need to finish the mitzvah of Hallel and drink 4 cups of wine before midnight. Many write that it is ideal to finish by then, but if one continues until a later hour he may still recite the beracha at the end of the Hallel. Some explain (see Binyan Shlomo ibid.) that Hallel is only Rabbinic and also that the beracha at the end of Hallel is not connected to the obligation to recite Hallel, but simply an added beracha of praise. It is also possible that all Tanaim agree that the mitzvos pertaining to discussing the laws and reenacting the story of Pesach (including Hallel and 4 cups of wine) apply throughout the night (the Gemara only explicitly mentions that korban pesach and matzah must be completed before midnight). Meshech Chochma (Parashas Bo 13:14) writes that certainly everyone agrees that discussing the hagadda all night is "praiseworthy". See also Haggada Shleimah (ch. 38) for a list of a number of practices mentioned in Rishonim based on the fact that the entire night is considered "Leil Shimurim" (a night of protection from Hashem), such as leaving the house-door open and not saying many of the standard tefillos for protection before going to sleep. It would seem that everyone can agree to these practices, even if one opines that the mitzvos of korban pesach and matzah need to be fulfilled before midnight.

6. *During what time of day were we redeemed from Egypt?* – The Gemara explains that we were "redeemed" (freed from our oppressors) at midnight, but we did not "leave" until day. (Daf al HaDaf quotes Zohar and Chida and that the night lit up at midnight as if it were day, but nonetheless, we did not leave Egypt until it was actually morning. See our notes on 4b regarding mentioning "redemption" at Maariv every night. See also Tur #693 for a dispute if redemption should be mentioned after reading the megilla at night, or if redemption mainly applies only during the daytime.) The Gemara continues to explain the aforementioned disagreement regarding the proper time to eat the korban pesach: everyone agrees that it was eaten (and commemorated as such for generations) before the full redemption; they only disagree if they finished even before the *partial* redemption or only before the *full* redemption (i.e. morning). It should follow, that on Pesach night throughout the ages, a primary focus of our commemoration of the redemption should be on the preparation immediately *before* redemption, since such was the case at the time when the original Pesach Seder occurred. Indeed, the main, full Hallel is recited with a beracha only the next day! (Some recite the Hallel at night with a beracha as well, but *everyone* agrees that the next day requires a beracha.) In other words, the Pesach Seder is not the climax of our Jewish experience, but the beginning.

1. *Why was it so important that Bnei Yisroel leave Egypt with great riches and why did Bnei Yisroel not want to do so?* – Taking riches from the Egyptians plays a prominent role in the exodus from Egypt: Hashem promised Avraham that they would do so, and then He made sure that this commandment was carried out by telling Moshe twice (Shemos 3:22, 11:2) and even "pleading" with him (as recorded in end of 9a). Hashem famously made this task easier for the Jews through the plague of darkness (when the Jews were able to search the belongings of the Egyptians in order to later know what to request from them), and during the exodus the Torah makes it clear that Bnei Yisroel indeed carried out this command. It seems that the reason that it was so important to leave with the riches of the Egyptians was not merely to make sure that the Jews would have great wealth, for Hashem could easily provide them with wealth in other ways (as He in fact did during the splitting of Yam Suf), but it was particularly important to make Egypt a barren wasteland, as explained in our Gemara through the word "וינצלו". Hashem wanted to display that when a kingdom attacks His people their success is only ephemeral, and in the end they lose everything that they originally gained. Pardes Yosef (on Shemos 11:2 ד"ה ובדבר"י) notes a similar point, that making Bnei Yisroel rich at Yam Suf would not have been a fulfillment of the promise to Avraham; the riches had to come directly from the Egyptians to the Jews. The Gemara records that the Jewish people nonetheless wanted to leave *without* the riches; they wanted to leave as soon as possible and did not want the "burden" of this wealth. The commentators explain (see Tzlach, Eitz Yosef in Ein Yaakov, HaEmek Davar Shemos 12:35, Or HaChaim Shemos 3:18) that if Bnei Yisroel would not have taken the Egyptians' riches, they could have simply left (for the Egyptians wanted them out at this point!), and they would have been completely free with no more troubles. But because they took the riches, the Egyptians later regretted sending them away and ended up chasing after them. Hence, the Jews were not free until a week later when the Egyptians drowned in the Yam Suf. But one can still be left baffled: why did Hashem have Bnei Yisroel "borrow" the Egyptians belongings and leave in a way that people can construe as theft and trickery? Why did He not orchestrate the demise of the Egyptians in another fashion? Indeed, numerous commentators (see Sanhedrin 91a; Rashbam, Ibn Ezra, and many others on Shemos 3:22) quote scoffers who refer to the Jewish people as cheats and thieves who fled with the Egyptians' money after promising to return in three days. And even though Chazal and the commentaries offer very good answers to the scoffers' question (see Sanhedrin ibid. that the Egyptians owed this money to the Jews; Rashbam ibid. that the Egyptians in fact did not *lend* the money but *gave* it; see also Seforno 3:22 and others), nonetheless why did Hashem write the Torah and orchestrate the events in such a fashion that could cause people to have this problem in the first place? (Moreover, see notes on 5b above that even taking something which is rightfully yours can sometimes be forbidden if it makes one appear as a thief.) Perhaps one can explain that Hashem wanted the Jews to leave in a fashion where they would indeed feel like runaway thieves, and the only way for them to justify their actions was by putting their faith in the command of Hashem who told them to leave in this seemingly ill-mannered fashion. In fact, Ibn Ezra (Shemos 3:22) writes that the reason that Bnei Yisroel were not considered thieves is due to the simple fact that everything in the world truly belongs to Hashem, and He has the right to take money from one person and give it to another person in any manner He desires. In other words, Hashem orchestrated that the only way that Bnei Yisroel could justify their actions was by putting full faith in Hashem; this was Hashem's goal! Hence we find that Bnei Yisroel's exodus displayed the triumph of Hashem's sovereignty over the world, but it also entailed the Jewish people themselves feeling like fugitives, with no hope besides cleaving to Hashem's will. This dichotomy can also be seen in the exact manner that Bnei Yisroel left Egypt: On one hand, Hashem made sure to take them out "b'etzem hayom hazeh" (in the middle of the day; Shemos 12:17) in order to display that the Egyptians had absolutely no control against His will (see Sifri on Parashas Ha'azinu 32:48). Similarly, the Medrash (Tanchuma Bo end of #7) relates that Moshe remarked to Pharaoh that the Jews will leave in the morning and not at night like thieves. The Gemara (bottom of 9a) also quotes Bamidbar 33:3 that the Jews left "b'yad rama" (upraised hand). But on the other hand, Hashem wrote the Pesukim in a way that implies that Bnei Yisroel were pushed out quickly at night (see Shemos 12:34 with Rashi). Indeed, the matzah also famously represents the fact that we left quickly, and the Torah stresses that everything was done with haste "בחפזון", as described on 9a. It seems that Hashem wanted to display His omnipotence as well as His closeness to Bnei Yisroel, but at the same time, to make sure that Bnei Yisroel did not feel that they were emancipated and now free from all bonds. Rather, Bnei Yisroel were rushed from the dominance of the Egyptians to the sovereignty of Hashem. Indeed, Maharal explains (Gur Aryeh Devarim 16:3) that Hashem made sure that Bnei Yisroel were rushed out of Mitzrayim and unable to wait for their bread to rise in order to show them that *He* was taking them out; they were not leaving on their own volition.

2. *Explanation of the conversation between Hashem and Moshe regarding Bnei Yisroel's future exiles* – Ramban (Shemos 3:13) explains that Hashem was informing Moshe that the best proof to Hashem's closeness to Bnei Yisroel is the fact that He is and will be with them throughout all difficult times. But Moshe remarked that even though this is true, it is difficult for man to relate to this point, for man does not like to think about future tragedies. Hashem "agreed" that even though the fact that He will be with us in all difficult times depicts greater love, nonetheless, Moshe should only speak to Bnei Yisroel about the current situation, for that is all that they can currently comprehend. (This

conversation parallels Eliyahu's plea to Hashem as well; he asked that Hashem not only cause the miracle, but also make sure that people comprehend it rather than misconstrue it.)

3. *Explanation of the disagreement in the Mishnah regarding the latest time that one can fulfill the mitzvah to recite Shema in the morning* – Tos. Yom Tov explains that the first opinion in the Mishnah understands that one is required to recite Shema by sunrise like the "vasikin", whereas the second opinion understands that "vasikin" is only the most ideal way to perform the mitzvah, but one can nevertheless fulfill the mitzvah until the last point when people still rise in the morning. R. Akiva Eiger doesn't like this explanation and therefore writes that the first opinion holds that Shema must be recited before the time when *most* people rise, i.e. before sunrise, whereas the second opinion says that Shema can be recited as long as *some* significant people are still rising, i.e. kings. (Regarding the question whether Shema must be recited by the beginning or the end of the third hour of the day, see our notes on 3b.)

4. *What color is techeles?* – Rashi here refers to techeles as "ירוק", green, leaning towards the color of a leek. Rashi also explains this way in the beginning of Parashas Terumah. Rashi in the end of Shelach adds that it is the color of the sky when it darkens towards the end of the day. The Gemara in Menachos 43b writes that techeles is similar to the sea which is similar to the sky. Tosafos in Succah 31b initially understand that to be blue, but they then quote the Yerushalmi that adds that the color is also similar to grass, which is green. Hence it seems that techeles is a blueish-green, but slightly closer to green than to blue. But Tiferes Yisroel here seems to understand that it is mostly blue. Rambam (hil. Tzitzis 2:1 with Sefer HaLikutim in back of Frankel ed.; Klei HaMikdash 8:13 with Mahari Kurkos) also seems to understand that it is mostly blue, like the bright sky, but it has a tint of green. Rambam in commentary on Mishnah here also seems to write this way (see notes 16 and 17 in Kapach ed.).

5. *What is the reason for the various opinions regarding the earliest time to recite Shema and put on tallis and tefillin?* – We have seen (see notes on 2b and 8b) that Keriyas Shema is patterned after a combination of the periods of night/day and sleep/awaking. The Gemara here (and explained further in Menachos 43b and Yerushalmi here beg. of 1:2) expounds upon the exact period that is considered "day" for this mitzvah and explains that it is based on the ability to distinguish between various phenomena. The most easily understandable is the opinion that connects the time to recite Shema with the ability to fully see the tzitzis, for the mitzvah of tzitzis represents all 613 mitzvos, and Shema entails accepting those mitzvos upon oneself ("kabbalas ol Malchus Shamayim"). The other opinions in the Gemara can perhaps be understood to represent the idea that one's renewed service of his Creator (which he accepts at the beginning of each day by reciting Shema) only fully begins at the point where he is able to distinguish between his surroundings, when he has a renewed and bright perspective on the world around him. The Ramban (quoted in Magen Avraham 58:6) adds that this time also relates to the period of "rising", explaining that most people don't rise until this time. (Nonetheless, in time of need one may recite Shema from alos hashachar, the beginning of the daytime, since that is nonetheless "day"; see notes on 9a. And as for "vasikin", see below.) Regarding the earliest time to wear tefillin, R. Yonah writes (quoted in Beis Yosef OC 30) that since the Torah refers to "seeing" tefillin, therefore, one should only wear them at a time when one can distinguish between various objects, as above. It can be explained that just as one accepts his renewed service through Keriyas Shema, one literally wraps himself in this mindset through the mitzvah of tefillin, and the times for these mitzvos therefore coincide. (For another ramification of the phrase "seeing" regarding tefillin, see Rosh hil. tefillin printed in the end of Gemara Menachos pg. 121a with note 10 of Maadanei Yom Tov.) The Levush (30:2, followed by Pri Megadim and Mishnah Berurah) adds another reason for this time, explaining that it is still considered "night" to a large degree at this early hour, and the Rabbinic decree to not wear tefillin at night (lest one fall asleep with the tefillin) still remains until the point when one can recognize his friend. As for the mitzvah of tzitzis, Rishonim here (see Rashba and others) explain that it begins at a similar time to that of tefillin since the idea of "seeing" is explicit in the Pasuk regarding tzitzis and all of the aforementioned reasoning applies. R. Moshe Feinstein (Igros Moshe OC vol. 4 #6 ד"ה ומה שהכרעתי) goes so far as explaining that this time is mandated by the Torah itself for the mitzvah of tzitzis, whereas it is only Rabbinic regarding Keriyas Shema and tefillin. (Others disagree, however; see Sho'el U'Meishiv telisa'ah vol. 2 #162 and Minchas Yitzchak vol. 9 #9.) The Rama (18:3), however, based on Mordechai and Raavya, writes that one can ideally perform the mitzvah of tzitzis as early as alos hashachar, explaining that one is already able to see at that point, and the Gemara only required the ability to see very clearly in order to perform the mitzvah of Keriyas Shema. (The difference in language of the Shulchan Aruch regarding the earliest time for tzitzis (18:3) and tefillin (30:1) and Shema (58:1) is also noteworthy; see there. But Poskim discuss how seriously to take this variance in language; see Einayim LaMishpat and others.) Yet other Poskim, however, strongly question and disagree with this opinion (see Gra quoted in MB on Rama and Igros Moshe ibid.). (Regarding leniencies for someone who needs to daven early due to work etc., see Igros Moshe ibid. and OC vol. 1 #10 and Minchas Yitzchak ibid. Regarding the earliest time for Tefilla in such a scenario, see also Pri Yitzchak #2 along with many others. See also further discussion in Hebrew essay printed in the back of this kuntrus. This entire issue is also complicated by the lengthy disagreement regarding the exact time for alos hashachar and "mi'sheyakir"; see Beiur Halacha beg. of 89 and note 2 in Dirshu ed. there.)

6. *When is "vasikin" and what is the obligation to daven at that time?* – The Rishonim disagree (see Beis Yosef 58:1 and Einayim LaMishpat here) regarding the exact time that the vasikin recited Shema and davened; some explain that they recited Shema at (or right after) sunrise and then davened, but the Shulchan Aruch (58:1) codifies that they said Shema right *before* sunrise and davened during (and immediately after) sunrise. The issue is further confounded by the fact that the Poskim disagree how to define "neitz hachama" (the time that we usually refer to as "sunrise"); see Beiur Halacha 58:1 (ד"ה כמו) with Piskei Teshuvos there. See also Teshuvos HaRambam (#255) who writes that "דיוק הזמן אינו מחוייב אלא הוא לפי מה שמתקבל על דעת המתפלל שהוא הוא הזמן" (one does not need to be completely exacting in the time, rather he should act according to that which seems sensible). The Rishonim disagree if davening at the time of the "vasikin" is "l'chatchila" (ideal) and doing anything less is considered only "bedi'eved", or if davening at this time is exceptionally laudable, but davening at "mi'sheyakir" is still considered "ideal" (see Beis Yosef 58:1 and Pri Yitchak ibid.). Practically, the Shulchan Aruch codifies that it is in fact considered "ideal" to recite Shema even as early as "mi'sheyakir". The Rishonim further disagree if the Pasuk on which the time of the "vasikin" is based (" ייראוך עם שמש") refers to the recital of Shema or to Tefillas Shacharis. Rashi seems to understand that it refers to Shema, but the Tur and Shulchan Aruch (see 89:1 and 58:1) seem to understand that the Pasuk refers to Shacharis. See Einayim LaMishpat that this disagreement is connected to the aforementioned disagreement regarding the exact timing for "vasikin" (if Shema is recited right before or after sunrise). One ramification of this disagreement concerns a situation when one will not be davening Shacharis until much later in the morning, if he should nonetheless recite Shema at sunrise.

7. *When should one ideally daven Mincha?* – Rashi writes that the ideal time is when there are "dimdumei chama" (last rays of sun before night), but Maharsha argues that we don't find such a halacha anywhere. See 29b.

8. *Are we supposed to run and give honor even to evil kings?* – See 58a.

9. *What is so special about being somech Geula l'Tefilla and how much does it apply at Maariv?* – See notes on 4b. Tosafos (here) write that it is especially important to be somech Geula l'Tefilla along with davening in the morning at the time of vasikin. This ideal time and form of davening work together to create a unique closeness with our Creator through Tefilla.

10. *In what way does the beracha of Hashkivenu refer to Geula?* – See notes on 4b.

11. *To what degree is Hashem sefasai tiftach considered part of Shemoneh Esrei?* – See notes on 4b.

12. *What does "olam haba" refer to?* – Rashi here uses the term "olam haba" when referring to the time of Mashiach. There are a few more places where "olam haba" refers to the time of Mashiach, but usually "olam haba" refers to the afterlife (see Einayim LaMishpat here; Yad Ramah (Sanhedrin 90a from pg. 336 ד"ה ואם תשאל through pg. 339 ד"ה ויש מקומות); Rash MiShantz (letter printed in the back of Yad Rama on Sanhedrin, pg. 19). See notes further on 17a.

13. *Is the Pasuk of "y'heyu l'ratzon imrei fi" part of ch. 18 or 19 of Tehillim?* – Maharsha (here) and Bach (on Tur beg. #117) explain that Dovid originally organized Tehillim as such that the first two Perakim ("ashrei ha'ish" and "lamah rigshu") constituted just one chapter, leaving "y'heyu l'ratzon" at the end of ch. 18. But when the Rabbis later added a 19th beracha into Shemoneh Esrei (see bottom of 28b), they also split the first chapter of Tehillim into two (as we have it today in our Sefer Tehillim), leaving "y'heyu l'ratzon" as ch. 19. (Apparently, splitting a chapter in Tanach does not constitute "changing" Tanach, for the Rabbis would never actually *change* any part of Tanach. See also Rashi and Tosafos on Megilla end of 17b; Bach ibid.; and Teshuva Me'Ahava vol. 1 #111 regarding the exact number of chapters in Tehillim.) Regarding a general approach in deciding between the Scriptural text as quoted in the Gemara and the text before us in the Tanach itself, see Artscroll Gemara here end of note 62 for sources that we assume like the text of the Tanach and not like that of the Gemara.

1. *Females knowledgeable in Torah* – Our Gemara relates a couple stories illustrating Beruria's depth in Torah knowledge. See Sdeh Tzofim (here) for numerous other examples of such knowledgeable women during the periods of the Gemara, Rishonim, and Acharonim.

2. *Are we allowed to daven for evil people to perish?* – See notes on 7a that even if we are permitted to *kill* a heretic, we may not *curse* him in order to "force" the hand of Hashem to kill him. See there further for a debate amongst commentators if our daily Tefilla in Shemoneh Esrei of "v'lamalshinim" is a request for evildoers to *die*, or for them to do *teshuva*, in line with our Gemara. Tos. HaRosh (here) adds that even though it is generally improper to pray for an evildoer to die (as he understands from 7a), R. Meir thought that when the evildoer is exceedingly bad or is bothering him tremendously it is permitted to pray for his death. Beruria, however, told R. Meir (and the Gemara seemingly accepts her opinion) that one should pray for the evildoer to teshuva even in such a situation. But it is possible that even according to the conclusion of the Gemara, if the evildoer is causing imminent danger to other innocent people and praying for him to do teshuva is not working, it would indeed be proper to daven for his demise. See also Megadim Chadashim here who quotes a few Acharonim who write that one may pray for the death of a *heretic*, while our Gemara is only referring to someone who sins but is not an absolute heretic. The commentators also raise a difficulty in praying for evildoers to do teshuva: Based on the dictum that "everything is in the hands of Heaven except for fear of Heaven", Maharsha asks how someone can pray for another individual to repent; it would seem to be a "tefillas shav" (a meaningless, and therefore improper, prayer) since repentance is not in the "hands of Heaven"! Some Poskim answer (see Igros Moshe OC vol. 4 40:13 and Megadim Chadashim) that the focus of the prayer is that Hashem should afford the evildoer with opportunities that will arouse his soul to repent, not that Hashem should bring about the actual repentance itself. Me'il Tzedaka (#7) writes that one can only pray for an evildoer to repent if the rasha is affecting *others* in some negative way (bothering them etc. as in our Gemara; see there further for a few other similar ideas) and therefore the prayer is in order to help others (or oneself). He adds that one can also pray for Hashem to help the rasha perform teshuva if the rasha first expresses some inner sign of repentance. Megadim Chadashim further quotes some Acharonim who explain that it is not considered as being brought about by the hands of Heaven since a *person* is davening for the Divine assistance, even though the sinner himself is not the one praying. For further discussion of this question, see R. Yisroel Reisman's "Pathways of the Prophets" (pg. 255-262).

3. *Is it proper to rejoice when evildoers die?* – The Gemara relates (here and bottom of 9b) that Dovid HaMelech sang praise to Hashem when his evil enemies perished. The Maharsha (9b) questions the appropriateness of this praise, since we know that Hashem did not allow the angels to sing praise when witnessing the demise of the Egyptians. The commentators explain as follows (see Maharsha and Maharal Sanhedrin 39b; Maharal in Gur Aryeh Bamidbar 18:8 based on numerous Gemaros etc.): It is certainly not "good" when anyone perishes, for Hashem truly wants only positive outcomes for all of His creations. Therefore, Hashem does not allow the upper realms (angels) to rejoice over the demise of evil, since this destruction is not good in its essence. Nonetheless, from the perspective of mankind, it is indeed a positive gain for the world when evil people desist, and therefore man can, and sometimes must, respond in jubilant song over the destruction of evildoers. This distinction also explains why Bnei Yisroel sang "Shiras HaYam" when crossing Yam Suf, whereas the angels (from the perspective of the Heavens) were not allowed to rejoice. Similarly, Gemara Megilla 10b relates that the Jews praised Hashem for His Divine assistance in conquering the enemy, but they left out the adjective that Hashem is "good" in that situation, since destruction is not an expression of His ultimate goodness. (This also explains why we are hesitant to pray for the destruction of evildoers, even though we ourselves are sometimes permitted to destroy them ourselves, as mentioned above.) The commentators further point out (see Chazon Ish OC 56:4 ד"ה ומ"מ and others) that even when man rejoices over the destruction of evil, one must do so as an expression of happiness over the increased honor of Heaven that was brought about through the demise of evil, but one may not do so out of personal aggrandizement, sheer nationalism, or other selfish interests. The commentators (Tzlach 9b; Ze'ev Yitrof on Pesach ch. 96) also quote the Zohar that even Hashem is happy over the destruction of evil if the evildoer has reached the point where he *deserves* to be obliterated and is not simply punished out of Divine mercy towards another individual. My Rebbe, R. Moshe Stav Shlit"a, explained that in such a situation the evildoer has exhausted all of his positive attributes and he is now "completely evil", and it is therefore not bad in any way to destroy him, for no "good" is lost through his demise. (For a different approach to the topic, see Chavas Yair and Chida quoted in Daf al HaDaf here. See also Hebrew essay printed in the back of this kuntrus for further elaboration of the topic.)

4. *Why do we rejoice over our terrible state of exile?* – The Gemara states that Bnei Yisroel gloat to the nation of Edom over the fact that we are more righteous than they are and that we will not have to endure Gehenom as they will. The Gra explains that it is precisely due to our exile that we are able to remain righteous, whereas Hashem would have otherwise allowed us to remain sovereign over our own land of Eretz Yisroel but succumb even further to evil and

receive terrible punishment in Gehenom. Therefore, exile is (to a degree) a reason for joy! It could be explained that the trials and tribulations of exile force us to focus on the need to improve ourselves, and when we do, we will eventually merit the afterlife as well as our land. (It should be noted that Metzudos Dovid and Radak on the Pasuk in Yeshaya on which this Gemara is based explain the Pasuk completely differently than our Gemara, writing that the Pasuk refers to the future time of Mashiach when the land will no longer be barren.)

5. *What do the five "worlds" of Dovid's praise represent?* – The commentators explain (see Pnei Yehoshua along with numerous kabbalistic commentators; see also Maharsha) that a person's soul (similar to the human psyche) is not static; rather, it changes and grows through various experiences. They explain that there are 5 levels to the soul: "nefesh", "ruach", "neshama", "chaya", and "yechida". Pnei Yehoshua writes (see also R. Tzadok HaKohen's Sichas Malachei HaShares pg. 24a-24b) that the first three levels of a person's soul are attained by all individuals: the "nefesh" is the life-force extant in all living beings; "ruach" allows for an individual to react to surroundings etc. (similar to the wind) and therefore mature and grow (respond to various magnificent creations, as Dovid expressed); "neshama" adds a level of understanding and wisdom to the individual, and it therefore begins to grow as the baby nurses from the place of "bina" of its mother, soaking up some of her innate wisdom and intuition. "Chaya" is only attained after one achieves a higher degree of character perfection and therefore lives with an outlook imbued with wisdom and propriety (i.e. he has conquered evil, as Dovid expressed). The highest level of the soul, "yechida", was only attained during one's lifetime by Moshe Rabbenu, but all tzadikim will attain these heights after death when they experience immense closeness with Hashem (see below). (Nefesh HaChaim 1:15 writes that only Moshe attained the level of "neshama", but it seems that the he may be referring to sub-levels within the "neshama"; see there 2:17 and 4:28.) The Gra (Beiurei HaGra on Berachos here #44) and others add that these five "worlds" correspond to the five characteristics of the soul listed in our Gemara. This idea can be explained as follows: the life-force ("nefesh") of the person drives ("fills") one's entire being; the "ruach" of a person allows him to see and experience; a person's ability to understand ("neshama") sustains one's inner desire to search, mature, and attain higher levels of being; the level of "chaya" is achieved through purity of character; "yechida" refers to an extremely close, private bond that one attains with Hashem. (The Gra, however, explains the correspondence in a slightly different order, writing that "sustaining" refers to "nefesh", "filling" to "ruach, and "seeing" to "neshama"; see there.) It is the individual's task to make his way up these levels and attain the greatest heights that he can.

6. *Looking at the place of ervah* – Sdeh Tzofim notes that our Gemara implies that there are negative effects even for a *baby* to see the place of ervah of a woman. He writes that the Satmar Rebbe and the Chazon Ish therefore disapproved of bringing boys, even when extremely young, to a place where women are not dressed (swimming pools etc.). (It should be noted, however, that our Gemara only refers to the actual makom ervah.)

7. *Which is better, life or death?* – The Gemara records that Dovid HaMelech sang praise when he recalled the phenomenon of death. We previously mentioned that his praise was due to the fact that a tzadik will attain tremendous closeness with Hashem ("yechida") only after death when he will merit to experience more of G-d's presence. This idea is explained by the Gra (Beiurei HaGra ibid.). Yet, it is well known that the Gra himself was deeply saddened when he was nearing the end of his life and could no longer serve Hashem in this world (see story quoted in essay #2 in the back of Halichos Shlomo on Tefilla). To reconcile the ostensible contradiction, my Rebbe, R. Mayer Twersky Shlit"a explained that while in this world, the Gra was completely enveloped in his deep desire to serve his Creator and therefore did not want to leave even though the next world would most certainly offer even greater closeness to Hashem. A similar idea can be used to explain the two seemingly contradictory halves of the Mishnah in Avos (4:17) regarding the uniqueness of our current world and the next: Our world is special for the fact that we can *serve* our Creator, and this service itself creates wondrous closeness (see Maharal on Avos there). Yet the spiritual heights and pleasure that one will attain in the next world far surpass all degrees of pleasure that one can experience in this world (see famous words of Ramchal in beginning of Mesillas Yesharim; see also Rashi and Meiri on Avos ibid.; R. Avraham ben HaRambam's Sefer HaMaspik l'Ovdei Hashem pg. 313 in Hebrew Feldheim ed.; Tzlach Berachos 16b ד"ה א"ר אלעזר). Nonetheless, when one is still in this world and enjoying serving G-d to his fullest, he craves the ability to continue to serve his Creator and is deeply saddened when forced to stop. (For further statements of the Gra on this issue, see Ruach Chaim on Avos ibid. with footnote #67 in R. Goldberg ed. These sources are also quoted in the Hebrew essay regarding honoring the deceased, printed in the back of this kuntrus.) It must be stressed, however, that the Torah repeatedly emphasizes the importance of life (e.g. a dead body contains the highest form of impurity; it is an obligation to care for one's health and to violate almost any mitzvah in order to save a life etc.) to teach us that one must not desire death even though he realizes that an even greater world awaits him after death. It is the love of life and the desire to serve G-d for as long as He permits that allows us to attain higher degrees of perfection and greater closeness to Hashem, both in this world and the next. Michtav Me'Eliyahu (vol. 4 pg. 221) develops this idea further, explaining that Hashem instilled a love for life into every person, and that this love of life is in truth a desire to utilize

each moment to provide further honor to Hashem's great name. Only people who have lost much of their innate spiritual makeup take their own lives lightly and unnecessarily put themselves into situations of danger.

8. *Which is greater, aggadeta or halacha?* – R. Yaakov Emden (notes in the back of the Gemara) points out that our Gemara depicts R. Yehoshua ben Levi as proficient in the depths of aggadeta (esoteric teachings of the Torah), but the Yerushalmi (Shabbos 16:1, 79b) and Maseches Sofrim (16:2) record that R. Yehoshua refrained from reading books of aggadeta and strongly warned against it. R. Emden explains that both are true: Aggadeta contains the deepest, most secretive ideas of the Torah, and it is therefore a great form of Torah study for those who can understand it. But if someone who is not fitting to properly comprehend the ideas learns aggadeta, he will be wasting his time at best, and he can sometimes even emerge with incorrect and harmful ideas. R. Yehoshua ben Levi therefore refrained from learning aggadeta unless he was taught by someone who knew how to explain the ideas properly and sufficiently (see commentary of Kisei Rachamim on Maseches Sofrim ibid. in the name of the Radvaz). This also explains the Yerushalmi (Maasros 3:4, 17b) that Z'eirah told his son to only learn halacha and not aggada, since aggada can be explained "one way and its opposite" and "you do not learn anything from it". Even though aggadeta is clearly an integral part of the Torah (see Maseches Sofrim ibid.), nonetheless, he felt that we do not understand it and therefore should not learn it.

9. *Comparing Hashem to man* – Nefesh HaChaim (2:5) points to our Gemara (five parallels between Hashem and the human soul) as one of numerous examples where the Torah and Chazal use the structure and character of man as the best model to understand Hashem. But he cautions not to (Heaven forbid) think that we can truly compare the two, for in truth Hashem is limitless and cannot be defined. These descriptions are simply to assist our understanding, not to actually define G-d in any way.

10. *Hashem's multifaceted governance over the world* – The Gemara describes Hashem as a masterful "compromiser". This is indicative of the manner by which Hashem runs the world in general: He often handles the multiplicity of variables in the world with a single action that takes care of all issues. In the story described here, Hashem both punishes Chizkiyahu and causes Yeshaya to visit Chizkiyahu through one act of bringing illness upon Chizkiyahu.

11. *Whose honor is greater: prophet or king?* – See Einayim LaMishpat here, Machazeh Elyon (10:4), and Nachalas Shimon (Melachim 2 vol. 2 #31) who discuss this issue at length. Einayim LaMishpat concludes by positing that a navi needs to display reverence and submission when in the presence of the king so that the entire nation will honor and follow the king fully. But the navi may be intrinsically greater, and he therefore does not necessarily need to appear before the king when called; the king may have to come to him. It could also be that they are equal in this regard, and therefore various prophets and kings acted differently in this situation. This point was therefore the center of the debate between Yeshaya and Chizkiyahu, as clear in the Gemara. (It should be noted that these great men were obviously not arguing for their own personal honor but for the honor of Hashem, for each person represented Hashem in a different way.) Meiri (here) similarly concludes that the navi and king are equal in this regard, adding that the navi also leads the nation to a degree, along with the king.

12. *Is one permitted to refrain from performing a mitzvah due to negative outcomes that he foresees stemming from the mitzvah?* – Nefesh HaChaim (1:22) famously quotes Yeshaya's response to Chizkiyahu as a directive that we may not make our own calculations regarding the consequences of mitzvos. Rather, we must follow Hashem's commandments and let Hashem decide the appropriate consequences. He further explains that before the Torah was given (during the time of the forefathers etc.), one *was* supposed to take the consequences of and the reasons behind mitzvos into account, but since the Torah was given we may no longer make such calculations. (See Nachalas Shimon Melachim 2 vol. 2 #31:12,15 who quotes from Sichos Mussar and Brisker Rav who also understood that Chizkiyahu's mistake was that he made his own calculations contrary to the letter of the law.) Nonetheless, my Rebbe, R. Tzvi Schachter (B'ikvei HaTzon #3 pg. 16) notes that this dictum must be modified, for Chazal write (Yevamos 90b and elsewhere) that the Rabbis and prophets are told to periodically suspend various mitzvos when absolutely necessary and appropriate, utilizing various halachic mechanisms and reasoning ("חלל שבת אחת כדי", "הוראת עשה", "עוקר דבר מן התורה" , "עבירה לשמה", "שישמור שבתות הרבה" etc.). He further points to the Nefesh HaChaim himself (in Sefer Kesser Rosh) who agrees that even *after* the Torah was given there were unique circumstances when it was permitted to violate the Torah for a greater good (i.e. Yael's "sin" in order to save all of Klal Yisroel, which R. Schachter understands to be only one of numerous reasons why the letter of the law was sometimes suspended; see also Teshuvos Minchas Asher vol. 2 #134 who applies this idea to a practical scenario). It should be added that in fact there are numerous instances throughout the Neviim and Kesuvim where Chazal and the commentators explain the actions of various tzadikim through the concept of "hora'as sha'ah" (temporary ruling against the standard law); see Avoda Zara 24b, Temurah 15b, Temurah bottom of 28b and many others. The Netziv (intro. to commentary on She'iltos) explains that during the era of prophecy, Rabbis (i.e. Kohanim, prophets, etc.) often ruled the halacha based on Divinely inspired insight and according to the unique personality and soul of the individual involved. It was only after the era of prophecy

ended that we no longer have the right to rule in such a fashion since we do not have the capacity to understand the depths of each person's soul etc. Seemingly based on this understanding, Yaaros Devash (vol. 2 #7, pg. 178b ד"ה אמנם) writes that Chizkiyahu's argument truly made quite a bit of sense: since he knew from a Divine source that his son would turn evil, the rules of hora'as sha'ah (or the like) should dictate that he refrain from having children. He explains that Chizkiyahu's mistake was not in his reasoning but in that he did not understand the awesome capabilities of repentance. He did not know that Menashe would eventually repent and that his existence would somehow be a positive force in the world. He explains that this was the meaning behind Yeshaya's response: teshuva comes from "kavshei d'Rachmana", the most hidden places of Heaven which are not fully comprehended by man. See also Takkanas HaShavin (pg. 7a) and Ben Yehoyada (here) for a similar explanation. Mishbatzos Zahav (Melachim 2, 20:1 pg. 487) records that the Ponevezher Rav and Chafetz Chaim also explained that Chizkiyahu's mistake was that he did not know that Menashe would do teshuva. See similar approaches quoted in Mishbatzos Zahav (ibid. bottom of pg. 488) and Nachalas Shimon (ibid. 31:14). (On an even deeper level, see R. Goldberg's ed. of Nefesh HaChaim pg. 108 that this hidden capability of teshuva accounts for the idea that negative, forbidden forces such as non-kosher etc. will eventually be permitted in the next world. These ideas are currently incomprehensible since we are not yet privy to seeing the "kavshei d'Rachmana"; that is, how bad can really be good.)

13. *Can one change a prophecy?* – Chizkiyahu responds to Yeshaya's tragic prophecy by remarking that teshuva has the ability to change Heaven's decree even when the decree is revealed through prophecy. This is codified in Rambam hil. Yesodei HaTorah 10:4. (It is interesting to note that here Chizkiyahu expressed great faith in the capability of teshuva, yet his mistake (as mentioned above) was due to his inability to fathom that his evil son would eventually repent and that that "decree" could turn out positive as well.) Chidushei HaGra (here) adds that Chizkiyahu nevertheless told Yeshaya to halt the disclosure of his prophecy, for once it is revealed it is much harder to change (since Hashem does not like to make His interference with the natural order of the world overly apparent). (For more on reversing prophecies, see notes on 4a.)

14. *Is it proper to pray for recovery from an illness even after doctors have given up hope?* – Our Gemara states that one should not refrain from asking Hashem for mercy even when death seems inescapable. Yet Poskim note that one must be careful when encouraging public prayer in such a situation, for a negative outcome could lead to disillusionment with the power of Tefilla in general (see Moed Kattan 18b; Halichos Shlomo Tefilla pg. 102-3). Many Poskim further point out that if a sickness is causing the individual terrible pain, it is sometimes even proper to pray for the person to die and thus end his misery (see Ran Nedarim 40a; Aruch HaShulchan YD 335:3). See Aderes Tiferes (vol. 4 #52) for a lengthy discussion of this topic, citing numerous sources in Chazal and Poskim.

15. *What is the source of the Bach's amendments to the Gemara?* – The Bach here (#2) quotes the continuation of the Gemara's story regarding Chizkiyahu based on the text of the Ein Yaakov (see Mesivta ed. of the Gemara for further explanation of the passage). Megadim Chadashim (below 24a) notes that a number of the Bach's amendments throughout Shas are based on the text of Ein Yaakov, which often contains a purer form of the text of the Gemara. He argues, however, that many of the Bach's additions and corrections to the prevalent text are based on his own reasoning and not on other editions of the Gemara or its commentaries. He also posits that the Bach did not intend to actually *change* the text of the Gemara but to simply provide comments to allow the text to flow more easily to assist one's study. (For further reading, see R. Dovid Cohen's introduction to his sefer "He'Akov L'Mishor" for various reasons for inaccuracies throughout the common text of the Gemara.)

Short Notes on Berachos 10b

1. *What is the proper response to dreams?* – Tashbetz (vol. 2 #128 and 129) quotes seemingly contradictory statements in the Gemara about this question and concludes that some dreams are true and others are not, and a dream therefore carries with it all of the regular rules of a "safek" (halachic state of unclarity): we must act stringently regarding matters that pertain to possible Torah prohibitions, but we do not make someone pay money due to dreams. Shivas Tzion (#52) writes that in fact *most* dreams are nonsense, and therefore we should only care about dreams in situations of possible danger as a matter of extra caution. (See Sdeh Tzofim here for a lengthy discussion of the topic.) Regarding our Gemara, the Acharonim question why the Gemara needs to instruct not to refrain from requesting Divine mercy after receiving an ominous dream, for the Gemara just said that even after one hears a negative *prophecy* he can still change a Divine decree through repentance! R. Ronshberg (notes in back of Gemara) explains that the Gemara is saying that someone should daven for mercy even if he *only* experienced a negative dream, since there is a chance that the dream is true. Mahartz Chayes writes that in fact this statement in the Gemara does not add to the previous statement, but the Gemara simply wants to quote another statement concerning this general matter.

2. *Davening facing a wall* – Gilyon HaShas cites the Yerushalmi (Sanhedrin 51b) that adds another explanation for Chizkiyahu's actions, learning from Chizkiyahu that it is proper to face a wall during davening. See our notes on 5b for the reason for this practice.

3. *What was Sefer HaRefuos and why did Chizkiyahu bury it?* – Einayim LaMishpat quotes various explanations in the Rishonim if the potions and procedures mentioned in this book were regular forms of health care or if they were forbidden, magical methods of healing (which were studied by some Chachomim in order to know the ways of the sorcerers when necessary). The Rishonim further disagree why Chizkiyahu buried the book: because people were relying too much on medicine and not on Hashem, or because people were misusing this forbidden material. He also quotes the related discussion in Rishonim regarding the propriety of using medicine is general.

4. *Why was Chizkiyahu permitted to drag his father's bones?* – Einayim LaMishpat cites a disagreement amongst Rishonim if one is required to afford honor to one's father if his father is evil. He explains that according to those who opine that a son must honor even his evil father, Chizkiyahu was nonetheless allowed to act as he did as a form of "hora'as sha'ah"; to discourage future sinners and to bring his people to repentance (see below further). He quotes others who explain differently, writing that Chizkiyahu did not actually *disgrace* his father; he merely buried him in a fashion similar to regular people as opposed to the manner usually afforded to a king.

5. *Why was Chizkiyahu incorrect for cutting the water supply etc.?* – The great Chizkiyahu HaMelech had good reasons for everything that he did. See Radak (Divrei HaYamim 2 30:2 and 32:30) who doesn't even understand why Chazal write that Chizkiyahu was incorrect! He explains that Chizkiyahu wanted to lengthen the year in order to provide Bnei Yisroel more time to do teshuva and come to Yerushalayim for Pesach. It is logical that this reasoning should trump the slight problem of lengthening the year during an unideal time. His cutting the enemy's water supply also seems to have been a wise move in order to protect the entire Jewish nation. In fact, Radak points to the language of the Pasuk itself and to a Medrash that imply that Chizkiyahu acted correctly, and Einayim LaMishpat quotes more Midrashim that imply that Chizkiyahu was correct. Even Chizkiyahu's sending the doors of the Mikdash to the enemy (Melachim 2 18:16) can be easily defended since he did so in order to save the nation. Moreover, according to some interpretations, he only gave the gold *covers* that were attached to the doors which were possibly not considered kadosh (see Einayim LaMishpat). Yet, Meiri (Pesachim 56a ואחר ה"ד) and Tosafos Yom Tov (Pesachim 4:9) explain that Chizkiyahu should have showed extreme trust that Hashem would help him without his needing to take any questionable action. Although most people most certainly wouldn't be reproved for such action since it was indeed wise (and therefore some Chachomim, along with the Medrash, approved of his decisions), nonetheless, Chazal held Chizkiyahu to a higher standard, stating that these actions were inappropriate for him. (See Mishbatzos Zahav on Shemuel 1 pg. 433 who explains Dovid's "sin" of cutting Shaul's cloak in a similar fashion.) Interestingly, each of the three actions for which Chazal *praise* Chizkiyahu also involved a degree of "sin" which Chizkiyahu permitting as a form of "hora'as sha'ah" in order to assist in Klal Yisroel's teshuva process. We described above that dragging his father's bones consisted of a degree of embarrassment of his father which he allowed in order to make a public statement against evil. Similarly, the "sefer refuos" (according to Rashi and others) was an exceptional tool to help people overcome sickness, but since it was being misused Chizkiyahu decided to forfeit its benefits for the sake of his nation's spiritual health. Destroying the snake made by Moshe Rabbenu had similar negative aspects: it was a remembrance of a great miracle (see Bamidbar 21:4-9 and Maharsha here) and a tool for healing throughout the ages (according to Aggadas Bereishis ch. 11). Yet, Chizkiyahu needed to do away with it for the same reason that Rashi explained regarding the burying of "sefer refuos" and also because people were using it as a sort of avoda zara (see Melachim 2 18:4). Chasam Sofer (OC #32) and Taama D'kra (both quoted in Mishbatzos Zahav on Melachim ibid.) explain that Chizkiyahu destroyed the snake along with the "bamos" (small altars, which they explain had kedusha

since they were constructed at a time when it was permissible to sacrifice upon them) as a "hora'as sha'ah", a necessary measure to prevent the nation from sinning. (See our notes on the bottom of 10a for further discussion of the concept of "hora'as sha'ah.") We see that both the actions for which he was lauded and those for which he was criticized were of similar nature: they were bold moves for the sake of a greater good. But Chazal understood that the latter three were unnecessary and due to a lack of complete reliance on Hashem, whereas the former three were indeed necessary and proper.

6. *Is a talmid chachom permitted to receive gifts and support from others?* – The Gemara states that there are two tracks regarding this issue and both are allowed: that of Shemuel who did not take from others and that of Elisha who did. The Rishonim debate this issue at length (see Rambam hil. Talmud Torah 3:10 and his commentary on Mishnah Avos 4:7; Tashbetz vol. 1 #142; Kesef Mishneh on Rambam ibid.; Beis Yosef on Tur YD #246). Nonetheless, even the Rambam agrees that there are situations when one may accept a gift (such as various scenarios where it is common to offer such a gift to friends etc. as a form of honor), and even the Tashbetz agrees that it is often praiseworthy to go above the letter of the law and *not* take from others. Both sides of the argument are very understandable. On the one hand, through refraining from taking from others, a talmid chachom ensures that he continues to serve Hashem "lishma", for all of the correct reasons. He also remains independent and less susceptible to stray from that which is true and right. Taking gifts can also lead to a disgrace of the Torah as people see that chachomim are dependent upon others. Indeed, Shemuel was extra careful not to take anything from others because he wanted to restore the faith and respect that people lost in their leadership during the era of the Shoftim. On the other hand, by accepting gifts from others, a talmid chachom has the ability to provide tremendous merit to his hosts and donors. Accepting from others can also forge a bond between the talmid chachom and the donor which allows the donor to become closer to the Torah (just as one gets closer to *Hashem* through offering korbanos). Michtav Me'Eliyahu (vol. 5 pg. 217) writes that one should initially follow Elisha's path; eventually, when his complete devotion to Torah learning brings him to lose all concern for material wealth, he can then act on the "higher level" set by Shemuel.

7. *Hashem protects holy people from impure things* – Hashem makes it that flies (impure creatures; see Maharsha) are repelled from holy people and places, for such is the law of nature on a more spiritual plane: the holy and the profane do not mix.

8. *Why is it forbidden to stand on higher ground when davening?* – The Gemara explains that standing on higher ground expresses a degree of arrogance. Meiri and Levush (90:1) add that it gives an appearance that one needs to be higher up in order for one's prayer to "reach" Hashem, an idea which hinges on heresy. Tur (98:4) writes another idea, explaining that we cannot have a blockage between our feet and the floor similar to the Kohanim during their service in the Mikdash. Levush and Mishnah Berurah (90:1) add yet another reason, noting that standing on a chair can hinder one's *intent* when davening, for he may be scared that he will fall. (It needs further understanding why the Poskim added reasons to that of the Gemara.) Poskim mention (see MB 90:5 and others) that it is permitted for the chazzan to stand on higher ground in order to ensure that everyone can hear him, yet some congregations have the custom that the chazzan stands on particularly low ground out of humility. Meiri adds that if the shul is built with some higher and lower ground as part of the regular floor then there is no prohibition to daven in that area even though it is raised; see further in Shulchan Aruch (90:2).

9. *How should one position his feet while davening?* – The Shulchan Aruch (95:1) codifies our Gemara that one should stand with his feet together, side by side similar to an angel. Beis Yosef explains that this position signifies a complete halt in movement and absolute focus on Tefilla. The Tur (95:1) quotes a dissenting opinion in the Yerushalmi, that one should station his feet one in front of the other, with his heal touching the toe of the second foot, just as the Kohanim would stand when walking up the ramp of the altar. Fascinatingly, this position provides a completely different setting for one's Tefilla. As opposed to standing still before Hashem, this position connotes slow but constant advancement *towards* Hashem. (See, however, Perisha on Tur ibid. for an alternative explanation.) It is possible to add that even though the halacha is in accordance with the opinion that one's feet are positioned side by side, our Tefilla nonetheless contains an aspect of the other opinion as well: we stand in awe before Hashem, but we also move closer and closer *towards* Hashem as the Tefilla progresses.

10. *Is one permitted to eat anything before Shacharis?* – There is a general prohibition against eating before *any* Tefilla or mitzvah in order to ensure that the mitzvah is performed in a timely fashion (see notes on top of 4b; see also Mishnah Berurah 89:19 for a possible additional reason), but many Poskim are more lenient regarding that general prohibition than they are concerning eating before Shacharis specifically. For example, see Piskei Teshuvos (232:3) and Siach Tefilla (89:17) for leniencies to eat before Mincha or Maariv if one has a set minyan etc. See also Piskei Teshuvos (235:6-8 and notes 49-50) regarding appointing someone to remind you daven etc. (See also our notes on 4b.) The Poskim generally do not record these same leniencies to permit eating before Shacharis. Some Poskim also differentiate between a light snack, which may be permitted before Mincha and Maariv but not before Shacharis. (See,

for example, language of Rambam hil. Tefilla 6:4-5 with commentaries. It should be noted, however, that a small minority of Poskim allow for light snacking even before Shacharis; see She'eilas Yaavetz vol. 1 #40; Piskei Teshuvos 89 note 223; Einayim LaMishpat here #3. But Yabea Omer vol. 5 22:1 records that the consensus of Poskim is not this way.) The strictness of this prohibition regarding Shacharis is based on the fact that Chazal provided a hint from a Pasuk to this prohibition in regards to Shacharis and explain that it is "arrogant" for one to satiate himself before serving Hashem first. A few Rishonim even understand the prohibition as being Biblical (see Ra'ah here and Poskim quoted in Piskei Teshuvos #89 note 209 and Einayim LaMishpat). For this reason (and other more esoteric reasons) many Poskim quote the Zohar that one may not even eat before *alos hashachar* (after he awoke from his night's sleep), even when it is too early to daven. (See Yabea Omer ibid. 22:5 for a list of Poskim on this matter, yet he proves that the Gemara, Rishonim, and most prominent Poskim disagree with the Zohar.) Nonetheless, Poskim record various leniencies even regarding eating before Shacharis, most notably that someone who has a difficult time concentrating on Tefilla may eat in order to enhance his ability to pray (see Shulchan Aruch 89:3-4; Shev Yaakov #8; list of Chasidic Poskim in Kobetz Or Yisroel vol. 32 pg. 56-61). The Poskim also allow drinking water, coffee, etc. for the same reason (see Poskim on Shulchan Aruch 89:3 and Kobetz Or Yisroel vol. 31 pg. 93). Drinking (or even eating) for this purpose is not considered "arrogant", but a necessary tool to serve Hashem more fully. As to what is considered "davening" for this purpose, the Beiur Halacha (89:3 ד"ה ולא לאכול) concludes that one should first say Shema and Shemoneh Esrei. But R. Yonasan Steif (Shu"t Mahari Steif #41) writes that in a time of need it is enough to merely say Birchos HaShachar and the first paragraph of Shema. (See also Einayim LaMishpat #3 ד"ה כל האוכל who quotes a number of Rishonim who write that this halacha depends on Keriyas Shema, not Shemoneh Esrei.) See also Hebrew essay printed in the back of this kuntrus for further basis for leniencies.

11. *Is Tefilla part of "accepting the yoke of Heaven"?* – According to the language of our Gemara (כל האוכל ושותה ואח"כ מתפלל... לאחר שנתגאה זה קבל עליו עול מלכות שמים) it seems clear that included in Tefilla is "accepting the yoke of Heaven". Einayim LaMishpat makes this point as well, writing that the *main* acceptance of the yoke of Heaven occurs through Keriyas Shema, but it only happens *completely* through Keriyas Shema along with Tefilla. (But see Einayim LaMishpat further that some Rishonim did not have this language in their text. See also the Gemara on the top of 21a that states that Tefilla does not include the "kingship of Heaven".) This idea can be found in a few halachos as well: a) Pnei Yehoshua (beg. of 11b) writes that when one recites the beracha of Ahava Raba, then Shema and Shemoneh Esrei, and only afterwards learns Torah, it is nonetheless considered as if he learned Torah *immediately* following Ahava Raba, for Tefilla does not constitute a disruption between Shema and Torah study since " קריאת שמע ותפלה חדא מלתא הוא" (Keriyas Shema and Tefilla are *one thing*). b) Tosafos 14b (ד"ה ומנח) explain (based on the Gemara beg. of 15a) that one must wear tefillin during both Shema and Tefilla since both together constitute a full acceptance of the yoke of Heaven. At the same time, just as Tefilla has an aspect of Shema, Keriyas Shema also has an aspect of Tefilla: a) Beis Yosef (47:7) explains that reciting Shema after Ahava Raba does not necessarily constitute learning Torah (to allow Ahava Raba to work as Birchos HaTorah; see Tos. 11b) because "Tefilla is not learning" and " קריאת שמע כדברי תפילות הוא" (Keriyas Shema is like words of prayer). b) Many Rishonim and Poskim equate the concentration required for Shema with the concentration required during Tefilla (see notes beg. of Perek 2; see also Kol Bo quoted in Beis Yosef 62:2 with note 2 in Mechon Yerushalayim ed. of Tur). (But see our notes on 16a that some Rishonim clearly distinguish between intent for Tefilla and Keriyas Shema, explaining that Keriyas Shema does not constitute standing before Hashem in prayer.) c) The Gemara (15a) refers to Keriyas Shema as "צלותא", praying (but some Rishonim do not have this text; see Tos. there, and see R. Yonah bottom of 8a in pgs. of Rif who notes a similar point). The Gemara (16b) also states that the Pasuk (Tehillim 63:5) "כן אברכך בחיי" (Thus shall I bless You) refers to reciting Shema; Shema is a form of blessing Hashem! d) Also noteworthy is the Tosefta (beg. of ch. 3, quoted in Rambam Sefer HaMitzvos aseh #10) that derives the proper timing for Tefilla from the prescribed timing for Keriyas Shema.

12. *Until when may one recite Birchos Keriyas Shema of Shacharis and why?* – The Gemara explains that even though the time to fulfill the mitzvah of Keriyas Shema ends with the third hour of the day, one may nonetheless read Shema with its berachos until a later point. The Poskim explain (Rashba quoted in Beis Yosef 46; MB 58:25 and 60:3) that the berachos of Shema are not strictly "birchos hamitzvah" (berachos over the performance of a mitzvah which can only be recited when one performs the mitzvah at the correct time). Rather, these berachos are a form of Tefilla and praise on their own right, and Chazal merely connected them to Keriyas Shema. (For another ramification of this point, see MB 59:25 regarding unnecessary pauses between Birchos Keriyas Shema and Shema itself. It should be noted that the Ramban Berachos 22b understands that the beracha before Keriyas Shema is indeed a birkas hamitzvah, but he would seemingly agree that it is *also* a Tefilla on its own right. See Teshuvos HaRashbash #174, cited in Beiur Halacha 239 mistakenly as #74, who writes this point almost explicitly.) Nonetheless, many Poskim note that it is certainly ideal to fulfill the mitzvah of Keriyas Shema along with its berachos, and the Poskim disagree whether one should do so even at the expense of davening with a minyan (see Beis Yosef ibid.; Beiur Halacha end of 46; Piskei Teshuvos 58:8). The Rishonim disagree until what point in the day one may recite these berachos: Rambam (hil. Keriyas Shema 1:13 and commentary to Mishnah here 1:5) writes that one can recite these berachos the entire day;

Shulchan Aruch (based on Rosh and Tur etc.) writes that one can only recite the berachos until the end of the fourth hour of the day, which is the end of the official "time for Tefillas Shacharis". Practically, one should certainly try hard to recite the berachos of Shema by the end of the fourth hour as codified in Shulchan Aruch, but some Poskim allow one to rely on the Rambam's opinion when absolutely necessary (see Piskei Teshuvos 58 note 99). The Acharonim discuss why it is that the Rambam allows one to recite the berachos of Shema the entire day even though one can only daven Shacharis in the morning. Kesef Mishneh (on Rambam ibid.) famously writes that the Rambam holds that according to Torah law, the mitzvah of Keriyas Shema can be fulfilled all day, and the cut-off point of the 3rd hour is merely Rabbinic. For this reason, someone who misses the Rabbinic cut-off can still recite Shema with its berachos since the Torah mitzvah still applies. But many Acharonim disagree with the Kesef Mishneh, explaining that Keriyas Shema is based on the time of "arising", not simply when someone is awake or "daytime". (See Einayim LaMishpat here for more on this discussion and for another novel approach to explain the Rambam. See also below and our notes on 2b for more on the question if Shema is based on "night and day" or "sleeping and arising".) Alternatively, the Rambam may hold that the berachos of Keriyas Shema are a Tefilla that applies the entire day (since they praise Hashem for creating light and Torah etc. which apply all day) even though Keriyas Shema itself applies only in the morning. There is a third opinion in the Poskim (see Beiur Halacha 58:6 quoting Mishkenos Yaakov and Piskei Teshuvos 58:12) that allows one to recite the berachos for Keriyas Shema until midday, just as one may daven Shacharis (in time of need) until midday (Shulchan Aruch 89:1). But those who require Shema to be said by the 4th hour (as mentioned above) seem to opine that the berachos of Keriyas are different in nature than the rest of Tefillas Shacharis. The rest of Tefilla is "request for Divine mercy" and therefore applies to a degree even after the prescribed time. Birchos Keriyas Shema, however, contain much more general praise for Hashem's creations etc., separate from the rest of Tefilla, and Chazal established this prayer to be said in the early morning alone (see Shevet Halevi vol. 10 #10). Also relevant to this discussion is the halachic debate regarding someone who missed Shema whether he can somewhat rectify the situation ("tashlumin") by saying it at a later time (see Shulchan Aruch 58:7 and Einayim LaMishpat here). Some Rishonim hold that this idea of "tashlumin" only applies to Tefilla since requesting mercy always applies to a degree, while Keriyas Shema is not strictly Tefilla.

13. *How do we calculate the "hours of day" concerning timing for Keriyas Shema and Tefilla?* – Most Poskim (see Shulchan Aruch 58:1 with Piskei Teshuvos note 19, based on Rambam's commentary to Mishnah here 1:5; Teshuvos HaRambam #134) assume that we calculate the "hours of the day" as "sha'os zemaniyos". That is, we break up the "daytime" hours into 12 parts, and each part is considered one hour. The Poskim famously debate when the "daytime" starts regarding this calculation: alos hashachar (Magen Avrohom) or neitz hachama (Gra). (See Piskei Teshuvos 58:3 for numerous Poskim on both sides of this debate.) Some Poskim disagree completely with these calculations and opine that we follow the regular hours of the day: midday is 12 noon and therefore the end of the 3rd hour is 9AM, regardless of time of year. They explain that since Keriyas Shema follows the time that people go to sleep and rise, it does not make sense to follow "sha'os zemaniyos", for people do not drastically change their entire sleep schedule based on the exact time of year. They also point to the Zohar who seems to write this way. Daas Torah (58:1) quotes Tos. HaRosh (Berachos 3b ד"ה כיון) who also seems to explicitly agree with this opinion. Pnei Yehoshua (Berachos Mahadura Basra 3a) even suggests that perhaps the Rambam himself changed his mind on this issue. Shach (YD 184:7, quoted in Shulchan HaTahor OC 58:1 and R. Yaakov Emden's Lechem Shamayim Berachos pg. 9) seems to understand that the Shulchan Aruch understood this way as well. R. Yaakov Emden (ibid.) writes that one needs to take the stringency of both opinions on this issue. Mishkenos Yaakov (#79) uses this opinion only as a means to provide some justification for people who are lenient. R. Yosef Chaim Zonnenfeld (Teshuvos, end of #23) similarly justifies those who are lenient on the matter and suggests that the proper time for Shema is later in our generation because people often sleep later than they did years ago. (See also Piskei Teshuvos 58:2.) In a related issue, Mo'adim U'zmanim (vol. 2 #155 note 1) writes that it is possible that in a place that is constantly daytime (such as the far north), Keriyas Shema (based on "sleeping and awaking") and Tefilla follow the hours of the day based on the above system, and one would therefore recite the nighttime Shema during the "sleep hours" even though the sun is out and it is thus technically "day". (See Nachalas Shimon on Yehoshua vol. 2 #36 for Poskim who discuss how to calculate "days" in regards to general halachos in such a place.) As for the generally assumed opinion that we follow "sha'os zemaniyos", it can be explained that "the time that people go to sleep and arise" only outlines the general guidelines of this halacha and helps define the general timeframe in this context. In other words, the time for Keriyas Shema follows Chazal's understanding of the *average* time for sleeping and rising (for those times have a particular nature of night/morning etc.; see notes on 2b and our discussion of the nature of "nighttime" in many of the previous pages), but one does not need to be concerned with the fact that there are times and places where people rise earlier or later in the morning.

14. *Do Keriyas Shema and Tefilla trump Torah study?* – The Rishonim (Tosafos, Rashba, Meiri) note that both Tefilla and Keriyas Shema, when recited at their proper time, take precedence over Torah study. But they quote a debate in the Yerushalmi (end of 1:2 here) whether this applies even to someone who studies Torah constantly ("toraso um'naso"). For more on this discussion, see Shulchan Aruch 106:2 with its commentaries.

1. *What is the crux of the argument between Beis Shamai and Beis Hillel regarding one's position during Keriyas Shema?* – The Gemara records Beis Shamai's retort back to Beis Hillel: if the Torah only required the timing of "sleeping" and "rising" as Beis Hillel opines, the Torah would have stated "בבוקר ובערב" and not "בשכבך ובקומך". Acharonim (Tzlach, Meromei Sadeh) ask the obvious question: Beis Hillel also expound the wording of "בשכבך ובקומך", explaining that this timeframe is different than that of pure "night and day", for Keriyas Shema depends on the time that people rise but not strictly on night and day (see Gemara 2b, 9a, 9b etc.). The Acharonim answer this question in various manners. But perhaps one can explain that Beis Shamai understood this point, but nonetheless, Beis Shamai were saying that once the Torah is clearly directing us to base the mitzvah on "sleeping and rising", it is more sensible to follow that directive completely and even position oneself in such a manner. Indeed, Beis Hillel also understand this reasoning, but they understood that the phrase "ובלכתך בדרך" clearly instructs us that it can be said in any position. Hence it can be explained that everyone agrees that Shema must serve as the bookends of our day (see 4b), but Beis Shamai understood that we must also physically express it as such, that it directs our rising and our sleeping, whereas Beis Hillel learn that Shema joins our day more naturally, during any activity.

2. *What is considered "involved in a mitzvah" and therefore relieved from the obligation to perform other mitzvos?* – See Einayim LaMishpat who quotes the various opinions of the Rishonim whether one needs to be actively occupied with a mitzvah or if even passive involvement in a mitzvah relieves one from his other obligations. (See Minchas Asher on Devarim 11:2 for an explanation of this disagreement.) Einayim LaMishpat also points to a discussion whether it is *forbidden* to pause one's current mitzvah in order to partake in another or if it is simply not obligatory. (Minchas Asher (ibid.) explains that haulting one's involvement in one mitzvah in order to perform another is considered a disgrace to the first mitzvah.) The Rishonim mainly discuss this topic in Maseches Succah (25a). See also our notes at the end of Perek 2 and beginning of Perek 3 below for more discussion of this topic in general and regarding a groom's obligation in mitzvos in particular.

3. *Does a mourner have a mitzvah to be sad, and how is he different than a groom who worries about his impending mitzvah?* – The Gemara states that a groom is absolved from the mitzvah of Keriyas Shema since he is worried about the mitzvah of consummating his marriage with his wife. Rambam explains (hil. Keriyas Shema 4:1) that his worries do not relate to actual preparation for the mitzvah, but that he simply worries about the possibility of something going wrong. (See also Kesubos 6b with Rashi and an alternative explanation in Rashi Succah end of 25a.) Seemingly, the Torah understands that it is normal and even proper to worry about accurately carrying out mitzvos to their fullest, and therefore such anxiety is itself part of the mitzvah (see Lehoros Nosson vol. 6 #108, but see Moreshes Moshe towards the end of 14:2 for a different explanation; see also our notes on 17b beginning of Perek 3). (It should be noted, however, that the Shulchan Aruch (70:3) writes that grooms today do not have this dispensation since even the general populace unfortunately do not properly concentrate during the recital of Shema.) The Gemara contrasts this case, however, to that of a mourner whose grief and apprehension are not considered occupation with a mitzvah and do not relieve him from his other mitzvah obligations. At first glance this is baffling, for it seems clear that a mourner is obligated to keep himself in his aggrieved state of mind, as explained clearly by the talmid of R. Yechiel M'Paris (Moed Katan 14b) and as seen from the fact that mourning does not apply on Yom Tov because the joy of Yom Tov is a contradiction to the mitzvah to mourn (see Sherashim B'Semachos #1 and more). It could be explained that even though the mourner is required to remain distressed, his misery is not supposed to prevent him from performing mitzvos. Quite the contrary; the Rambam writes (see hil. Aveilus 13:12; hil. Taaniyos 1:1-3 and 5:1; see also Sefer HaChinuch #264) that one of the key reasons that the Torah commands one to mourn is in order to bring him to teshuva and *more* intense service of Hashem! That is, certainly the mourner must remain in a solemn state, but this experience brings him to more intensity and care in his performance of mitzvos from the depths of his broken soul. Rashi (Succah end of 25a) adds that the mourner expresses anguish in order to give honor to the deceased, but he is not required to experience debilitating sorrow. (See further discussion of this matter and regarding the essence of mourning in Divrei Sofrim in an essay at the end of hil. Aveilus; Nitei Gavriel hil. Aveilus vol. 1 pg. 26 and onward; Gesher HaChaim vol. 2 #16; Even HaEzel hil. Avel 1:1 and 5:2; Reshimos Shiurim Succah 25a.)

4. *Why doesn't a mourner wear tefillin?* – Einayim LaMishpat quotes two different reasons offered by Rashi in various places: a) he makes himself appear as if he is not a mourner by adorning himself in such glory; b) it is not befitting to the tefillin to be worn by a mourner. Einayim LaMishpat offers various possible halachic ramifications of this debate. It can be added that a mourner is compared in numerous places to the deceased himself, which clearly would add to the lack of beauty illustrated by the mourner. (See, for example, beginning of 3rd Perek of Moed Katan for a comparison between a metzora, someone who is excommunicated, and a mourner. Chazal write explicitly that the former two are considered "dead", and it is therefore sensible to describe the mourner this way as well. See also

Maharal in Netzach Yisroel ch. 41 and Chidushei Agados to Sanhedrin 22a, and see Shem MiShemuel beginning of Ki Sisa.)

5. *Is one permitted to act stringently against the accepted halacha?* – The Gemara is clear that it is forbidden for one to act "stringently" in accordance with Beis Shamai's opinion against the opinion of Beis Hillel. Chidushei HaGra comments that there are numerous scenarios in which one is not obligated to do something but is nonetheless considered righteous for doing so. For example, in a case where Beis Hillel does not require a particular action but nevertheless agree that it is a good thing to do, it is indeed praiseworthy for someone to act stringently on the matter. But there are other examples where there is no reason whatsoever to be stringent, and in such cases acting stringently is foolish at best ("כל הפטור מן הדבר ועושהו נקרא הדיוט"). (See also Shnos Eliyahu, Tiferes Tisroel Boaz #8, and Tos. Yom Tov on Shabbos 1:9 who write similarly. See also Tos. Yom Tov Beitza 2:6, but Chidushei R. Nachman ben HaRamban Beitza 21b explains that Mishnah differently.) The Gra explains the various opinions in our Gemara based on this idea: one opinion understood that Beis Hillel agreed that acting as Beis Shamai is indeed a mitzvah although not required, while others understood that such action is forbidden since Beis Hillel held that it was completely meaningless, and therefore someone who acts in such a manner was clearly demonstrating a lack of faith in the halacha and the halachic system. (The Rashbetz here explains the first opinion in our Gemara differently: the halacha is only like Beis Hillel when Beis Shamai's opinion contradicts that of Beis Hillel, but if one can fulfill both opinions, then the halacha does not require to act like Beis Hillel. See also Tos. HaRosh and R. Peretz here.) The Ra'ah here concludes that it is forbidden for one to act "stringently" in accordance with an opinion against the accepted halacha, for doing so gives off an appearance that one is disagreeing with his teachers and the halachic deciders. But he notes that a Rav himself may act stringently in accordance with his own opinion, but he may do so only in private as not to publicly disagree with the accepted halacha (in accordance with the Gemara in Yevamos 15a). (It should be noted, however, that many understand that during the era of the Sanhedrin one was not allowed to act "stringently" according to his own opinion against Sanhedrin's ruling even privately. But see Dibros Moshe Yevamos 12:1 ד"ה והנה לכאורה who disagrees; see also Rashi Horios 2b ד"ה וקא טעה and various commentaries there. Magen Avraham 63:2 qualifies that one may not be stringent against his Rebbe's opinion *in the presence of his Rebbe* unless he has clear proof against his Rebbe's reasoning.) Nonetheless, the Rav of a particular community often has the right to rule according to his minority opinion for his own town (see notes on 9a). The Ritva (Shabbos 130a ד"ה ולא עוד) adds that it is part of the mitzvah of "lo sassur" for the members of a community to follow their Rav's minority opinion. In fact, the Gemara states (Yevamos 14a) that even Beis Shamai ruled according to their own opinions, but the Chachomim wanted to establish the halacha in accordance with Beis Hillel for future generations and therefore ruled out Beis Shamai's opinion for anyone who was not already part of that group (see Pri Megadim in Eshel Avrahom 63:2; see also Eruvin 13b). (Nonetheless, if the *Sanhedrin* rules against that Rav, he may no longer rule for others according to his opinion. Also, if the Rav himself discussed the issue with the other Chachomim of his generation and they rule against him, it is possible that he must concede to the majority opinion and no longer rule in accordance with his own opinion. See wording of Ritva ibid. and Pri Chadash OC 496:11. See also Sefer Tal Chaim on K'lalei Hora'ah vol. 1 #1 pg. 58 and vol. 2 #1 who argues that the Rambam's opinion was that even Beis Shamai was not allowed to follow their own opinion. Nonetheless there are times when an opinion will not be completely "ruled out", but remain a minority opinion. See ramifications of this point in Ediyos 1:4-5.) For further exploration, see Chomer B'kodesh and Piska Tava by R. Yosef Dovid Cohen regarding acting stringently against the accepted halacha and concerning a Rav or community following different rulings than most other communities. See also Tal Amarti by R. Tal Doar (ch. 37:5,8,10) regarding acting "stringently" against the ruling of *other* Chachomim besides Beis Hillel, particularly Poskim during generations following the Mishnah and Talmud. And see Hebrew essay printed in the back of this kuntrus regarding the heightened honor and authority that the Torah affords to one's particular Rav or Beis Din.

6. *Is one permitted to stand for Keriyas Shema during Shacharis?* – It is clear from the Gemara that one is not allowed to stand for Keriyas Shema in the morning (or sit during Keriyas Shema at night) in order to act in accordance with Beis Shamai's opinion, as explained above. Many Rishonim write that one who does so does not fulfill his obligation, and he is required to recite Shema again. (See Tosafos here and Succah 3a; Einayim LaMishpat here #3; our notes on 9a; but see Rashbetz and Gra here who disagree.) From the simple reading of the Gemara (and see wording of Meiri), one could conclude that it is only forbidden to stand in order to give deference to Beis Shamai's opinion, but standing for another reason would be permitted. R. Avharam ben HaRambam (Sefer HaMaspik Feldheim ed. appendix #1 pg. 300) goes further and writes that it is *better* to stand because standing is a more ideal form of prayer. He adds that we are not very concerned today that someone may conclude that the halacha is like Beis Shamai, for Beis Hillel's rulings have already spread throughout the nation, and no one follows Beis Shamai anymore. But Hagahos Maimoni (on Rambam hil. Keriyas Shema 2:2) quotes that there were some people who would stand because they believed that it is better to accept the yoke of Heaven in a standing position, and he writes that such is a custom of fools and is completely incorrect, for we never find Beis Hillel saying such a thing. The Tur (63:2) similarly quotes R. Amram Gaon who writes that someone who stands in order to be stringent upon himself is incorrect. The Beis Yosef (there)

explains that Beis Hillel never said to do such a thing, and therefore such action is incorrect since it appears that one is acting in accordance with Beis Shamai. Chidushei Hagahos (on Tur, quoting Maharlach) explains R. Amram Gaon differently, writing that it is better to sit since one can have more intent in such a fashion, but not because it appears that he is acting in accordance with Beis Shamai. The Shulchan Aruch (63:2) codifies the words of R. Amram Gaon. Nonetheless, Aruch HaShulchan (63:3) writes that if someone wants to stand simply out of comfort and the like, it is permitted. It is possible that this holds true also for someone who wants to stand because it helps his intent (because he is tired etc.); he only may not stand if he does so out of principle because it is objectively better. But the Pri Megadim (Eshel Avraham 63:2) writes that even standing in order to improve someone's intent and the like is incorrect, since doing so could give off the appearance that he is acting like Beis Shamai. He adds further that even standing for Keriyas Shema during *Maariv* is not allowed because someone may end up doing so during Shacharis as well. But it seems that many Poskim did not make these extensions of the Pri Megadim and allowed one to stand for various reasons such as those mentioned in the Aruch HaShulchan (see Ishei Yisroel ch. 20 notes 98-99 and Piskei Teshuvos on MB ibid.). The Poskim (see Piskei Teshuvos ibid.) further write that one is certainly permitted to stand *well before* reaching Shema, for doing so does not give off the appearance of ruling like Beis Shamai. Nonetheless, the Aruch HaShulchan and others (see Piskei Teshuvos) write that according to *kabbala* it is better to sit during Keriyas Shema. Darkei Moshe (on Tur ibid.) and Raavad (on Rambam ibid.) write this way as well (although most probably in order to increase intent and not for kabbalistic reasons).

7. *Is one permitted to make changes to the text of Tefilla?* – The Mishnah states that one is not allowed to "shorten or lengthen" the berachos (the Rishonim disagree regarding the exact meaning of the Mishnah, but the essential idea is true according to everyone). Yet the Rishonim disagree if Chazal mean to prohibit any small changes, or only certain more substantial changes. The Rashba proves from numerous implications in Chazal that one may indeed make some changes to the exact wording of the berachos or tefillos as long as he keeps a few specific ideas listed in Chazal and the basic structure of each beracha. The Ritva and Ra'ah write that one may only *temporarily* add to the berachos of Tefilla for a specific reason, but one may not add or subtract on a permanent basis. The Roke'ach (beginning of his Siddur) writes that there is deep meaning to each word and letter of the Tefilla written by the Anshei Kenesses HaGedolah, and one may not add or subtract even one letter from their text. As a corollary to this debate, the Rishonim further disagree whether there is a point to "counting" the letters of various berachos in the Tefilla. The Rashba here (and others) writes that there is no need to keep the exact amount of letters and words of the various berachos, but Roke'ach (ibid.), Siddur R. Shlomo M'Girmayza (pg. 81), and many others state that there is great depth to the exact number of letters in the various berachos. This debate runs throughout the commentary of various Rishonim and commentaries on the Siddur. Nonetheless, the Beis Yosef (end of #113) points out from the Abudraham that much of the original language of the various Tefillos have changed over time (albeit slightly) due to error or otherwise, and therefore counting letters *today* is often futile since we often do not know the exact amount of letters that were originally extant in the Tefilla. The Mishnah Berurah (beg. of siman 68 and 101:4 in Beiur Halacha ד"ה יכול) seems to codify both the Rashba and his opponents. He seemingly understands that it is technically permitted to make changes to the language of the Tefilla, but one should nevertheless only do so with good reason. He therefore utilizes the Rashba's opinion only to offer basis for the custom to add some hymns to the Tefilla at various points of the year. The Poskim are generally very hesitant to make changes to the Tefilla, and we usually rely on the custom as printed in our current siddurim (see for example Beiur Halacha ibid.; Piskei Teshuvos #119 note 15; see also R. Yisroel Reisman's fascinating articles on some historic corrections to the Siddur in "Pathways of the Prophets" pgs. 237-254 and 263-271). In a case when one incorrectly changes the language of a Tefilla, the Kesef Mishneh (hil. Berachos 1:6) explains the Rambam's opinion: if someone changes the form of the beracha completely (deleting the opening or closing beracha etc.), he does not fulfill his obligation to recite the beracha and he must repeat the beracha properly, but if someone kept the structure and merely changed some wording, he fulfills his obligation and does not need to say the beracha again. Magen Avraham (64:3) quotes this Kesef Mishneh as practical halacha. But the Kesef Mishneh quotes the Ramach who seemingly did not understand this distinction. Gra (quoted in Frankel ed. of Rambam hil. Keriyas Shema 1:7) also does not agree with this distinction, and he writes that the Rambam changed his mind from that which he wrote in hil. Keriyas Shema and concludes that one always fulfills his obligation, even when reciting a beracha incorrectly. The Mishnah Berurah (64:1) cites this disagreement between the Magen Avraham and Gra. He notes that these are also the two opinions quoted in Shulchan Aruch (187:1). (As somewhat of an aside, see also Rashba and Peirush Rashbetz here who discuss at length the exact structure of numerous berachos.)

1. *Why do we mention the night during the day and the day during the night?* – See our notes on 26a (beginning of Perek 4) that regarding some things the night follows the day, whereas regarding other parts of life the day follows the night. We see that day and night do not stand on their own; rather, they are constantly either a continuation of or a preparation for the periods of time that precede and follow them. It can be explained that we mention the night during the day and the day during the night to mention and enhance this connection. Similarly, "day and night" represent propitious and less propitious times of history. We realize that these points in history are not comprised of isolated events, but the "night" leads into the "day" and vice versa, and it is the same G-d who controls each point in time.

2. *What are the parameters of utilizing the beracha of Ahava Raba as a beracha for learning Torah?* – Tosafos quote the Yerushalmi that Ahava Raba can only serve as the beracha for learning Torah if one learns Torah immediately after reciting Ahava Raba. Tosafos understand that this is not the case regarding the standard Birchos HaTorah which work even if one does not follow these berachos with Torah study (see below). The Rishonim explain (see Tos. HaRosh and others) that since Ahava Raba is essentially a beracha for Shema, one can only demonstrate that he is utilizing this beracha as a beracha for learning Torah if he learns immediately after davening. Tosafos seem to also understand that the beracha of Ahava Raba (as opposed to the standard Birchos HaTorah) only covers one's Torah learning after davening, but if he takes a break and later returns to his study he needs to recite Birchos HaTorah before continuing to learn. As opposed to the real Birchos HaTorah that provide full praise etc. for the mitzvah of Torah study, Ahava Raba is a mere substitute and therefore does not have the "power" to fulfill his obligation even after he takes a break from his study. Many other Rishonim disagree (see further in Tos. HaRosh and others) and hold that even Ahava Raba can last for the entire day, similar to Birchos HaTorah. Nonetheless, Divrei Yetziv (vol. 1 #51:3) notes that it is certainly ideal to recite the real Birchos HaTorah which Chazal instituted as the most proper and direct beracha for the Torah. (He equates Ahava Raba to the beracha of "She'hakol" which works if said before any food, but ideally one should recite the proper beracha for each specific food.) Also, since Ahava Raba is essentially a beracha for Shema and not strict Torah study, the Poskim further discuss if Ahava Raba covers Torah study even if one does not have intent for it to do so (see MB 47:14 and others). Nonetheless, it should be noted that the fact that Ahava Raba works as Birchos HaTorah illustrates that Keriyas Shema itself is a form of Torah study. It is for this reason that some Poskim hold that the mere recital of Shema after Ahava Raba constitutes bona fide Torah study, and one does not have to learn Torah again after davening in order for Ahava Raba to take effect as Birchos HaTorah (see Raavad quoted in Rashba; Shulchan Aruch 47:8). R. Yosef Dov Soloveitchik (שעורים לזכר אבי מורי vol. 2 #1) proves this same idea from the Yerushalmi (quoted in Tosafos 2a) that states that Keriyas Shema can serve as Torah study before prayer. (He explains that Torah study is an essential component of Tefilla, for it too has an aspect of being "service of the heart". See notes on 3b that Torah study itself can sometimes even serve as a form of *Tefilla*. Regarding the general idea of Keriyas Shema as Torah study, see Yerushalmi here end of 1:2 that R. Shimon bar Yochai holds that someone who is constantly immersed in Torah should not disrupt his Torah study in order to recite Keriyas Shema, since Keriyas Shema is also "study", and one does not disrupt one study for another. See also Gemara 14b that refers to the Pasuk of "ודברת בם" as referring to Torah study (see Rashi there ד"ה שזה ללמוד), yet that Pasuk is also the source for the mitzvah to recite Shema, as recorded in Rambam Sefer HaMitzvos aseh #10. See further sources in Einayim LaMishpat 10b #5 ד"ה ואולם and 21a ד"ה והנה התוס', Pesicha #9 of Chadashim Gam Yeshanim, and our notes on 2a.)

3. *Does one need to learn Torah immediately after reciting Birchos HaTorah, and what is unique about Birchos HaTorah?* – The Rishonim disagree whether one needs to learn Torah directly after reciting Birchos HaTorah (see Tosafos here; Beis Yosef and Shulchan Aruch 47:9). Some Poskim opine that Birchos HaTorah work in a similar fashion to all other berachos recited before performing a mitzvah ("birchos hamitzvah"), and therefore one must perform the mitzvah immediately after reciting the beracha. Beis Yosef (ibid.) writes that others disagree, explaining that Birchos HaTorah differ from the beracha recited on all other mitzvos. He explains that since Torah study is a constant obligation (unless there is another pressing need), the Birchos HaTorah are always viewed as "attached" to the mitzvah of Torah study which is ever present. To put this idea differently, Birchos HaTorah can be seen as a beracha on one of the constants of life itself, similar to the various berachos that one recites in the morning which thank Hashem for His various creations. The Poskim write a similar idea regarding the question whether one who remains awake all night must recite Birchos HaTorah once again in the morning. Some write that Birchos HaTorah are similar to the rest of the berachos that we recite each morning, and therefore a new beracha must be said (see MB 47:28). This idea can be seen further in the Rambam who does not record Birchos HaTorah with his laws of Torah study (which would be the proper place to record this ruling if these berachos were standard birchos hamitzvah), but with his laws of prayer (hil. Tefilla 7:11), along with the rest of the berachos recited each morning. R. Binyamin Feller (in Yeshurun vol. 9 pg. 302) notes this point and explains that Birchos HaTorah are not only birchos hamitzvah, but they were instituted also as a general Tefilla for the Torah, recited each day along with other praises of Hashem's creations. He adds that this idea explains the custom that the Rishonim quote in the name of Rashi (see Hagahos

Maimoni on Rambam ibid. #20) to rise early in the morning to say Birchos HaTorah and learn, and then to recite Birchos HaTorah again at shul along with the other berachos recited before davening. He explains that the first recital of Birchos HaTorah (before alos hashachar) acts as a regular birkas hamitzvah, but the second recital acts as a Tefilla along with the rest of the berachos that one recites each morning. See also Siddur Chasidei Ashkenaz (quoted in Shitos Kamai here pg. 233) who rules this way and explains very similarly. A similar idea is further illustrated in the discussion of women's recital of Birchos HaTorah. Some Acharonim explain (see Chidushei HaGriz end of hil. Berachos; Kehillas Yaakov Berachos #22 along with many others) that women can recite Birchos HaTorah even though they do not have an obligation to learn Torah because Birchos HaTorah are not standard birchos hamitzvah, but more general berachos of praise for the Torah. Igros Moshe (OC vol. 1 #21) further notes that according to one opinion in our Gemara, the beracha of "asher bachar banu etc." is the sole beracha for learning Torah, even though that beracha does not contain the language of a standard birkas hamitzvah ("אשר קדשנו במצותיו וצונו") at all. Since the mitzvah of Torah study is constant, it may not *require* the standard language of a birkas hamitzvah; rather, a beracha of praise can serve as the beracha for this mitzvah. (This idea is true according to the conclusion of our Gemara as well. Einayim LaMishpat ד"ה והנה יש להתפלא notes that the Rishonim lump all of the Birchos HaTorah together, and those who opine that one needs to recite the berachos again after taking a break from study say to recite all of the berachos, even "ashar bachar banu etc.". That is, even when these berachos are clearly serving as birchos hamitzvah, the beracha of praise must nevertheless be recited, for this birkas hamitzvah was written in a manner of praise.) It should further be noted that even though most Rishonim write that Birchos HaTorah are considered birchos hamitzvah and explain women's ability to recite Birchos HaTorah differently than the Acharonim mentioned above (see Beis Yosef ibid. and 47:14 based on Agur; Teshuvos Maharil HaChadashos 45:2 with footnotes; Rishonim on Eruvin 96a, Rosh Hashona 33a, and Kedushin 31a; Rishonim quoted below regarding making another beracha after pausing Torah study), they may nevertheless agree that Birchos HaTorah are also unique just as the mitzvah of Torah study is unique, as explained.

4. *Does one need to recite Birchos HaTorah again after taking a break from his study?* – The Rishonim disagree (see Tosafos here; Beis Yosef 47:11) whether one is required to recite Birchos HaTorah again after taking an extended break from his Torah study. According to some Rishonim, since the mitzvah to learn Torah is constant one can never truly see himself as taking a break from Torah study. Beis Yosef quotes the Agur with a somewhat similar idea, explaining that Torah study applies even while partaking in other pursuits (in the bathroom etc.) since one must be cognizant of the numerous halachos that dictate one's practice even in those scenarios (see also Teshuvos Maharil HaChadashos 45:2). That is, one must always have the Torah's laws on his mind; Torah study constantly exists. The Rosh (see also Tosafos and Tos. R. Yehuda) compares this mitzvah of Torah study to the mitzvah of living in a succah: the beracha made before eating in a succah covers all of one's activity in the succah until his next meal, even in a situation where he takes an extended break from sitting in the succah. It can be explained that the mitzvah of succah is similar to the mitzvah of Torah study in regards to this very idea: both are constant mitzvos that dictate all of one's activity and therefore always apply. This idea also relates to the debate amongst the Rishonim whether the beracha reads "על דברי תורה" or "לעסוק בדברי תורה". Some Rishonim explain (see Rishonim in Beis Yosef 47:5 and Einayim LaMishpat ד"ה ואף הברכה) that "על דברי תורה" refers not only to the study of Torah but to the practical application of that study throughout one's day of mitzvos and service of Hashem. Hence, the mitzvah of Torah study is constant not only in thought but also in how it manifests itself in action. Nonetheless, some Rishonim rule that only those who immerse themselves constantly in Torah view Torah study as this continuous pursuit, while other people need to make a new beracha after pausing their study (see Poskim quoted in MB 47:22).

5. *Does the second beracha of Keriyas Shema begin with the words "ahava raba" or "ahavas olam"?* – The Gemara records a disagreement regarding this issue, and various Rishonim have varying texts of the Gemara and therefore disagree how to rule the halacha (see Rif). The Beis Yosef and Shulchan Aruch (60:1) record that the Sefardi custom is to say "ahavas olam", whereas the Rama (with MB 60:2) notes that the Ashkenazi custom is to recite "ahava raba" in the morning and "ahavas olam" at night to fulfill (to a degree) both opinions in the Gemara (see Tosafos).

6. *Which topics of Torah require a beracha to be recited before learning them?* – The Gemara records a debate if Birchos HaTorah need to be said only before learning Pesukim or even before studying various parts of the Oral Torah etc. The commentators explain the Gemara's deliberation and conclusion in various manners: a) R. Yonah understands that a beracha only needs to be said before learning Pesukim, and he explains the Gemara's conclusion that even Gemara and Medrash require a beracha because they are *based* on Pesukim. It is possible to explain the reasoning behind his opinion by noting that it is only with regards to the Written Torah that the exact *words* are essential, whereas regarding the Oral Torah, the words are not the essence, but it is the *ideas* that matter most. Since Chazal instituted the Birchos HaTorah for uttering the *words* of Torah (see below), one is therefore only required to recite the berachos before learning Pesukim. Moreover, only the words of the Pesukim can be said to be completely objective and the "cheftza (entity) of Torah", whereas the Oral Torah refers to the explanation of the Torah, and an explanation depends,

by definition, on one's finite understanding, and not all people understand each concept alike. The Birchos HaTorah are recited over the objective, everlasting "cheftza of the Torah", not merely on its study and personal understanding. (See also 13a beginning of Perek 2 that some Rishonim similarly understand that the obligation of "והגית בו יומם ולילה" requires one to learn the actual words of the Written Torah each day and night.) Based on R. Yonah's understanding, the Aruch HaShulchan (47:8) is unsure if one is required to make a beracha before studying aggada and kabbala, since those parts of Torah do not discuss halachos based upon Pesukim. Yet it could be argued that aggada etc. also expound Pesukim and therefore surely require a beracha. b) Others (Levush and Shulchan Aruch haRav 47:2) explain the conclusion of our Gemara as saying that we make a beracha on *all* parts of Torah, not only on Pesukim. The Aruch HaShulchan (ibid.) points out that according to this explanation one would certainly make a beracha on aggada etc. Others conclude this way as well (see Piskei Teshuvos 47 notes 31-32). Most Poskim (Shulchan Aruch 47:4) write that one does not need to recite a beracha before merely *thinking* about the laws and concepts of the Torah. The Gra (on Shulchan Aruch) disagrees based on the fact that it is a mitzvah to learn Torah even through thinking alone, so even thinking about Torah should require a beracha. (And more, the Gemara on 6b relates that the *main* reward for learning Torah depends on the degree that one toils to understand.) The Gra further asks why the Shulchan Aruch rules (47:3) that one needs to recite a beracha before *writing* Torah; how is this different than thinking? The Aruch HaShulchan (47:10) answers that even though it is certainly a mitzvah to think about Torah, the Pasuk of "והגית בו יומם ולילה" refers mainly to speaking Torah, for it is through speech that a person studies Torah in action, not just in his mind. Similarly, the Maharal (Gevuros Hashem end of ch. 62) writes that a beracha is only recited before performing a mitzvah with action as opposed to with mere thought. The Aruch HaShulchan continues that it is for this reason that the beracha refers to using one's *mouth* to learn Torah ("בפינו ובפי עמך"), and the Gemara (Eruvin 54a) censures people who learn silently with their minds but do not utter the words of the Torah. He adds that writing Torah is the main way that it is taught and kept for all generations, and therefore it also requires a beracha. It can be added (based on the above) that Birchos HaTorah are recited before partaking in the "cheftza of Torah" which is expressed in an objective, even semi-tangible fashion through speaking or writing. But abstract thought, although a tremendous mitzvah, lacks in its expression of the concrete, eternal nature of the Torah. The Poskim further disagree whether one recites a beracha before reciting words of Torah without understanding them. The Maharal (ibid.) writes that the beracha was instituted for "involvement" (esek) in Torah, not for understanding it. He explains that it is for this same reason that one can recite the beracha before reading the Megilla or Hallel even though he does not understand them. This opinion can be further understood based on the above; Birchos HaTorah are recited on the everlasting Torah itself, not necessarily on its main mitzvah, the in-depth study of Torah. (Maharil HaChadashos 45:2 also rules like Maharal. But others disagree with the Maharal, while some draw a distinction between the Written Torah and Oral Torah regarding this issue. See Yabea Omer vol. 1 26:9 and Piskei Teshuvos 47 note 30.) The Poskim further disagree whether Birchos HaTorah need to be said before reciting Pesukim in the form of Tefilla (see Shulchan Aruch and Rama 46:9). There too, it can be argued that it is a "cheftza of Torah" even though it is not being "studied".

7. *How many birchos haTorah are there?* – The Rosh here (#13) cites a disagreement amongst Rishonim (and variant texts of the Gemara) whether "הערב נא" is its own separate beracha or the ending of the first beracha; that is, whether there are a total of two or three birchos haTorah. This disagreement is quoted in Beis Yosef, Shulchan Aruch, and Rama (47:6) with the following ramification: if the paragraph of "הערב נא" is the ending of the first beracha then one needs to place a "vav" at the beginning of the word "והערב" in order to join it to the first beracha. The Mishnah Berurah (47:12) raises another ramification of this issue, explaining that according to those who opine that the two first berachos are really one, one should respond "amen" only after the conclusion of "והערב נא". This is indeed the general practice. But some Poskim write (see Piskei Teshuvos on MB ibid.) that most Rishonim and Poskim hold that there are indeed three berachos, so if one listens to another person's recital of the berachos in order to fulfill one's own requirement to say the berachos, then he should indeed split the berachos by responding "amen" before "הערב נא" as well. (It is interesting to note that the Gemara originally assumed that there is only one beracha of Birkas HaTorah, but R. Papa (see Gilyon HaShas) concludes that we should recite all the berachos due to the disagreement regarding the wording of the beracha. As an aside, see also Sdeh Tzofim who points to numerous places where R. Papa concludes in a similar fashion, establishing the halacha to satisfy all opinions.)

8. *Notes on the meaning of Birchos HaTorah* – a) We already mentioned the debate whether the first beracha reads "על דברי תורה" or "לעסוק בדברי תורה" and whether it embraces only *learning* Torah or also *acting* upon that learning through performing mitzvos. We also mentioned that the Maharal notes that we use the word "לעסוק" because a main part of the mitzvah includes active *involvement* in the Torah, not just cerebral study. Similarly, R. Yeduda ben Yakar (quoted in Shitos Kamai here pg. 236) adds that we use this word because it connotes *complete* involvement in Torah. He writes that to the degree that one involves himself in other pursuits he will have that much more difficulty in studying Torah to its fullest. b) Most commentators (see Abudraham and R. Yonasan M'Lunil here; see also famous intro. to Iglei Tal) explain the beracha of "והערב נא" as a request to *enjoy* Torah learning and therefore allow one to perform this mitzvah with real love for the mitzvah. Tzeida L'Derech (quoted in Shitos Kamai here pg. 234) explains

that our request for the Torah's sweetness refers to our desire to *understand* the Torah, as opposed to bitter foods which do not rest peacefully on one's pallet. It seems that the Raavad (Hasagos on 5b of Rif) also understands this way, for he writes that the beracha is a request that we do not make mistakes in our study. R. Yehuda ben Yakar (ibid.) explains the root word "ערב" here completely differently than the other commentators, writing that it refers to our request for the Torah to *guard* us from doing evil etc. (similar to ערב meaning cosigner and ערבות meaning camaraderie). c) The Rishonim disagree whether the conclusion of this beracha reads "*hamelamed* Torah etc." Einayim LaMishpat here #5 quotes Teshuvos haRambam who writes that this language is incorrect, "for Hashem does not teach us, rather He commanded us to learn it (ourselves)". Nonetheless, a similar language appears in the beracha of Ahava Raba ("והאר עינינו"; "ותלמדם חוקי חיים"), and it refers to Hashem's Divine assistance, even though the person himself is commanded to try his hardest as well. d) Tzeida L'Derech (ibid.) explains that the final beracha of Birchos HaTorah (which the Gemara states is the most special) refers to the fact that Hashem lovingly gave us the Torah so that we can perfect ourselves and continue to rise above the character of all other nations.

9. *What did the Kohanim and the nation daven during the time of the Beis HaMikdash?* – The Gemara records the Mishnah in Tamid that the Kohanim (during the 2nd Beis HaMikdash) davened a truncated Tefilla. The Rishonim explain (see Rashi here; Rosh and others in Tamid) that the Kohanim had to daven very early and also had to truncate their davening in order to have ample time to perform all of their service in the Mikdash (avoda), but they nevertheless made sure to daven some parts of the Tefilla in order to accompany their service with some prayer and to daven for the acceptance of the avoda. Moreover, according to Rambam's commentary on the Mishnah in Tamid (Kapach ed.), the Kohanim's Tefilla was actually a beracha to Bnei Yisroel, distinct from regular Tefilla. According to Rashi (here, as explained by Shita LeRashbi) the Leviim and Yisroelim who were present in the Mikdash would also recite this Tefilla along with the Kohanim, not as their own personal Tefilla which they would daven later at the proper time, but as an additional Tefilla for the acceptance of the korbanos. The commentators debate what the rest of the nation davened during that time period. Some write (see Tashbetz vol. 2 #161; R. Yehuda ben Yakar on "Modim"; Otzar HaTefillos intro. to Shemoneh Esrei) that due to the fact that the Beis HaMikdash was in existence, the numerous requests in Shemoneh Esrei for the building of the Beis HaMikdash etc. were recited differently during that time; they asked Hashem to *accept* their korbanos, not to *build* the Mikdash. But others (see R. Dovid Cohen's Ohel Dovid vol. 3 on Ezra ch. 3) suggest that the nation davened for the 3rd Beis HaMikdash even as the 2nd Beis HaMikdash stood, since the 2nd Beis HaMikdash lacked a strong presence of the Shechina and numerous miracles. As for the era prior to the Anshei Kenesses HaGedola (1st Beis HaMikdash and earlier), it is clear from Pesukim and Chazal (see Medrash quoted in Shibolei HaLeket #18; sources quoted in Nesiv Bina's intro. to Shemoneh Esrei; Otzar HaTefillos) that Tefilla always existed, and even the ideas discussed in the Shemoneh Esrei were already around. But the *exact text* of the Shemoneh Esrei was not established until the period of the Anshei Kenesses HaGedola. Otzar HaGeonim (Berachos pg. 77, 33a #203) records that during the era of the first Beis HaMikdash, *everyone* davened a Tefilla similar to the Tefilla of the Kohanim during the Second Beis HaMikdash (described in our Gemara). See also Tashbetz (ibid.) who discusses what they davened during earlier eras.

1. *To what degree are the fulfillment of the mitzvah of Keriyas Shema and Birchos Keriyas Shema dependent upon each other?* – Even though it is obviously ideal to recite the berachos in the order instituted by the Chachomim (see also Piskei Teshovos siman 60 notes 22-23), the Gemara states that one nonetheless fulfills his obligation even by reciting the berachos of Keriyas Shema out of their proper order. Yet the Poskim debate if one fulfills his obligation to recite Birchos Keriyas Shema if he omits one of the berachos altogether. (Meiri here and Toras Chaim by R. Yaakov Sofer 60:4 record a disagreement but favor the opinion that he does fulfill his obligation; Beiur Halacha 60:3 ד"ה שאם הקדים also rules this way; but see Machatzis HaShekel 60:1 who may disagree.) The Poskim (Meiri, Pri Megadim, Toras Chaim ibid.) offer consequences of this debate in cases when one can recite only *one* of the berachos (i.e. he only knows how to recite one or only has time for one); should he recite just one or would that constitute a "beracha l'vatala" (reciting a beracha in vain)? The Tur (66:2-3) quotes a further disagreement amongst the Rishonim whether one fulfills his obligation of *Keriyas Shema* if he omits one of the *berachos* of Keriyas Shema. The Poskim (Beis Yosef and Bach end of 66) add that this same disagreement applies to the berachos recited *after* Keriyas Shema ("emes v'yatziv" and "emes v'emunah"). Certainly everyone agrees that he fulfills his *Torah* obligation in these scenarios, for the Birchos Keriyas Shema are only Rabbinic in nature, but they nevertheless disagree on a Rabbinic level. One possible consequence of this debate may be found in a situation where one is unable to daven Shemoneh Esrei until later but he nonetheless wants to recite Shema by its proper time; should he recite Shema alone and recite the berachos later or should he recite the Shema with its berachos now (see Beiur Halacha 60:2 ד"ה ונ"ל)? The Poskim generally assume that we rule in accordance with the opinion that one indeed fulfills his obligation of Keriyas Shema even without reciting Birchos Keriyas Shema (see Beis Yosef and Bach and Beiur Halacha ibid.; MB 66:54). But many Poskim nonetheless write that one only fulfills the obligation of Keriyas Shema to its fullest if he also recites the berachos of Keriyas Shema, so it is certainly ideal to recite the berachos of Keriyas Shema by the proper time as well (see Beis Yosef and Bach ibid.; Aruch HaShulchan 60:2). (There seems to be a disagreement how to understand the various opinions in this debate. Some write that one side (R. Hai Gaon) holds that an individual does not fulfill the obligation of Keriyas Shema at all (on a Rabbinic level) without reciting the berachos, whereas the other Rishonim opine that he fulfills his *basic* obligation, but not the mitzvah to its fullest. But others seem to understand that *all* Rishonim agree that he fulfills his basic obligation; the Rishonim only disagree whether or not one fulfills his obligation to its fullest. See seemingly contradictory remarks in Beis Yosef ibid. and Beis Yosef 60:2-3 and MB 66:53 and Beiur Halacha 60:2 ibid. See also Machatzis HaShekel and Levushei Serad 60:1.) Shulchan Aruch (60:2) writes that when one eventually does recite Birchos Keriyas Shema he should ideally repeat Shema along with them. The Poskim debate the reason for this ruling; some explain that this second recital of Keriyas Shema is to enhance one's fulfillment of *Keriyas Shema*, while others explain that it is said in order to enhance one's *Shemoneh Esrei* that follows. Ramifications of these varying reasons include: a) a scenario in which the time for Keriyas Shema has already passed; b) a situation where one already davened Shemoneh Esrei (see MB 60:4 with Beiur Halacha ibid.; MB 66:53). One can offer an alternatively reason for this halacha, explaining that this recital of Shema is not meant to enhance Shema or Tefilla but to enhance the *berachos* of Keriyas Shema. That is, even though the berachos were instituted as their own unique Tefilla (see notes on 10b) and can be said without reciting Shema at all (according to Rashba quoted in Beis Yosef 60:2-3), nonetheless some Rishonim may understand that one should indeed recite Shema after saying the berachos (see Beis Yosef end of 46), and the Shulchan Aruch therefore writes that it is ideal to satisfy that opinion as well.

2. *Is it proper to recite the Aseres HaDibros in Tefilla, and what is unique about the Aseres HaDibros?* – It is clear from our Gemara that the Aseres HaDibros (10 Commandments) *should* ideally be recited as part of our regular Tefilla, but since doing so may give the appearance that only these commandments are from Hashem as opposed to the rest of the Torah (Heaven forbid), the Chachomim therefore did not include their recital in our prayer service. (See Megadim Chadashim here regarding *which* "heretics" made such a claim. See there further on רש"י ד"ה מפני for a discussion of whether or not Bnei Yisroel heard all 10 Commandments directly from Hashem at Har Sinai.) Nonetheless, the Shulchan Aruch (1:5) writes that it is a good practice to recite the Aseres HaDibros each day, but the Rama notes that they should not be recited as part of the congregational Tefilla, and the Mishnah Berurah adds that they should not be said even by an *individual* as part of the formal Tefilla. Piskei Teshuvos (1:17) discusses the propriety of the practice of many shuls to display the Aseres HaDibros on the Aron HaKodesh and the like. Some Poskim note (see there note 150) that this used to be the practice of Reformers, but today this is less of an issue since many completely Orthodox shuls carry on this practice and it is therefore not a statement of dissent. The Poskim have a similar debate regarding standing during the public Torah Reading of the Aseres HaDibros (see Piskei Teshuvos 146 note 30). It is important to realize that the fact that the Aseres HaDibros were part of the service in the Beis HaMikdash and that Chazal wanted to put them into everyone's daily service illustrates the great importance of these Pesukim. And more, Tosafos (end of 12b) cite the Yerushalmi that we in fact hint to the Aseres HaDibros in our Tefilla, for they can all be found in Shema. Indeed, Chazal write that all of the mitzvos in the Torah are hinted to in the Aseres HaDibros (see Rashi

Shemos 24:12), and many Rishonim organize their count of the 613 mitzvos according to the Aseres HaDibros (see R. Dovid Cohen's Maasas Kapai end of vol. 2 "קונטרס סדר תרי"ג להרמב"ם" for numerous sources).

3. *How important is one's intent during the beginning of a beracha?* – Rashi understands our Gemara as asking whether one needs to intend to recite the proper beracha while saying the generic, opening portion of the beracha ("buruch ata Hashem etc."). Many Rishonim (see Rishonim quoted in R. Yonah, Tos., Rosh, and others) challenge Rashi's explanation, questioning why intent is important at all and remarking that as long as one says the correct words he fulfills his obligation. Rashi seemingly understands (see R. Yonah) that although reciting the correct words is crucial, one can only truly be considered as recognizing Hashem's gifts if he knows for what he is currently thanking Hashem, for without that understanding his words are meaningless. On the other hand, Rashi's opponents seemingly opine that one's understanding can be more general (see Raavad quoted in Rosh), and that one's obligation is to offer words of thanks, but it is not absolutely essential to truly intend to do so. Even though it is obviously better to have full intent during all mitzvos, it is nonetheless only essential that one simply *performs* the mitzvos. They invoke the general principle that "mitzvos einan tzrichos kavanna" (mitzvos do not require intent), i.e. action is crucial; intent is merely an ideal addition. But on the opposite extreme, Rambam (hil. Berachos 8:11) seemingly goes even further than Rashi and writes that *only* the intent during the beginning of the beracha is crucial. That is, as long as one has proper intent during the initial section of the beracha he fulfills his obligation even if he utters the wrong words for the conclusion of the beracha. The Shulchan Aruch (209:1) rules in accordance with the Rambam, but the vast majority of Poskim disagree with him, and the Mishnah Berurah therefore rules that one does not fulfill his obligation in such a situation and needs to make a proper beracha again. R. Shlomo Zalman Auerbach (Halichos Shlomo on Tefilla ch. 22 in Orchos Halacha #24) writes that it is sensible that even Sefardim do not follow the Shulchan Aruch on this issue, for this opinion finds almost universal disagreement. (The Acharonim discuss other difficulties and contradictions within the opinion of the Rambam; see Einayim LaMishpat here #3 ד"ה ועתה נבא and Halichos Shlomo ibid.)

4. *Can one correct the wording of a beracha after he has already finished reciting it?* – The Rif (as explained by Rosh and other Rishonim) understands the Gemara as asking exactly this question. The reasoning is as follows: on one hand, one can argue that once the beracha was completed the statement is over and it is impossible to go back and fix it. And even if one tries to correct his mistake, the incorrect words may have constituted too much of an interruption in the beracha, making his beracha invalid. But on the other hand, since he corrects his beracha immediately, it is possible to see his entire statement as one long sentence. And even though he added some unnecessary words in the middle, since they were nonetheless words of praise they do not ruin the beracha (see Acharonim quoted in Dirshu ed. of MB 209 note 3). The Shulchan Aruch (209:2 with Mishnah Berurah) rules that correcting one's beracha indeed works regarding Rabbinic berachos. Beiur Halacha (there) adds some situations where one can fix his misspoken beracha even for berachos obligated according to the Torah. (For more explanations of our Gemara according to various Rishonim, see Einayim LaMishpat at length.)

5. *If one is unsure if he recited a beracha correctly, should he recite it again?* – The Rishonim here disagree how to rule regarding a case where it is unclear if one fulfilled his obligation to recite a beracha. Some Rishonim opine (see Tos. and others) that one needs to recite a beracha again in such a situation. They are seemingly of the opinion that the prohibition to recite a "beracha l'vatala" (beracha in vain) is only Rabbinic and that it is worse to eat with a possibility of not having recited a beracha than it is to possibly recite a beracha twice. Even though reciting a beracha is only a Rabbinic obligation (and generally one is not required to perform Rabbinic mitzvos unless one is clearly obligated to do so, as opposed to in a case of "safek"), these Rishonim explain that reciting a beracha before eating is a strict obligation due to the fact that eating without reciting a beracha is tantamount to stealing from Hashem and the like (see 35a below). (See Moreshes Moshe ch. 11 for sources in Rishonim and Acharonim regarding these points along with a number of other approaches to explain Tosafos's opinion.) But most Rishonim (see Rif quoted in Tosafos; Beis Yosef end of 209:2,3; Moreshes Moshe ibid.) rule that one is *not* obligated to recite a beracha again in this case of doubt, just as one is not obligated to perform most Rabbinic mitzvos in situations of uncertainly. Some Rishonim add (see R. Yonah here; Beis Yosef end of 67:1) that due to the possibility of reciting a "beracha l'vatala" it is forbidden to be "strict" on oneself and recite the beracha again. The Acharonim write that this point is certainly true according to the Rishonim who hold (see Teshuvos HaRambam P'er HaDor #105 and note 4 there) that reciting a "beracha l'vatala" constitutes a Torah prohibition. The Mishnah Berurah notes (Shaar HaTziyun 215:21) that even the Rishonim who understand the prohibition of beracha l'vatala as Rabbinic nonetheless agree that it is a very strict prohibition since Chazal refer to it as part of the severe prohibition of uttering Hashem's name in vain. The Acharonim further explain (see Shevet HaLevi vol. 7 #29; Kehillas Yaakov Berachos #5) that one is permitted to continue eating even though there is a possibility that he did not recite a beracha since the obligation to recite a beracha is only Rabbinic and the Rabbis did not prohibit eating in such a situation. Minchas Shlomo (vol. 1 18:9) adds that the Rabbis only forbade eating before reciting a beracha in order to ensure that people recognize Hashem before eating. Hence in a situation where one is forbidden to make a beracha, there is no reason for the food to be prohibited. (See also Gan

Shoshanim #14 ד"ה בגמ' ברכות commenting on the Gemara on 17b, and see our notes on 20b.) Nonetheless, Poskim write (see Aruch HaShulchan 202:2 and others) that when one finds himself in a state of doubt, it is praiseworthy to find a way to fulfill the obligation of making a beracha with certainly while also making sure to avoid a possible beracha l'vatala (such as listening to someone else reciting the beracha for himself and the like; see Piskei Teshuvos 209:7 and 213:4). Some Poskim write that one can even purposely cause a "break" (hefsek) in his meal in order to obligate himself to recite another beracha and thus relieve himself from his doubt (see Igros Moshe OC vol. 4 40:1; Piskei Teshuvos 167:19; see also Mishnah Berurah 206:10.)

6. *If one recites the beginning of a beracha incorrectly, can he correct his mistake by reciting the end of the beracha properly?* – The Poskim disagree (see Beiur Halacha 59:2 ד"ה ולא אמר) how to understand the conclusion of our Gemara. The Shulchan Aruch seems to rule that one needs to correct both the beginning and end of his beracha (that is, he needs to say "יוצר אור" at the beginning of the beracha and "יוצר המאורות" at the end). But the Gra and others rule that it suffices to merely finish the beracha properly ("יוצר המאורות") even if the beginning of the beracha was recited incorrectly. Practically, many Poskim (see Dirshu ed. of MB ibid. note 6) rule in accordance with the position of the Gra, both in this scenario and numerous others (mistakes made in Shemoneh Esrei etc.; see there).

7. *Reciting "ha'etz" for wine or "birkas hamazon" for fruit or mezonos foods* – See Einayim LaMishpat based on Tosafos and Gemara here.

8. *To what degree does one who omits "emes v'yaztiv" fulfill his obligation of Keriyas Shema?* – Tur (end of #66) concludes that one indeed fulfills his basic obligation of Keriyas Shema, but in a less than ideal fashion. See also notes above (beginning of amud).

9. *What do the various praises mentioned in "emes v'yatziv" refer to?* – Einayim LaMishpat cites a disagreement amongst the Rishonim if one is allowed to shower Hashem with various praises during Tefilla. (Adding such praise to formal prayer such as Shemoneh Esrei is certainly forbidden.) According to those who opine that one is forbidden to add praise, he quotes commentators who explain that the myriad of praises in the prayer of "emes v'yatziv" do not refer to Hashem but to the truthfulness of Shema or Shemoneh Esrei (see Tosafos and Tanya Rabbasi #4 quoted in Shitos Kamai here). According to the other commentators, however, these praises can refer to Hashem Himself.

10. *What is the proper manner of bowing during Tefilla?* – The Gemara states that one should bow at "baruch" and stand erect for Hashem's name. Bowing displays one's fear of Hashem and his extreme humility before Him; standing erect expresses our confidence that He listens to our prayers and desires to fulfill our needs (see R. Yonah here; Mabit in Beis Elokim, Tefilla ch. 8). The Poskim disagree if one should straighten himself *as* he says Hashem's name or *before* doing so (see Dirshu ed. of MB 113 note 16 and Piskei Teshuvos 113 note 17). Regarding the procedure for bowing, the Mishnah Berurah (113:12) writes that one should bend his knees while saying "baruch" and then bend his body while say "ata". But other Poskim write (see Shaarei Teshuva and Be'er Heitev 113:5; Piskei Teshuvos 113:3) that one bends his body during "baruch" and then bends his head downwards at "ata". Some write (see Piskei Teshuvos ibid. note 14) that one can fulfill all opinions by bending one's knees along with slightly bending one's body during "baruch" and then further bending one's body and head during "ata". Regarding bowing during "Modim", the Mishnah Berurah (ibid.) writes that one bows his torso all at once, but other Poskim rule (see Dirshu ed. ibid.; Me'ir Oz 113:7) that one bows his knees at Modim as well. (R. Schwab explains that bending one's knees and torso is a fulfillment of Tehillim 35:10 that "all of one's bones" should be involved in prayer; see R. Schwab on Prayer pg. 410.) When straightening oneself, the Shulchan Aruch (113:6) rules that one first lifts his head and then his body, but many Chasidim and Sefaradim follow the Arizal (see Piskei Teshuvos ibid. note 15) to first lift one's body and only then lift the head. The Shulchan Aruch further codifies (113:5-6, based on Gemara 12b) that one should bow quickly, but get back up slowly. He warns, however, against bowing too low (below one's waist). The Poskim explain this ruling in numerous fashions: it displays arrogance, disrespect, can be indecent, etc. Yet a couple Rishonim write that bowing in an extreme fashion is indeed praiseworthy (see Meir Oz 113:5 who quotes many commentators on this issue; see also Piskei Teshuvos ibid. note 19).

1. *Does one need to repeat Shemoneh Esrei if he says "האל הקדוש" or "מלך אוהב צדקה ומשפט" during Aseres Y'mei Teshuva?* – The Rishonim disagree about this point (see Beis Yosef 118 and 582:1 and Einayim LaMishpat). Some write that the disagreement in our Gemara was never meant to make one repeat Shemoneh Esrei, but most others disagree. Some Rishonim write that it is only problematic if one does not mention the word "melech" at all (that is, if one says "האל אוהב צדקה ומשפט", which many had the custom to say during the year), while others write that even "מלך אוהב" etc. does not suffice, for that language only implies that the *people* act with propriety, not that the *King* sits in judgement. Practically, the Shulchan Aruch (ibid.) rules that one must repeat Shemoneh Esrei, whereas the Rama (siman 118) writes that one only repeats Shemoneh Esrei if he does not mention "melech" at all, but if he says "מלך אוהב" etc. then he does not need to repeat.

2. *Does one need to repeat Shemoneh Esrei if he forgot to add the other insertions ("זכרנו" etc.) during Aseres Y'mei Teshuva?* – Tosafos cite a debate amongst the Rishonim regarding this issue. Most Rishonim opine that one does not repeat Shemoneh Esrei for omitting these insertions since these additions were not instituted by Chazal but by the Geonim, and they are therefore not as strict. Some Rishonim even opposed saying these extra sentences altogether because we generally do not make these types of requests during the first and last three berachos of Shemoneh Esrei. But most Rishonim defend the practice (see Beis Yosef 582:4-5 and 34a below).

3. *Why does Hashem respond to Tefilla recited for the sake of another individual?* – Minchas Yitzchak (vol. 8 #53) quotes numerous commentators (Maharal, Chasam Sofer, Maharam Shik) who explain that when someone truly feels pain and even makes himself sick (as stated in our Gemara) because of his fellow's difficulties and anguish, he shows that the punishment expressed in this illness is not directed not at his friend alone, but it affects him as well. By doing so, he inspires Hashem (kaviyachol) to reevaluate whether the reason for this illness warrants the extreme anguish of not just the immediate victim but also of all those who deeply feel the victim's pain. Hence, by feeling another person's sorrow, one "attaches" himself to that friend, and his Tefilla is not simply recited for his friend but for the two of them together, as two limbs of the same body. (This idea also explains some of the importance of the general concept of "nosei b'ol chavero", because when one feels his friend's pain he "carries the burden" with him and can literally lessen the punishment itself.) See Sefer Shome'ah Tefilla (by ר' ישעיה בראווער, vol. 2 ch. 45-53) for more on the topic of davening for others. It is important to note that the most essential prayers are the ones that one prays for *oneself*, as the Maharal (Be'er HaGolah #4) notes from Bereishis Raba (53:14). Hashem brings hardships on an individual in order that he repent (see 5a), and therefore the most critical response to such hardships (yissurin) is to repent and personally foster one's relationship with Hashem through one's own Tefilla and performance of mitzvos.

4. *Were Do'eg and Achisofel talmidei chachomim, worthy of Dovid's prayer?* – Rashi explains that Dovid davened profusely for Do'eg and Achisofel because they were talmidei chachomim. Megadim Chadashim questions Rashi, pointing to a number of Gemaros that write that Do'eg and Achisofel were resha'im, evil people whose Torah knowledge was only superficial and who used their knowledge for wicked purposes. He writes that perhaps Dovid only davened with such passion for Do'eg and Achisofel before he knew of their malicious intent. (But see Mishbatzos Zahav on Shemuel 2 6:1 who cites Tiferes Tziyon who explains that Dovid knew of Achisofel's poor character early in his reign.)

5. *Why is feeling embarrassed of one's sins so significant?* – Michtav Me'Eliyahu explains (vol. 4 pg. 222 and 263) that the feeling of embarrassment finds its source in the spiritual aspects of one's psyche. That is, when one senses that he has slipped from his spiritual capabilities and that his actions contradict his true essence, he becomes embarrassed of his own state of being. Orchos Tzadikim (shaar 3) adds that the degree that one experiences embarrassment depends on one's level of "daas" (maturity of thought). This explains why infants never feel embarrassed, toddlers feel only slight embarrassment, righteous adults experience embarrassment even for small infractions, and wicked individuals almost never feel ashamed at all. Michtav Me'Eliyahu proceeds to explain that when someone feels deeply ashamed of his wicked ways, he achieves atonement for his sins due to the fact that his inner spiritual psyche (which houses his sense of shame) takes over his persona. That is, his embarrassment is an expression of the fact that his spirituality is his essence. Orchos Tzadikim and Michtav Me'Eliyahu both explain that there are various forms of embarrassment. The most basic level is to feel ashamed to sin in front of others, but ideally one should acquire a sense of deep shame within oneself and in front of one's Creator. But someone who feels absolutely no shame even before others has stooped to an exceedingly low level of impurity and is completely out of touch with the sense of spirituality hidden in the deep recesses of his psyche (see also Michtav Me'Eliyahu vol. 3 pg. 215).

6. *Why would it have been appropriate to include the Pasuk from Parashas Balak in Keriyas Shema?* – Rashi here explains that the Pasuk that the Gemara quotes (Bamidbar 24:9) refers to going to sleep and awaking with the recital of Keriyas Shema, as we express our confidence in our safety (just like a lion sleeps without fear) due to our reliance

on Hashem. Mesoras HaShas (on the side of the Gemara) quotes a variant text in which the Gemara quotes an earlier Pasuk in Parashas Balak (23:24). Rashi on that Pasuk quotes the Tanchuma which explains that the Pasuk describes Bnei Yisroel's rising like a lion in the morning to say Shema and to perform mitzvos and the fact that they do not sleep at night until they say Shema again and put their full faith in Hashem. Daf al HaDaf here quotes the Sfas Emes (Parashas Balak) and Pnei Yehoshua (here) who add a further reason to recite Parashas Balak, pointing to a Pasuk in Micha (6:5) that states that we should remember the story of Balak each day. Daf al HaDaf further quotes some who write that we recite "Ma Tovu etc." each morning since this Pasuk stems from Parashas Balak and thus fulfills the requirement cited in the aforementioned Pasuk in Micha. (He further quotes some Poskim who were against reciting "Ma Tovu" since it was originally said by the evil Bilaam, but quotes others who strongly disagree, pointing to our Gemara which clearly states that it is indeed appropriate to include Parashas Balak in our daily Tefilla.)

7. *When is there a problem to "split" Parshiyos and Pesukim?* – The Gemara states that Chazal were not permitted to isolate a Pasuk from Parashas Balak and add it to Keriyas Shema because of the dictum that we do not split sections of the Torah that Moshe was not originally told to divide. The Gemara elsewhere (Taanis 27b and Megilla 22a) records that we may not divide *Pesukim*, but a prohibition against dividing larger sections (Parshiyos) is not mentioned. In fact, Meromei Sadeh here quotes the Turei Even who cites numerous places where we indeed divide Parshiyos. Meromei Sadeh answers that we only may not *begin* in the middle of a Parasha, but we may *end* in the middle of a Parasha. He further quotes the Turei Even who writes that we are permitted to stop in the middle of the Parasha if we plan to continue the rest of the Parasha later, but Meromei Sadeh argues that this reasoning does not suffice to explain why we are permitted to stop in the middle of a Parasha during the Torah Reading on Mondays and Thursdays; he therefore prefers his own reasoning (ibid.). (Meromei Sadeh seemingly considers the reading on Shabbos a completely new reading because it does not continue where the congregation ends on Monday or Thursday. See also Magen Avraham beg. of 282 and Levushei Serad there for a parallel discussion.) The commentators discuss numerous situations where we indeed "split" both Parshiyos and Pesukim, and they explain various scenarios in which this prohibition does not apply. Magen Avraham (ibid.) writes an essential distinction, explaining that we may divide Pesukim during Tefilla for the sake of making requests and singing Hashem's praises. (It seems that Keriyas Shema does not fall under this category since Keriyas Shema is not simply a Tefilla, but a more formal "reading", similar in some senses to Torah Reading and the like; see Emek Beracha bottom of pg. 9). One can also add (see Ha'elef L'cha Shlomo OC #43) that there is no prohibition against splitting Pesukim during simple conversation or when ones wishes to merely prove a point from a Pasuk while studying Torah. Indeed, the Gemara itself often quotes partial sections of Pesukim in order to teach various halachos etc. Chazal only prohibited dividing Pesukim when reciting them in a formal manner, such as Keriyas HaTorah, Keriyas Shema, or when formally learning or teaching the Pesukim. Zecher Yehosef (vol. 1 #38 top of pg. 56b) posits further that even one who is specifically learning or teaching the Pesukim is only forbidden to pause in the middle of a Pasuk if he is learning/teaching in a very formal manner, i.e. in public or with the "trop" (the special tune used during Torah Reading). (Some Poskim make a similar distinction regarding the prohibition against reciting the Written Torah by heart; see, for example, Kol Bo in Beis Yosef #49.) But Igros Moshe (OC vol. 2 #56; see also Beis HaLevi intro. to vol. 1, quoted in Megadim Chadashim 17a pg. 181) seems to understand that this prohibition applies even when studying Torah in a regular fashion. See Sdeh Tzofim (here and Taanis 27b) and Kobetz Yeshurun (vol. 7 pg. 617) for further distinctions recorded in Poskim. See also Einayim LaTorah who discusses whether this is a definite "prohibition" or a mere propriety. (See also our notes on 14b.)

8. *Heresy and Avoda Zara are the same concept* – The commentators note that the Gemara initially records that there are 5 ideas mentioned in the third paragraph of Shema, but it then continues to list 6. Many commentators explain (see Tos. HaRosh; see also Raavya and Einayim LaMishpat) that "heresy" and "avoda zara" are the same concept, i.e. a betrayal of the underlying tenets of the Torah. Indeed, the Rambam (hil. Avoda Zara 2:2-3) codifies these two sins together: a) not to read books of avoda zara; b) not to read or think about heresy. He explains that both can easily bring someone to abandon the basic tenets of our religion and Hashem's commandments altogether.

9. *What is prohibited based the Pasuk of* לא תתורו אחרי לבבכם ואחרי עיניכם? – The Gemara records that "אחרי לבבכם" refers to thinking heretical thoughts (see parameters in Rambam hil. Avoda Zara 2:2-3), whereas "אחרי עיניכם" refers to "הרהור עבירה", literally "sinful thought". Mitzvas HaMelech (on the Rambam's Sefer HaMitzvos lo saaseh #47) explains the various opinions of the Rishonim regarding the latter prohibition: a) The Rambam (Sefer HaMitzvos ibid.) understands the prohibition of "אחרי עיניכם" as referring to a general over-occupation with worldly pleasures. (For further explanation of the Rambam's opinion, see the Hebrew essay printed in the back of this kuntrus.) b) Other Rishonim understand this Pasuk as prohibiting staring at women with promiscuous intent (Smak; see also Igros Moshe Even Ha'Ezer vol. 1 #69) or in a way that could lead to sin (R. Yonah). Mitzvas HaMelech further points to a disagreement whether "לא תתורו אחרי לבבכם ואחרי עיניכם" constitutes two separate prohibitions out of the 613 mitzvos (Smak; R. Yonah) or whether both of these prohibitions are lumped together into one mitzvah (Rambam; Smag).

10. *What was the argument between the Chachomim and R. Elazar ben Azarya/Ben Zoma regarding mentioning Yetziyas Mitzrayim at night?* – Most Rishonim explain that the Chachomim did not say the third paragraph of Keriyas Shema at night at all (Chidushei HaRashba and Ritva based on Gemara 14b; Machzor Vitri vol. 1 pg. 292, Commentary on the Hagadda, hil. Pesach #95; Shibolei HaLeket on Haggada), but some write that they indeed recited it but held that it was only Rabbinic in nature (Raavad quoted in Rashba and Meiri). Those who opine that they did not recite this paragraph also write that they did not say the paragraph of "emes v'emunah", but simply recited the first two paragraphs of Shema followed by a short Tefilla and/or the words "דבר אל בנ"י ואמרת אליהם ה' אלקיכם אמת" (see Rashba and Machzor Vitri ibid.; but see Shibolei HaLeket ibid.), and then the final two berachos after Shema. Some commentators explain (see Peirush HaRi"d on the Haggada; Shibolei HaLeket ibid.; Einayim LaMishpat beg. #3) that the Chachomim agreed to Ben Zoma after hearing his argument, but others seem to learn (see Ritva on the Haggada) that they kept their opinion. Either way, the halacha concludes that one must mention Yetziyas Mitzrayim at night, either because the Chachomim agree or because we rule in accordance with R. Elazar ben Azarya. The Poskim disagree, however, if this requirement is Biblical or Rabbinic. Some Poskim understand that even the requirement during the *day* is only Rabbinic since the language of the Pasuk does not imply an absolute command. See Einayim LaMishpat for a lengthy discussion of this matter and for a debate regarding distinctions between this mitzvah and the mitzvah to discuss/mention Yetziyas Mitzrayim on the first night of Pesach.

11. *Why will we need to remember Yetziyas Mitzrayim even during the time of Mashiach?* – Maharal (intro. to Netzach Yisroel) explains that that which Am Yisroel gained through the servitude and redemption from Mitzrayim stays with us and defines us forever. When we eventually (hopefully in the very near future!) merit the final Redemption, we will be riding on the coattails of Yetziyas Mitraim, advancing to the next stage while bearing the persona that enriched us during Yetziyas Mitzrayim. It is for this same reason that we mention Yetziyas Mitzrayim each day and night throughout Galus, for it was that experience that defined us as a people. The story of Yetziyas Mitzrayim serves as a constant reminder that without Hashem we are mere slaves, contemptible and lowly. But because of Hashem we became a great, holy nation, "ממלכת כהנים וגוי קדוש" (see our notes on top of 9b), and this identity remains with us forever.

1. *What is the difference between the names "Yaakov" and "Yisroel", and why does the name "Yaakov" remain as opposed to the name "Avram"?* – Kedushas Levi (Parashas Toldos 25:22) explains that the names "Yaakov" and "Yisroel" represent two aspects of Yaakov Avinu's personality and soul. On the one hand, Yaakov forever remained the same pure, reserved individual that he was in his younger years (יעקב איש תם יושב אהלים). This attribute is represented by the name "Yaakov", from the word "heel", the lowliest (yet foundational) part of one's body. But on the other hand, Hashem forced Yaakov to spread his wings and become the father of the entire Jewish nation by raising a large family of twelve holy sons with varying personalities. This flourishment is represented in the name "Yisroel" (which contains the name of Hashem Himself), and it is this name that defines Yaakov's children as "Bnei Yisroel". (See also the end of the Maharal's intro. to Netzach Yisroel and end of ch. 3 of Gevuros Hashem for a similar idea.) In contrast, Avraham embodies the attribute of "chesed" to its fullest extent, as he spent his life opening himself up and connecting to others while he displayed the path of Hashem to the entire world. Therefore, his original, more limited name of "Avram" became completely obsolete; he must only be referred to as "Avraham", for anything less is a corruption of his personality. (The extra letter in his name also adds a letter from Hashem's name into Avraham's character, and Bereishis Raba 12:9 utilizes this name to say that the world was created for Avraham ("בהבראם" read homiletically as "באברהם"). See also note 129 in Gur Aryeh Bereshis ch. 21. See also note 42 on the Ritva's commentary on the Haggada printed in the back of Musad HaRav Kook ed. of Ritva on Pesachim that the name "Avram" is insulting to Avraham since it was his name before he became Jewish and opened himself to the entire world.) Based on the above, it is possible to explain that Sarah, Avraham's partner in his life's mission, also underwent a similar name change for the same reason. Nonetheless Sarah remained more hidden and grounded in their home (see Rashi Bereishis 18:9), and it is therefore not a distortion of her personality to refer to her with her more limited, private name of "Sarai". (Daf al HaDaf here writes that most of the world still knew Sarah as "Sarai", yet her "main" name, as far as describing her essence, became "Sarah".) Interestingly, Kedushas Levi adds that Yitzchak never underwent a name change, for Yitzchak always remained more closed off to the world, symbolizing immutable inner strength. (For an alternative explanation for the significance of the name "Yaakov", see Ritva ibid. with note 45 that in the End of Days the Jewish people will reign after all other nations finish their reign, just as Yaakov entered this world after Esav, holding onto his "heel".)

2. *What are the halachic ramifications of Avraham's name change?* – a) The commentators question (see Einayim LaMishpat) why the vast majority of Poskim did not codify the prohibition against calling Avraham by his original name, "Avram". Some explain (see Acharonim quoted in Sdeh Tzofim here) that the Poskim understood that this is not an absolute prohibition, but only a praiseworthy custom. Others explain that the prohibition only applied during Avraham's lifetime and therefore does not apply today. (See Mishmar HaLeviim here end of #23 for R. Yechezkel Abromsky's brilliant reading of the Gemara according to this approach. See also Ben Yehoyada here.). One can possibly explain differently, that the Poskim understood this Gemara as aggada and not as truly prohibiting this reference. The Gemara is teaching that understanding and referring to Avraham as "Avram" is a complete misunderstanding of the monumental transformation that occurred when Hashem changed his name. Nemukei HaGriv and Maharatz Chayes (notes in back of Gemara) understand this Gemara literally but write that we do not rule in accordance with this Gemara. Einayim LaMishpat further points out that the Tosefta here (1:14) also seems that there is no prohibition. b) Nonetheless, many Poskim write that the name "Avram" is written in official documents (get, kesuba) as "Avraham" unless one has a specific family tradition to name "Avram" (see Sdei Chemed vol. 3 "chaf" #83; Maharatz Chayes Gittin 50a; Sdeh Tzofim here). c) Another ramification of our Gemara is codified by the Rambam (hil. Bikkurim 4:3) who writes that a convert can refer to himself (in the context of bringing the first fruits) as the progeny of Avraham Avinu, since Avraham was the father of many nations (אב המון גוים). (See Einayim LaMishpat further regarding this halacha as well as the status of converts pertaining to various berachos and promises. See also note 44 on the Ritva's commentary on the Haggada in the back of the Musad HaRav Kook ed. of the Ritva on Pesachim.)

3. *Who is referred to as a "navi"?* – Maharatz Chayes questions the wording of our Gemara, pointing out that the Chachomim speaking in the Pasuk quoted here from Nechemia were not listed by Chazal as Neviim (see Rashi Megilla 14a). He further quotes the Yerushalmi that refers to them as part of the Anshei Kenesses HaGedolah, but not as Neviim. (See Mishmar HaLeviim here end of #24 who asks a similar question on a few other Gemaros.) It is possible that the Gemara refers to these Chachomim as Neviim because they had a tradition that they were indeed Neviim, but they were not included in the list of Neviim because their prophecy was not relevant for all future generations. Indeed Gemara Megilla 14a writes that there were hundreds of thousands of prophets in the history of Jewish nation (see also Shemuel 1 19:20-24), but the list of Neviim only includes those Neviim who were sent by Hashem to express their prophecy for all eternity.

מאמרים/Essays

- קונטרס פרי עמלינו -

א.   ביאור למה מחמירים כל כך בכבוד המת [ברכות ג:]

ב.   האם ראוי לינשא לגיורת (בענין אהבת וקדושת גרים) [ברכות ח:]

ג.   הזמן המוקדם בשעת הדחק למצות טלית תפלין ק"ש ותפלה [ברכות ט:]

ד.   שמחה ותפילה על מפלתן של רשעים [ברכות י.]

ה.   איסור אכילה ועשיית מלאכה קודם שחרית [ברכות י:]

ו.   ביאור החיוב שלא להחמיר נגד הלכה פסוקה (ובענין כבוד דיינים ובית דין) [ברכות יא.]

ז.   שיטת הרמב"ם בגדר מצות לא תתורו אחרי אחרי לבבכם ואחרי עיניכם [ברכות יב:]

8.   The Jewish Politician – Are we to scoff at evil or work with it? [Berachos 7b]

Essays from the Bnei Chabura

9.   Does Keriyas Shema depend on "sleeping and awaking" or "night and day"? [Berachos 2a] – *Rabbi Ranan Amster*

10. Kaddish D'Rabbanan: What is it and when is it said? [Berachos 3a] – *Dr. Jonathan Mazurek*

11. When is it imperative to daven in shul as opposed to one's home? [Berachos 6a] – *Dr. Jonathan Dobkowski*

סימן א' – ביאור למה מחמירים כל כך בכבוד המת

מצינו שהתורה מרחיקה לכת בחומרת כבוד המת עד שבהרבה דברים מקפידים יותר בכבוד המת מבכבוד החיים. כגון הא דאיתא בברכות (ג:), "א"ר זריקא א"ר אמי אריב"ל, אין אומרים בפני המת אלא דבריו של מת". ופי' בתוס' הרא"ש וז"ל, "מפני כבוד המת אין ראוי לספר כלום אלא בדבריו של מת". וכעי"ז בשטמ"ק קצת באו"ל, "מפני שיהיו עסוקין בהספדו. ויש מפרשים שמפני שהמת יודע כל מה שאומרים לפניו עד שיסתם הגולל ומצטער כששומע שמדברים שלא מצרכיו, וכתיב ועשית הישר והטוב, ואין טוב כשמצטער המת." ולא מצינו שהקפידו חז"ל כן בשאר דברים, דאין איסור לשאר גומלי חסד לספר בפני מי שנעשה החסד בשבילו (כל זמן שאין זה מגרע ממעשיהם), ולא אמרינן צער להזולת שיש כששומע שלא מדברים שלא מצרכיו וכדומה. וכיוצ"ב איכא עוד הרבה דברים שמפליגים בכבוד המת, כגון הא דאסרו חכמים לעשות מצוות בפני המת משום "לועג לרש" (ע' ברכות הנ"ל ושם יח.), ולא מצינו הקפדה זו בעודו בחיים ואף במקום שלא היה אפשר לו לעשות המצוה. וכן עם רב מבטלים ממלאכתן ומלימוד תורתן כדי להלוות המת, ואפי' למת שאינו ת"ח ושבחייו לא היה מצוה לכבדו (ע' כתובות סוף יז. ועוד), ואינו כן בשאר חסדים. ועוד למדו חכמים (ע' ברכות יט:) דכדי לקבור מת מצוה משום כבוד המת מבטלין מצוות מצוה של מילה ופסח, וגם כהן גדול ונזיר מטמאין את עצמן, ולא מצינו כן בשאר מצוות התורה. וכל זה צ"ב למה החמירה התורה כ"כ בכבוד המת. ויש להעלות כמה טעמים לחומר ענין כבוד המת, ונראה שהטעמים מתחלקים כפי דינים שונים של כבוד המת וכמו שיתבאר.

א: שפלות מצבו של המת

הנה בענין "לועג לרש" הנ"ל, אפשר לבאר שצותה התורה להקפיד על כבוד המת משום שפלות מצבו של המת, שהוא נמצא עכשיו חפשי מן המצוות וגופו טמא מאבי אבות הטומאה. (והוא גרוע אף מגוסס, דאפי' גוסס עוסק במידה מסויימת. והנה ע' בספר עלי שור להגר"ש וולבה זצ"ל (ח"א עמ' ש') וז"ל, "גוסס הרי הוא כחי לכל דבר (אבל רבתי פ"א) - לרבות מחשבות... אדם חושב בשעת גסיסתו כל אותן המחשבות שהעסיקוהו עד כה - קפידות קטנטנות, שנאה ונקמה וכו'." ונמצא דמחשבות רעות באותה שעה הן בבחינת "עבירה", ולהיפך באדם קדוש שמחשבותיו טהורות ומעולות כמו בכל חייו, ויש בהם ריבוי כבוד שמים ועליית האדם.) **וכיון שהמת חשיב "רש" יותר מכל חי, לכן מחמירים בכבודו** - א', מפאת כבוד הבריות ומעלת האדם דרך כלל, וב', כדי שלא יהי' המת ככלי ריק שאין לנו חפץ בו. ולכן אין אומרים שום דבר בפני המת שאינו מעניינו של מת כדי להראות שעניניו חשובין בעינינו עד למאד. וכן נזהרין טובא שלא יהיה בזיון למת, וכמו שמצינו דמשו"ה התירה התורה אף לכהן גדול ונזיר ליטמא למת לקברו כיוצ"ב (ע' ברכות יט:) כדי שלא יהיה המת מוטל בבזיון (ע' תוס' ב"מ ל: ד"ה אלא). ועוד אמרו רז"ל (ברכות יח.), "כל הרואה המת ואינו מלווהו עובר משום לועג לרש עושהו", דמי שרואה אדם אחר בשפלות נוראה כזו ואעפ"כ ממשיך כמנהגו ואינו חושש, הרי הוא כאומר שלא אכפת ליה בחסרון הזולת, וזה גופא חשיב "לעג". (ונר' דדבר זה אינו תלוי בדין בגמ' סנהדרין (מו:) אם קבורה משום בזיונא או כפרה, דנר' דכו"ע מודי דאיכא גדול בזיון כשהמת עצמו רוצה ליקבר ואינו קוברו, אבל דנה הגמ' שם בציור שאין המת רוצה ליקבר די"ל דאין הבזיון למת בכהאי גוונא גדול כ"כ לחיוב לקוברו עכ"פ מיד. ע' היטב בלשון תוס' הרא"ש שם (ד"ה קבורה) ובאגרו"מ (יו"ד ח"א סי' רמ"ט ד"ה וצריך), ואכ"מ.)

ובעיקר ענין לועג לרש, כתב הריטב"א (ברכות יח.) ד"ה לא יהלך) וז"ל, "שהמת פטור מן המצות ודואג כשרואה שאחרים עוסקים במצוה והוא אינו יכול". וכעי"ז מבואר בכל בו (סי' קי"ד) לענין שאר המת ביזוי וז"ל, "קשה לנפש כשתראה הגוף מתבזה". וכן ע' בספר חסידים (סי' תתשס"ג) וז"ל, "הנשמה רואה מה שעושין לגוף אחר מיתה... לכך קשה רימה למת, לא שכואב לו, אלא הנשמה קשה לה זילות הגוף." וע"ע בשטמ"ק הנ"ל דהדיבור בפני המת גורם צער למת. אבל ראיתי מהגרא"ז שז"ל (הליכות שלמה תפלה מילואים סי' ב') שביאר באו"א וז"ל, "נר' דהענין של לועג לרש הוא לא מחמת צערו של מת, שהרי המתים יודעים שהם חפשים מן המצוות, רק השרשת דרך ארץ בין החיים שלא להתהדר בכך שהם מחוייבים במצוות בפני המתים", עע"ש. וע"ע בתוס' יו"ט (אבות ב:ז) דנר' דנחלקו גדולי האחרונים בשאלה זו אם המת או נפש המת מרגיש בצער, או שרק החיים מרגישים בצערו של המת, ע"ש.

ונמצא דבזיון המת יש בו משום **צער המת עצמו** (לפי רוב מפרשים הנ"ל), ויש בו גם **פחיתות כבוד שמים מחמת זלזול בצלם אלקים** (כמו שביארו המפרשים בענין כבוד הבריות דרך כלל). ויש בזה גם ענין כבוד החיים, שהחיים מתבזים ע"י שהמת נסרח ונתבזה (ע' סנהדרין מו: ובמ"ב שיא:ז). והוא גם כבוד להמת עצמו בעודו בחיים שידע שינהגו בו בכבוד גם לאחר מיתתו.

[ויש להעיר בדרך אגב קצת בהא דאמרינן שהמת נקרא "רש" משום שהוא חפשי מן המצוות. דהנה אמרו רז"ל (אבות ד:יז), "יפה שעה אחת בתשובה ומעשים טובים בעוה"ז מכל חיי העולם הבא, ויפה שעה אחת של קורת רוח בעוה"ב מכל חיי העולם הזה". **ונר' דנחלקו המפרשים בביאור המש' אם עוה"ב עדיף או עוה"ז עדיף**. דהנה כתב המהר"ל שם (דרך חיים ד:יח)

וז"ל, "יש לך לדעת איך התשובה ומעשים טובים הם יפים מכל חיי העוה"ב, והוא דבר עמוק. וזה כי מצד התשובה ומעשים טובים אשר הם בעוה"ז, האדם מתעלה מן עוה"ז הגשמי להיות אל השי"ת. והנה מתנועע האדם אל השי"ת כאשר האדם הוא בעל תשובה, ואשר הוא מתנועע אל דבר הוא נחשב עמו לגמרי ביותר. כי המתנועע אל הדבר הוא מצד הדבר שאליו הוא מתנועע כאילו הוא דבר אחד עם מי שאליו התנועה... כי בעוה"ז שיש תשובה ומעשים טובים, והאדם עושה מצוה תמיד לשוב אל השי"ת, דבר זה נחשב יותר דבק עם השי"ת מצד זה מכל חיי העוה"ב. שהדבר הזה מה שיש לו חיי עוה"ב כבר הגיע למדריגתו אשר ראוי לו בעוה"ב. ואינו דבר זה כמו מי שהוא בעל תשובה ומעשים טובים שהוא שב אל השי"ת, שמצד שהוא מתעלה אל השי"ת הוא עם השי"ת לגמרי." וכתב שם בביאור המ' דעוה"ז אכן עדיף לענין המעלה, אבל עוה"ב יותר טוב לענין התענוג וקורת רוח וז"ל, "יפה מעלת עולם התשובה ומעשים טובים בעוה"ז מכל מעלת חיי עולם הבא... שבעוה"ב אין קנין מעלה, ומצד קנין מעלה, עוה"ז יותר במעלה מן עוה"ב... יפה קורת רוח שיש בשעה אחת בעוה"ז מכל חיי העוה"ב, כלומר שבכל חיי העוה"ז לא נמצא הקורת רוח שיש בשעה אחת של העוה"ב." ויסוד הזה ידוע מהסיפור שאומרים על הגר"א זצ"ל (כעדות הגרד"ל בספר עליות אליהו העל' קי"ז, הו"ד בהליכות שלמה תפלה מילואים סי' ב'), שבשעת פטירתו "אחז בציציותיו ואמר בבכיה, כמה קשה להפרד מעולם המעשה הזה אשר ע"י מצוה קלה כי"ז של ציצית אדם יזכה יחזה פני שכינה, ואיפה נוכל למצוא זאת בעולם הנשמות אף אם יתנו כל כוחותיו עבורו." וכן איתא בדרשת מהר"ח (לתלמידו הגר"ח מוואלזין, הו"ד ברוח חיים ד:יז העל' ס"ז) וז"ל, "העולם אומרים שגם עוה"ז הוא עולם וגם בעדו יש לחשוב. ובאמת צדיקי עולם העובדים את ה' מאהבה בלא שום כוונה זולתי שרצונם לעבוד את ה', להם נאה לומר כן. כאשר כן שמעתי כמה פעמים מפי קדשו של רבינו הגאון החסיד מו"ה אליהו מווילנא ז"ל נ"ע, מה העוה"ב חשוב ואין ערך ודוגמא כלל נגד שעה אחת בעוה"ז בעסק התורה והמצוה, מאחר שבעוה"ב אי אפשר לעבוד ה'." וע"ש בספר רוח חיים בזה דחילק בין העובד לשמה והעובד שלא לשמה וז"ל, "כי העובד על מנת שלא לקבל פרס כמו שאמר דוד וכו', כי ביקש דוד שיותן לו גמולו בזה העולם. והוא שיחיה ויזכה לשמור דבר ה', וזה יקר בעיניו מכל נהרי עדן. ואם על מנת לקבל פרס, אמר יפה שעה אחת כו' בעוה"ב מכל חיי עוה"ז." ולפי"ז מובן היטב למה מת נחשב "רש".

אבל ע' ברש"י ובמאירי במש' אבות הנ"ל דנר' דעוה"ב באמת עדיף מעוה"ז. וכ"כ ר' אברהם בן הרמב"ם לגבי איש כשר שמת (ע' לקמן שהבאנו דבריו). ועכ"פ י"ל שהמת חשוב כ"רש" מצד אחד כ"ז, דרק בעוה"ז אפשר לאדם לעשות עוד מצוות כדי לקבל עוד שכר לעוה"ב.

ובאמת גם בדעת הגר"א נר' דצ"ל כעי"ז. דהנה ע' בארורי הגר"א (ברכות י. אות מ"ד) על הא דאיתא שם דדוד המע"ה הסתכל ביום המיתה ואמר שירה וז"ל, "שאם זוכה ליחידה כמ' 'הראני נא את כבודך' ואמר לו 'כי לא יראני האדם וחי' וכו', ולעתיד יזכו בה וכו' וזהו שמחה של לויתן'. וכן נר' מהא דאמרו רז"ל (אבות ד:כא) ש"העולם הזה דומה לפרוזדור בפני העוה"ב". וידועין דברי הרמח"ל (מסילת ישרים פ"א) וז"ל, "שהאדם לא נברא אלא להתענג על ה' וליהנות מזיו שכינתו שזהו התענוג האמיתי והעדון הגדול מכל העדונים שיכולים להמצא. ומקום העדון הזה באמת הוא העוה"ב." וע"ע בצל"ח (ברכות טז: ד"ה א"ר אלעזר) וז"ל, "שיבח דוד את המיתה כי הוא הטוב האמיתי, וכמבואר במדרש במעשה בראשית (בר"ר ט:ה), 'וירא אלקים את כל אשר עשה והנה טוב, זה המות'... שהנשמות הוא התכלית הטוב האמיתי, ואז ניכר חסדו האמיתי של הקב"ה, ועל זה רמזו רז"ל (בר"ר ויחי צו:ה) שהחסד עם המתים הוא חסד של אמת, כי כל טוב העוה"ז הבל הוא... ולכן הטוב והחסד האמיתי הוא אחר המיתה, ואז עיקר התענוג הוא הדביקות בקב"ה ונהנין מזיו השכינה." ושמעתי ממו"ר ר' מאיר טברסקי שליט"א ד**גם הגר"א לא כיוון לומר דעוה"ז באמת עדיף מעוה"ב**, וכוונת דבריו אינן אלא ממבט מי שנהנה מעבודתו בעוה"ז, דמי שעובד ה' לשמה בעוה"ז הנאתו מרובה כ"כ עד שהוא אינו רוצה להפרד מהאי הנאה כלל, ואינו רואה באותה שעה איך אחר דבר שום דבר יכול להיות עדיף מעבודתו.

ונראה דצ"ל כעי"ז גם בדעת המהר"ל, דאע"פ שבפירושו על אבות הנ"ל כתב דע"י תשובה ומעשים טובים בעוה"ז הוא "יותר דבק עם השי"ת מצד זה מכל חיי העוה"ב", עכ"פ מפורש בדבריו במקו"א דמעלת האדם לאחר מיתה גבוה הרבה יותר ממעלתו בעוה"ז. וז"ל (הספדו על הגה"ר עקיבא גינצבורג, נדפס בסו"ס גו"א על במדבר בדפוס הישן עמ' קע"ח-קע"ט וקפ"ב, וע"ע בענין זה בבאר הגולה באר ב' העל' 33 במהדו' החדשה). "למה שולט המיתה בצדיק. אבל טעם זה כי לא נחשב המיתה פחיתות לצדיק, אבל נחשב לצדיק עליה כאשר הצדיק נלקח למעלה, כי לפני זה היה למטה בארץ במקום שהוא פחות ושפל מאד ועתה נלקח למעלה. ואף כי משה רבנו ע"ה אף כאשר היה בחיים היה מדבר עם השכינה, מ"מ לא היה במחיצה עליונית לגמרי, וראוי לצדיק שיקנה מעלה זאת, ואין מגיע האדם לדבר זה רק כאשר נלקח מן העוה"ז... וכמו שאמר שלמה (קהלת ד:ב) 'ושבח אני את המתים שכבר מתו מן החיים אשר המה חיים עדנה'... כי האדם הצדיק המיתה מעלה לו, כי הצדיק מתבקש להיות בישיבה של מעלה ואין דבר יותר עלוי אל הצדיק מדבר זה. ובודאי על זה אמר שלמה ושבח אני את המתים שכבר מתו."]

מאידך גיסא יש למת מעלה מסויימת מעל כל חי וכמ"ש המהר"ל (באר הגולה ריש באר ו', עמ' קנ"ה במהדו' החדשה) וז"ל, "כי המת נסתלק מן הגוף, וכאשר נסתלק מן הגוף ונשאר הנפש בלבד וראוי לכבוד". וכ"כ הגה"ר משה שטרנבוך שליט"א בספרו טעם ודעת (דברים כא:כג) וז"ל, "ע' ברמב"ן (כוונתו לספורנו בדברים שם) שכל עצם נבדל מחומר יקרא עצם אלה-ים, ומזה המין הוא עצם הנפש השכלית באדם הנקרא צלם אלה-ים... ובהיות שהבזיון הנעשה למת אחר מיתה הוא בזיון לנפש השכלית אשר היא עצם הנבדל הנשאר אחר מיתת הגוף אמר שהיא קללת אלה-ים ע"ש. ולמדנו בכאן ענין כבוד המת שהוזהרנו ע"ז בחומר כ"כ, כי הוא כבוד לנפש - חלק אלוקי ממעל - השוכנת באדם, ולא דמי לבזיון האדם החי שהוא מתיחס לאדם בכללותו, היינו גוף ונפש שדבוקים יחדיו, אבל אחר מיתת הגוף שוב אין הוא סובל בזיון הזה, ואך הנפש הנשארת אחר מיתת האדם, והבזיון לה בזיון לאלקינו ית'." נמצא דאע"פ שמצד א' המת איקרי "רש" משום שאין לו יכולת לעשות מצוות וכמ"ש לעיל, עכ"פ גוף המת, כיון שאין בו חיות גשמית, מזכיר לנו נפשו השכלית שהיא למעלה מהחומר. ולכן צריכין אנו לנהוג בו קדושה יתירה משום שכל ניוול שנעשה למת הוא "בזיון לאותו העצם הנצחי הנקרא אלקים" (לשון הספורנו שם).

וכן ע' בכל בו (סי' קי"ד) שהאריך לבאר טעם מצות קבורה וז"ל, "נאמר ונשאל למה החמירה תורה בטומאת מת, שהנוגע בנבלה או בשרץ יטהר ביומו והנוגע במת יטמא שבעה ימים... והלא קבורת מת מצוה גדולה עד שהקבלה אמרה שמת מצוה דוחה שאר מצות. זו תמיה גדולה על שתי מצות שהן סותרות זו את זו, והלא מגעו מצוה גדולה וטומאתו חמורה באה להזהיר האדם שלא יגע אל מקום במת. ועוד צריך להתבונן בחיוב מצות קבורת המת, והלא אם יקבר הגוף או לא יקבר הכל הולך אל מקום אחד. ונשיב להשיב על שתי השאלות הקודמות. נאמר שחשבוב קבורת המת הוא לשני טעמים - האחד על דרך מדה טובה, והוא שישא אדם פנים למי שנהנה ממנו וכו', וכן ראוי שלא יתועב אחר שהנפש גרה בו... וכן קשה לנפש כשתראה הגוף מתבזה... וכן בא על דרך זה חבוב קבורת הגוף ושאר הכבוד הנעשה לו במותו, והוא כחיבוב תשמישי קדושה שהן נגנזין. מצורף אל זה שקרובי המת מוצאין נחמה בכבוד ההוא... והטעם השני, והוא החזק והצריך לאמונתנו בתחיית המתים, כי אלו היו משליכין גוף האדם המת כאחת הנבלות, היו בני אדם אומרים נמשל כבהמות נדמו, ולא היו מקבלין אמונת התחיה כמו שהן מקבלין עם קבורתו בראותם כי יבנו לו בית וילבישנו, וכ"ש בראותם כי יקברוהו אצל אבותיו ובני משפחתו להיות עתידים לעמוד יחד בני המשפחה... ועל הדרך הזה היא ההקפדה ברוב כבוד גופות המתים. ולפי שלא יתעה האדם ברוב הכבוד הנעשה למת ושלא יעלה על לבו כי הוא המכוון באדם, אמרה תורה שהנוגע בו יטמא שבעה ימים להשיג הכונה ולדעת כי לא בשוקי האיש ירצה, כי אין הרצון הראשון בגוף כי אם בנפש הנשארת... לפי שסבת העונות היה הגוף, והוא נושא העונות. ולכן הנוגע בו יטמא שבעה ימים לדעת ולהבין שמגעו היה ככלי טמא... עוד טעם אחר על ענין טומאת המת שהפליגה התורה בענין טומאתו, ידוע כי ענין הטומאה ענין בזוי והמאסת הדבר, כל זה להראות שכל מה שנתיקר הגוף בעוד נפשו בו לא נתיקר רק לכבודה אשר תשכון בקרבו, אך אחרי הפרדה (הנפש) ממנו יחשבוהו (הגוף) ככלי שאין חפץ בו." הרי לן כמ"ש, דמצד א' גוף המת הוא מעולה ביותר ודינו "תשמישי קדושה", אבל מאידך גיסא הוא גם שפל ביותר "ככלי שאין חפץ בו".

ויותר מזה כתב החת"ס (ח"ו סי' י), שגוף המת יש בו קדושה ממש. וז"ל, "צריך להבין מאי טעמא התירו לעשות ממטפחת תכריכין למת מצוה (מגילה כה:), נהי שזו היא גניזתן, מ"מ תשמיש קדושה איך ישתמשו בו חול. וצ"ל דהאי דנמי תשמישי קדושה, דאדם ישראל הוי כס"ת, כדאמרי' מגילה (כט) 'כנתינתה כך נטילתה', ובמס' מ"ק (כה.) 'הא למה זה דומה לס"ת שנשרף'. ואע"ג דבחיי אדם אינו רשאי לשמש בתשמישי ס"ת, משום שאין הקב"ה מייחד שמו על הצדיקים כל זמן שהם חיים, ואל תאמין בעצמך תנן, משא"כ אחר שכיפרה עליו מיתתו, עמך כולם צדיקים." וכיוצ"ב כתב החת"ס עוד וז"ל (ח"ב יו"ד סי' של"ו), "כל העכו"ם חושבים בפירוד הנשמה מהגוף, נשאר הגוף בלי שום לחלוחית רוחניות... וע"כ מנתחים אותו ואינם חוששים לבזיונו... וע"כ מותר בהנאה ואין עכו"ם במותם קרוים עוד אדם לפי דעתם ואמונתם. אך בנ"י מאמינים גם 'אדם כי ימות באהל', עדיין במותו נקרא אדם פנימי ולא פגר (קערפער), כי גם בגופו שהיה נרתיק לנשמה נשאר בו לחלוחית קדושה ונוהגים בו כבוד, ואומרים עליו 'קללת אלקים תלוי'."

וכעי"ז איתא בתשו' דעת כהן (הל' אבלות סי' קצ"ט) וז"ל, "בענין המתים הדרושים בשביל הנתוח של למוד הרפואה, ולדעתי מאחר שניוול המת הוא אחד מהאיסורים המיוחדים לישראל, שהקב"ה צוה אותנו על קדושת הגוף כמו שאנו מוזהרים ממאכלות אסורות לא מצד הטבע של הגוף אלא מצד הקדושה המיוחדת לישראל, שקראם השי"ת גוי קדוש, והגויים כשם שאינם מקפידים על המאכלות רק באופן טבעי ככה אין להם שום טעם על הגוף שלא יתנוול בשביל איזה מטרה טבעית כמו הרפואה. ע"כ אנחנו צריכים לקנות בכסף מלא גויות מתים מאה"ע בשביל המטרה המדעית. ואין לחוש בזה משום שנאת הגויים, כי הישרים שבהם יבינו שסו"ס אומה זו שנבחרה להביא את אור הקודש של ידעת ד' אמת בעולם וסובלת ע"ז צרות מרובות לאין שיעור, היא ראויה ג"כ לאיזה פריבילגיה של קדושה... וענין המכירה והמסירה של הגופים בחייהם לא יוכל להועיל, כי איסור ניוול המת הוא מצד צלם אלקים שבאדם שהוא מיוחד לישראל ביתר בהירות מצד קדושת התורה, וחלק גבוה מי יתיר." (וכעי"ז כתבו כמה וכמה פוסקים בענין נתוחי מתים, ע' נוב"י (מהדו"ת סי' ר"י) ואגרו"מ (ח"ג סי' ק"מ) ועוד. וע' בספר רץ כצבי (עניני פוריות ויוחסין עמ' קכ"ח-קל"ב) שהביא עוד מדברי הפוסקים בענין זה. אמנם

ע"ע בספר נחלת שמעון (שמואל א' ח"ב סי' נ"ט) דאיכא כמה ראשונים דכתבו דלפעמים יש לחתוך ואף לשרוף את בשר המת כדי לחנטו וכיוצ"ב כששיש בזה תוספת כבוד למת. אבל עע"ש מה שהקשו כמה פוסקים על זה, וצ"ע.) וכן ע' בשו"ת שרידי אש (ח"ב סי' קכ"ג סוד"ה חמישית) וז"ל, "אנו יודעים ורואים שכל מי שיש בו אף זיק של אמונה דתית הוא מבקש שישמרו ויכבדו את גופו המת, ורק אלה שכבה בלבם כל רגש דתי ויש להם השקפת עולם חומרית מבקשים שישרפו את גופם."

 וע' במהר"ל דכתב כיסוד דברי החת"ס הנ"ל להסביר אף ענין טומאת מת וז"ל (הספד הנ"ל, עמ' קפ"ב-קפ"ג). "יש לשאול, כי אם נאמר כי המיתה אל האדם אין זה פחיתות וחסרון מעלה רק שבח הוא לצדיק, א"כ למה המת מטמא וצוה בכהנים הקדושים שלא יטמא למת... כי **לא מחמת החסרון שיש במת הוא מטמא.** אבל הטומאה הוא למת כי הנפש שיצאה מן המת הוא נבדל מן חיים ואין החיים עם המתים במחיצה אחת, וכל אשר קרב אל הדבר שהוא נבדל ומרוחק מן העולם הוא מקבל טומאה ונעשה מרוחק מן הבריות, כמו שהוא עשה קרב אל דבר שהוא רחוק ונבדל מן העולם ולכך הוא מתרחק ג"כ... שאין הטומאה רק מצד שהוא מרוחק, ולפעמים הוא פחיתות של הדבר שהוא מתרחק ממנו ולפעמים אף אם הוא דבר שיש לו מעלה מ"מ מפני שהוא קרב אל הדבר שהוא מרוחק, ולכך מקבל טומאה ונעשה מרוחק, ומצד הזה המת מטמא ואין זה חסרון כלל... וכך אמרו במס' ידים (ד:ו) וכו', עצמות חמור טהורים ועצמות יוחנן כהן גדול טמאים, אמרו לו לפי חיבתן היא טומאתן שלא יעשה אדם עצמות אביו ואמו תרוודן וכו', אף כתבי הקדש **לפי חיבתן היא טומאתן...** על כרחך אתה צריך לומר לא בשביל שיש חסרון במת הוא מטמא רק בשביל שהמתים והחיים אין להם חבור יחד והחיים נבדלים מן המתים ולכך כאשר הוא מתחבר לדבר שהוא רחוק ונבדל ממנו כאן הרחקה ממנו וזהו הטומאה... ולפיכך אמר ג"כ מה שספרי הקדש מטמאין, אין זה מפני פחיתות ח"ו, רק בשביל כי האדם מובדל מן ספרי קדש, שיש בספרי קדש החכמה האלקית והאדם מובדל ומופרש מזה, ולכך כאשר מתקרב ונגע בספרי קדש יש בהם טומאה כאשר אמרנו."

וכן ע' בכתבי ר' בחיי (קונטרס שלחן של ארבע שער ד', סוף עמ' תק"ו במהדו' מוהר"ק) שביאר שגוף האדם הוא "עיקר גדול" במעלת האדם ומשו"ה יהיה האדם עם גופו בגן עדן. (וידוע שנחלקו בזה הקדמונים, ע' ברמב"ם וראב"ד הל' תשובה פ"ח ה"ב ואכ"מ.) וז"ל, "[כלי הגוף בגן עדן] אינם לבטלה, כיון שמקבלים השכר והתענוג ביחד כשם שטרחו בתורה ובמצות בגוף ובנפש ביחד. שהרי הקב"ה אינו מקפח שכר כל בריה, ורוצה הוא שיקבל הגוף שכרו ולא יהיה עשוק במשפטו. כי **אע"פ שהנפש עיקר, מכל מקום אין הגוף טפל, כי הוא עיקר גדול,** כי הוא הכלי שהנפש מראה פעולותיה בו, ואין לה כח להוציאם לפועל זולתו." ואם כן ראוי שיהיה הגוף מעותד למתן שכר עם הנפש יחדיו. (וע"ע בדברי הרמב"ן בשער הגמול, ח"ב מכתבי הרמב"ן מהדו' מוהר"ק עמ' ש"ה.)

ג: כבוד חיי המת בכללותם

הזכרנו לעיל הא דאמרו רז"ל דמבטלין ממלאכה ומתלמוד תורה להלוויית המת. ונראה לבאר חשיבות הענין, דאין זה מפאת זהירות מ"ביזוי המת" (שהזכרנו לעיל בענין "לועג לרש"), דכיון שקוברין אותו אין כאן ביזוי. אלא מצוה זו היא כדי **להוסיף** כבוד גדול למת. וכעי"ז כבר מבואר בהדיא בגמ' סנהדרין (מו:), דלענין קבורה דנה הגמ' מפאת "ביזוי", אבל לענין הספד דנה הגמ' בענין "יקרא", דהיינו הוספת כבוד למת ולחיים. ומסתבר דגם הלוויית המת דומה להספד לענין זה. (וע"ע בסנהדרין שם דמבואר עוד, דכיון שאין בזה "בזיון" למת היה היה מקום להסתפק שכבוד ההספד באמת אינו משום המת כלל אלא משום המשפחה וכו', ע"ש.)

ונראה דעיקר כבוד זה אינו מפאת גילוי נפש השכלית של המת שהזכרנו לעיל, דענין זה הזכירו הפוסקים כטעם שלא לבזות את המת ע"י התעצלות מלקוברו או ע"י ניתוח גופו וכדומה, ובנוגע לענינים אלו כתבו הפוסקים דאינו יכול למחול כיון דבזיונו לאו דיליה הוא, ע"ש. אבל הספדו (ולכאו' הה"נ הלוייתו) אכן שייך ביה מחילה (רק דדנה הגמ' סנהדרין הנ"ל אי עיקרו משום כבוד המת או כבוד משפחתו וכו'). ולכן נראה שהטעם שהורו חכמים להפליג בכבוד זה הוא משום **דשעה זו היא הזמן הראוי לכבד חיי המת בכללותם.** ומשו"ה מכבדין את המת בענין זה כפי מעלתו הפרטית (ואם הוא אדם כשר או ת"ח מפליגים בזה ביותר, ע' כתובות יז.).

(אמנם יש להעיר דכשקרוביו המת אינם משתתפים בהלוויה כתב האגרו"מ דיש בזה גם ביזוי המת. וז"ל (יו"ד ח"א סי' רמ"ט ד"ה ולכן יש), "שאם לא ילווהו הוא בזיון להמת שיאמרו שאינו חשוב להם". אבל אי-השתתפות של שאר אינשי "אינו בזיון להמת" אלא הם מוסיפים "כבוד יותר להמת" (שם ד"ה ולכן אם) וכמ"ש. והא דהזכרנו לעיל דמי שרואה מת ואינו מלווהו חשיב "לועג" ואינו חסרון כבוד בעלמא, שאני התם שהמת שהמת בפניו וכשאינו חושש עליו הוי כלעג, אבל כשאין המת בפניו אין בזה ענין של בזיון אלא אי-הוספת כבוד וכמ"ש.)

ד: הסתכלות כללית בענין המיתה

חוץ מהכבוד שנותנים למת בפרט מכל הטעמים הנ"ל, נר' דישנו עוד ענין כללי שצריך האדם להכיר בכל התנהגותו עם המת ובענין המיתה. הנה ז"ל המהר"ל (נתיב גמ"ח פ"ד עמ' ק"ס), "אמר ר' יהודה (ברכות יח.), 'הרואה את המת ואינו מלוהו עובר משום לועג לרש חרף עושהו'... דע כי אם חרף לסומא לא שייך בזה חרף *עושהו*, כי הסומא אינו כמנהגו של עולם, ואם הוא סומא הרי חסרון זה מצד האדם. אבל מי שלועג לרש, שאין הרש מצד עצמו שהרי גלגל הוא שחוזר בעולם, ולפיכך דבר זה הוא מצד הבריאה, לכך חרף עושהו שהרי בהנהגת העולם כך הוא. וכן המיתה הוא כמנהגו של עולם, ואם אינו מלוה אותו לפי שאינו מקפיד על כבודו, נאמר עליו שהוא לועג לרש, שכך העולם אשר ברא הש"י נוהג במיתה, לכך חרף עושהו מי שברא העולם בענין זה." הרי לך דענין "לועג לרש" אינו מפאת בזיון לאותו מת לחודיה, אלא הרי הוא מבזה גם עצם ענין המיתה שברא הקב"ה, שהוא מראה שהוא אינו מזדעזע כלל מענין המיתה. וכעי"ז משמע קצת מדברי התשב"ץ (חשק שלמה על משלי יז:ה) עה"פ לעג לרש וכו' וז"ל, "שלא יתגאה החי על המת להראות שיש לו מעלה מצד חיותו, כי הוא יתברך הממית והמחיה וכו'".

ועע"ש בהמשך דברי המהר"ל וז"ל, "א"ר יהודה אמר רב, כל המתעצל בהספדו של חכם ראוי לקברו בחייו' (שבת קה:)... כי כל כך חזק וקשה במדת הדין מיתתו של ת"ח עד כי מי שהוא מתעצל בהספדו של ת"ח ראוי לקברו בחייו, שראוי שיפגע בו מדת הדין הקשה... וכל זה כאשר לא נתן לב על מדת הדין הקשה שפגע בת"ח, לכך ראוי שיפגע בו מדת הדין הקשה לגמרי." ונראה לבאר שהמתעצל בהספדת ת"ח, חוץ ממה שפוגע בכבודו של אותו ת"ח, יש בזה חסרון גדול גם במה שהוא אינו מכיר מידת הדין של הקב"ה שנתגלתה ע"י המיתה. והיינו **שצריך האדם להכיר חומר ענין מיתה ולהתנהג עם המת בכובד ראש ובריצינות** כראוי לו.

והענין נתפרש עוד יותר בספר המספיק לעובדי ה' לר' אברהם בן הרמב"ם (מהדו' פלדהיים נספח ב') וז"ל, "סוד האבלות המצווה, שהיא לתועלת החיים כדי שיתעוררו על האבלות ויתבוננו בגלל מצבם, ויזכרו המות המפסקת ההנאות אשר רוב בני אדם טרודים בהן כל חייהם... ואמרו (מו"ק כז:) שצריך האבל בשלשה ימים הראשונים לדמות המות וסיבתה וקרבתה 'כאילו חרב מונחת לו על כתיפו וכו' [מכאן ואילך כאילו] עוברת כנגדו בשוק'... וקבלתי מאבא מארי זצ"ל' (וע' רמב"ם הל' אבל פי"ג הי"ב) בפי' 'כאילו היא עוברת כנגדו בשוק', שחייב אדם לזכור המות תמיד ולהעמידו נגד עיניו כדי להתעורר עי"ז." הרי מבואר דישנה באבלות תועלת רב לחיים (ובכלל זה כל מה שמדברים על המת במשך ימי האבלות), שיתעוררו לתשובה ומעשים טובים ע"י זכרון המיתה והכרת ההפסד וכו'. ונראה דהתועלת הזאת קיימת (עכ"פ במקצת) בכל המנחמים והמשתתפים בקבורה ובהלויה וכו', וכל מי שמצטרף לאיזה דבר השייך למת צריך להכיר ענין זה ויתעורר על ידו.

ויש להוסיף לזה מש"כ בספר עלי שור (ח"א עמ' ד"ש) שהסביר האיך צער האבלות מביאו לעלות בעבודת ה'. וז"ל, "כל אדם מרגיש בזמן אבלותו דחיפה להתקרב למצוות ומעשים טובים, אפי' פורקי עול שומרים את 'הקדיש', מניחים טלית ותפילין ומתפללים. ממה נובע דחיפה זאת. יש לזה טעם עמוק. חז"ל אומרים, שלשה שותפים יש באדם - אביו ואמו והקב"ה. והנה ילד רגיל לראות רק אביו ואמו, את השותף השלישי אינינו רואה. אבל כשהוריו עוזבים אותו והולכים לעולמם, אז לבו אומר לו (בכח האמונה השרשית החיה בלב כל אדם מישראל) להשליך מעתה יהבו על השותף השלישי.

[ועע"ש בדברי ר' אברהם בן הרמב"ם הנ"ל שהאריך לבאר עוד תועליות חשובות במצות אבלות, דיש בה עוד כמה עניני כבוד המיוחדים לכל מת בפרט. וז"ל, "וישנו עוד ענין באבלות, והוא שהתורה מתקנת טבעינו הפגומים במדות רעות... ישנם אנשים עם טבע גס ומדות אכזריות עד כדי כך שאחד מהם מסוגל לקבור בנו בלי להתרגש... ובגלל זה מערכת התורה מתקנת ומתקנת טבע הגס ע"י חיובי האבלות... אב ואם, שהאבלות עליהם לכבודם, ועבור הפסד תועלותיהם וברכותיהם, שמכללם הפסד מצות כבוד או"א ומוראם שהיא מהמצוות החשובות ביותר... ולכן האבלות על הבנים בגלל הפסד תועלותם לעתיד בתור ממלאי מקומו, כמו שהאבלות על ההורים לכבוד תועלותם בעבר ע"י ההולדה. או [שהנפטר הוא] החבר הקרוב העוזר לו ברוחניות וגשמיות והוא אחיו... והאבלות על האחים עבור הפסד חברתם ועזרתם, והבעל או האשה כהאא... אם הנפטר מכלל השלמים הקיימים הזוכים להנעימות, על נפש המתאבל עליו להתאבל עבור שאינו נמצא עוד אצל החיים ועבור הפסד ברכתו ותועלתו ברוחניות, לא עבור הפסד חייו שנפסקו... שהעולם הבא עדיף להנפטר מעוה"ז... ואם הנפטר מן החסרים כמו הקטנים בשנים, על נפש המתאבל להצטער על שנאבדה הצורה הנעלה האלקית לפני שלמותה... ואם הנפטר מן התועים והפושעים וכו' שחטאו סובל תשובה לפני מיתתו כמקוה ברוב הפושעים, וא"כ על נפש המתאבל להצטער על שנעדר לפני תשובתו, ועל העונש שישיגנו ע"י רבונו בגלל חטאיו, ועל שהפסיד הטוב השלם עבור מרדו."

ובעיקר העניין אם אבלות היא לתועלת החיים או המתים, ע' הג' הגרעק"א (יו"ד סי' שד"מ ס"י בהגה"ה) שהביא מח' רמב"ם ורמב"ן אם אבלות יקרא דחיי או יקרא דשכבי. ויש בזה כמה נפק"מ בפוסקים, ע"ש ובפתחי תשובה ובחת"ס (יו"ד סי' שכ"ו). אבל ע' בספר שרשים בשמחות (עמ' פ"ג ואילך) שכתב להקשות על הגרעק"א, וכתב דאבלות דאורייתא "אינו ענין של כבוד חיים ולא כבוד מתים, אלא אבלות מדאו' מגזיה"כ להצטער על סילוק קרובו, ואינו נמדד במדת הכבוד של זה לזה", ע"ש.

וע"ע ברמ"א (יו"ד סו"ס של"ה) דפסק ע"פ הרמב"ם פי"ד אבל דניחום אבלים קודם לבקור חולים משום שניחום אבלים הוא גמ"ח עם החיים והמתים. ויש להאריך, ואכ"מ.]

<u>ה: פעמים שכבוד החי גדול מכבוד המת</u>

הנה הסברנו בארוכה גודל ענין כבוד המת, דנר' דמקפידין בכבודו יותר מכבוד החי. אמנם מצינו דכשכבוד החי סותר את כבוד המת, מעדיפים כבוד החי. כך איתא במס' שמחות (פי"א), "המת והכלה שהיו מקלסין ובאין זה כנגד זה, מעבירין את המת מלפני הכלה, מפני שכבוד החי קודם את המתים". וצריך להבין מדוע באמת כבוד החי עדיף.

ונראה להסביר דאע"פ שהפליגה התורה בכבוד המת מה שלא מצינו בכבוד החי, לימדנו רז"ל שזהו רק כשלא תהי' פחיתות כבוד לחי משום הכבוד שנותנים למת. אבל **לדחות כבוד החי כדי לתת כבוד למת אינו ראוי**, דכמו דחיים עדיפי ממות, כמו"כ צריכים אנו להעדיף החיים מעל המתים כשצריכין לבחור א' מהן. אבל כשדנין בענין כבוד המת בפנ"ע בלי סתירה לכבוד החי, יש באמת להפליג בכבוד המת מכל הטעמים שהזכרנו.

ועל דרך זה אפשר ליישב גם קושיית היד אליהו (סי' נ"ד) וז"ל, "יש לדקדק קצת, דהא בפני ת"ח צריך לעמוד אפי' העוסק בתורה... ולבטל מלאכה אין צריך ואינו רשאי כמ"ש תוס' בקידושין ל"ג... ולהלוויית המת אין העוסק בתורה צריך לבטל (כשיש למת כל צרכו), [אבל] ממלאכה צריך לבטל (כמבואר ביו"ד שס"א:ב). סתרי אהדדי וצ"ע." וע"פ הנ"ל נראה להסביר, דכבוד המת עדיף מכבוד התורה (ולכן מבטלין מלאכה לכבוד המת ולא לכבוד ת"ח) רק כשע"י כבוד המת לא תהי' פחיתות לכבוד התורה, אבל **לבטל מלימוד התורה כדי להוסיף כבוד למת אינו ראוי, דיש בזה זלזול לתורה** (אא"כ המת עצמו חכם הוא ויש בו ג"כ משום כבוד התורה), ולכן אין מבטלין ת"ת לכבוד המת אע"פ שמבטלין לכבוד ת"ח.

ואפשר להסביר עוד, דהחילוק זה הוא כעין הא דפירשנו לעיל, דמצד א' המת שפל משאר בשר אינשי, אבל מאידך גיסא הוא מעולה טפי מכולם. ולכן מצד א' מפליגין בכבודו, אבל כשיש סתירה בין כבודו וכבוד שאר בנ"א וכבוד התורה, מעדיפין כבוד שאר בנ"א וכבוד התורה, דודאי צריכין לבחור לעולם בחיים ולא במות.

סימן ב' – האם ראוי לינשא לגיורת (בעניין אהבת וקדושת גרים)

איתא בברכות (ה:) וכעי"ז בפסחים (קיב:), "אמר להו רבא לבניה וכו', דלא תנסבו גיורתא". ופי' הרשב"ם (פסחים שם), "משום דאמרינן גיורא עד עשרה דרי לא תבזי ארמאה באפיה (סנהדרין צד.)". ופירוש בהג' יעב"ץ (ברכות שם) וז"ל, "ואולי ר"ל הטעם משום הזרע שנשאר בו רושם מטבע השורש וכמ"ש אל תאמן בעבד עד י' דורות, ואמרו גיורא עד עשרה דרי לא תבזי ארמאה באפיה... [אבל] יקשה מרחב הזונה ורות ואשתו של טרנוסרופוס (שנישאת לר' עקיבא) וזונה שבכרכי הים שנשאה אותו תלמיד הזהיר במצות ציצית ודכוותייהו, אלא שאין מביאין ראיה מנביאים וחכמים ששימשו ברוח הקודש, והושע נצטוה לקחת אשה זנונים."

ועוד ציין היעב"ץ לגמ' הוריות (סוף יג.) דמבואר דהכל רצין לישא גיורת, ומשמע דלא כגמ' ברכות הנ"ל דאינו ראוי לינשא להן. אבל ע"ש ברש"י דכבר הרגיש בזה וז"ל, "שמתרצין לישא גיורת מלישא משוחררת". הרי פי' דאין הכל רצין לישא אותן יותר משאר ישראל, אלא הכל רצין לישא אותן יותר ממשוחררות. וכ"כ בהג' יעב"ץ שם וז"ל, "רוצים בגיורת יותר במשוחררת אם אין אשה אחרת מצויה להם אלא א' משתי אלה, מיהו בדאפשר לא קמיירי דודאי עדיפא, דהא אמרו (ברכות הנ"ל) לא תנסוב גיורתא. ועוד משום דרוב בנים הולכין אחר אחי האם (ב"ב קי.). אבל מ"מ ודאי אין כל גיורות שוות, ויהושע בועז וזולתם יוכיחו שהניחו בנות ישראל ובחרו להם בגיורות, עם שאפשר שכבר נשאו נשים גם מבנות עמם."

הרי נראה מהגמ' דאינו ראוי לינשא לגרים מפאת טומאתם. אבל מאידך גיסא מצינו כמה גדולי עולם שבאו מגרים, וצ"ב בפשר הדבר. ועוד יש לע' האיך י"ל דאינו ראוי לינשא לגרים, והרי נצטוינו לאהוב את הגרים, וצ"ב למה זה אין זה בכלל.

א: אהבת הגר

הנה כתב החינוך (מצ' תל"א) וז"ל, "שנצטוינו לאהוב הגרים, כלומר שנזהר שלא לצער אותם בשום דבר, אבל נעשה להם טובה ונגמול אותם חסד כפי הראוי היכולת... והפלגת האהבה שהפליגו בהם עד שאמרו שהשווה הכת' אהבתם לאהבת המקום, שבהם נאמר ואהבתם ובאהבת המקום ואהבת... ועובר עליה ומצער אותם או שמתרשל בהצלתם או בהצלת ממונם או שמקל בכבודם מצד שהם גרים ואין להם עוזר באומה ביטל עשה זה, ועונשו גדול מאד."

נמצא לפי החינוך שחייבה התורה לעזור לגר ביותר. ומדברי הרמב"ם מבואר עניין נוסף וז"ל (קובץ תשו' הרמב"ם סי' ק"ס, אגרות ושו"ת שס"ט), "חובה שחייבתנו התורה על הגרים גדולה היא. על האב ועל האם נצטוינו בכבוד ומורא, ועל הנביאים לשמוע להם, ואפשר שיכבד אדם ויירא וישמע ממי שאינו אוהבו. ועל הגרים צונו באהבה רבה המסורה ללב, ואהבתם את הגר כמו שצוונו לאהוב את שמו שנא' ואהבת את ה' אלקיך." וגדר הדברים נראה דכלפי ישראל דעלמא צריך רק לרצות בטובתו, אבל כלפי גר חייב להוסיף עוד אהבה וכבוד משום שמזכיר גדלותו ומסירות נפשו להשי"ת. ונ' דמטעם זה האריך הרמב"ם בתשו' הנ"ל בהכרת מעלת הגר וז"ל, "אדם שהניח אביו ואמו ומקום מולדתו ומלכות עמו וידם הנטויה והבין בעין לבו ובא ונדבק באומה זו שהיא היום למתעב גוי עבד מושלים בו והכיר וידע שדתם דת אמת וצדק והבין דרכי ישראל והכיר הכל ורדף אחרי ה', ועבר בדרך הקדש ונכנס תחת כנפי השכינה ונתאבק בעפר רגלי משה רבע"ה וכו', וחפץ במצותיו ונשאו לבו לקרבה לאור באור החיים ולעלות למעלת המלאכים ולשמוח בשמחת הצדיקים ולהתענג העוה"ז מלבו ולא פנה אל רהבים וכו'. והכרת מעלות אלו הוא היא יסוד האהבה. [העירו כמה אחרונים דיסוד שיטת הרמב"ם כבר מדוייק בקרא במש"כ ואהבתם את הגר. וז"ל הגר"י קמנצקי זצ"ל (אמת ליעקב פר' קדושים יט:יח), "ולכאו' מ"ש ציווי זה מאהבת רעים. וצ"ל משום דהתם כתיב ואהבת לרעך, בלמ"ד, וכאן כתיב 'את הגר', והרי זה כמו באהבת ד' – את ד' אלקיך, וכמו שביאר רבינו המלבי"ם כאן דהיכא דכתיב בלמ"ד היינו רק שיעשה לחבירו מה שחפץ בעדו... משא"כ באהבת הגר שכת' 'את' דהיינו שיהיה הוא הפועל, וזהי האהבה הפנימית." (ושו"ר בספר מצות המלך לר' עזריאל צימענט שליט"א, עש' ר"ז ענף ג' אות ג', שכ"כ והביא כל מה שהזכרנו.) וכמו שמצות אהבת ה' היא להכיר גדלות הבורא ית', כמו"כ (להבדיל) מצות אהבת הגר היא להכיר ולכבד מעלת הגר.]

אבל נראה דאין עניין אהבה זו דצריך לרצות להיות יחד עם הגר ולדבר אתו ולדומה כמו "חבר", שלא צוותה התורה אהבה כזו לא כפלי גר ולא כלפי שאר ישראל. אלא **אהבה שחייבתה התורה יסודה בהכרת מעלת הזולת**. ולכן אין חיוב לכל ישראל להשתדל לינשא להם בעצמן, וכמ"ש מאחר שיש להם קצת פסול יחוס וכמ"ש.

ועכ"פ הסביר לי מו"ר ר' משה סתיו שליט"א דאדם שרוצה להתחתן לגר לשם שמים כדי לחוס עליו ביותר ע"י אותו קירוב ודאי שקיים בזה מצוה רבה מהטעם הנ"ל בספר החינוך שהוא עושה לו חסד גדול. אבל מאידך גיסא צריך אדם לשקול הדברים מפאת עניני יחוס כנ"ל וכמו שמבואר עוד להלן.

הנה מפורש בגמ' ופוסקים שגר אינו מיוחס כשאר ישראל, ומותר לגר לישא ממזרת (ע' רמב"ם איסו"ב פט"ו ה"ז ועוד). ועוד כתבו המפרשים ד**נשאר ביה קצת טומאת הגוים**. וכגון הא דהובא בספר משבצות זהב (על מגילת רות ג:ג, עמ' פ"ט) בשם הב"ח בספרו משיב נפש על מגילת רות שהביא לשון זוה"ח רות זוה"ל, "תא חזי זוהמא דגוי אע"ג דאגייר קשה לפרוש מיניה זוהמא עד תלתא דרין". ועוד ראיתי בספר הנ"ל (א:יז, עמ' מ"ד) שהביא מר' משה דוד וואלי זצ"ל תלמידו של הרמח"ל וז"ל, "שהמנוחה בגן עדן שוה ליהודית ולגיורת, כי הגיורת אינה מתדבקת אלא בנפש, והיהודית לפני ולפנים". וע"ע בשל"ה (הגה"ה סוף מס' שבועות, עמ' קצ"ה.) וז"ל, "כי הגרים הם רחוקים ממדור עצם השכינה אף שנתגיירו... והנה יתרו לא היה בשעת מתן תורה אף שכבר נתגייר, והטעם כי ישראל קבלו התורה פנים בפנים מן השמים שהוא תפארת ועל הארץ מלכות שהוא הפנימיות, ויתרו לא זכה לזה." וכיוצ"ב ראיתי בספר שערי אהרן (יתרו עמ' תרכ"ח) שהביא מהרא"ש הטעם שהוצרך הכתוב לפרט חיוב גר במצות שבת וז"ל, "וא"ת והלא ישראל גמור הוא שהרי קבל עליו כל המצות. וי"ל דס"ד אמינא הואיל ומצות שבת חביבה היא על הקב"ה שקראה אות, שלא תהיה נוהגת אלא בישראל גמור שהורתו ולידתו בקדושה, צריכה." (וכעי"ז יש לפרש בשאר דוכתי דמצינו שריבה הכתוב או ע"י איזה דרשה להוסיף גר לכמה מצות ודינים (ע' רשימה ארוכה באנציקלופדיה תלמודית ערך גר). דה"א דפטורים משום פחיתות קדושתם. וע"ע זבים רפ"ב ובתוס' מנחות סוף ע"א: ועוד.) ועוד מזה הביאו האחרונים חידוש שנר' שנר' גדול מהמתרגום יונתן (דברים כג:ז) דאין מרחמין על מואבי אף אחר שנתגייר. (וע"ע בספר חבצלת השרון פר' בשלח עמ' שמ-שמ"ג.) וגם הגר עצמו מרגיש קירוב לעמו שבא ממנו וכמ"ש רש"י (פר' יתרו יח:ט) ע"פ המדרש וז"ל, "ויחד יתרו... נעשה בשרו חדודין חדודין, מצר על אבוד מצרים. היינו דאמרי אינשי גיורא עד עשרה דרי לא תבזי ארמאה באפיה." (ועע"ש במהר"ל בגו"א.)

אבל מאידך גיסא מצינו שהחמירה התורה ביותר בחיוב לאהוב ולכבד את הגר וכמ"ש. ועוד הרי גר שנתגייר כקטן שנולד דמי, וכל הטמטום הנ"ל לא נאמר אלא בנוגע לעצם קדושתו הנסתרת מעיני האדם, אבל עיקר דינו כישראל גמור לכמעט כל דבר. וגם כלל גדול הוא דלפום צערא אגרא, וגר הרי בא ממ"ט שערי טומאה והעלה את עצמו עד שמתדבק בקדושת ישראל, וא"א לשער גודל שכרו. ולא עוד אלא שהעירו המפרשים **שעיקר מסורת התורה היה דוקא ע"י גרים.** וז"ל השל"ה (סוף מס' שבועות, עמ' קצד:), "עוד יש חקירה לדעת על מה זה רוב נתינת התורה היה ע"י אחיזה בגרים – משה רבינו ע"ה היה מתדבק ליתרו שהוא גר, אונקלוס הגר תירגם התורה, בתורה שבע"פ אמרו רבותינו ז"ל (ע' סנהדרין פו.) סתם משנה ר' מאיר, סתם ספרי כו', וכולה סתימאה ע"י ר' עקיבא, ור' עקיבא היה מגרים מסיסרא, וכן ר' מאיר מניברון קיסר (גיטין נו.)... רצה הש"י ע"י התורה לייחד הכל מלמעלה למטה ומלמטה למעלה לגלות היחוד, וזהו צריך להיות ע"י האדם כי נשמתו משמים ממעל וגופו מארץ מתחת, ובקיום המצות במעשה ודיבור ומחשבה אז מייחד התחתון עם עליון כי נזדכך גופו עם נשמתו... על כן הוצרכה התורה ולהיותם נתונה בנגלה ובנסתר דהיינו הנגלה בבחינת הגוף והנסתר נמסר פה אל פה והוא בחינת הנשמה... ומאחר שהיה נתינת התורה ע"י האדם להתייחד עליון ותחתון להראות היחוד לבל ידח ממנו נידח היתה ההשגחה להיות ה' עוז לעמו יתן ה' יברך את עמו בשלום, ושלום לרחוק שנתקרב שהן הגרים להכניסם תחת כנפי השכינה. ובפ"ק דע"ז, שני אלפים תורה מתחילין מן 'ואת הנפש אשר עשו בחרן', 'ואת הנפש' פי' רז"ל אברהם מגייר את האנשים ושרה את הנשים." ונמצא דגריעותן היא היא מעלתן, דדוקא משום שהם בדרגה נמוכה במעלות הקדושה הם מסוגלים עוד יותר להראות יחוד ה' ולשמש יסוד למסירת התורה מדור דור. וע"ע בפרי צדיק (ריש פר' יתרו סוף אות א') שביאר עוד דעיקר תושבע"פ בא מכח גרים וז"ל, "איתא מהאר"י הקדוש דר"ע היה שורש תורה שבע"פ. ובגמ' נסדר ענין מתן תורה בפר' ר' עקיבא במס' שבת... הוא מטעם דר"ע שורש תושבע"פ שהיה בן גרים, ותושב"כ ותושבע"פ הם באמת אחד. ומטעם זה נכתב ג"כ מתן תורה בפר' יתרו ופר' הגר שהוא מענין תושבע"פ... ואיתא בגמ' (גיטין נז:) מבני בניו של סיסרא למדו תינוקות בירושלים, ובספר המפתח לר"נ גאון (ברכות כז:) הובא גירסא 'ומאן אינון, ר' עקיבא'. ואיתא בספר עשרה מאמרות להרמ"ע אשר ר' עקיבא בא מסיסרא שבא על יעל אשת חבר הקני והיא בא מיתרו. ועל כן נתחדש ע"י יתרו ג"כ פר' מינוי הדיינים ונקרא על שם זה יתרו שייתר פרשה פרשה... וכן נקרא כל פרשה של מתן תורה יתרו שממנו יצא ר"ע שהיה שורש תושבע"פ." יעו"ש. ואפשר להוסיף טעם למה תושבע"פ שייכת באופן מיוחד לגרים, משום שכח הגר הוא כח החידוש שהוא עיקר תושבע"פ, שהגר הפך כל חייו ובא מטומאת העמין להאמין לעם הקדוש, ויש לו הסתכלות מחודשת השונה משאר העם.

ונמצא לפי"ז דיש להן חסרון מצד א' ומעלה מצד אחר. ומש"ה דאמרו בגמ' דרך כלל לימנע מלישא אותן, אבל מאידך גיסא מצינו כמה גדולי עולם שנישאו להם וכמ"ש. וראיתי בספר נחלת שמעון (יהושע ח"א, הוספה סו"ס כ"ה) דהוסיף עוד דברים עמוקים בענין זה וז"ל, "והטעם דמשה רבינו ע"ה נשא את צפורה שלא היתה מבנות ישראל כבר ביאר המהר"ל (בגבורות ה' פרק י"ט). דמשה רבע"ה היה שקול נגד ששים רבוא מישראל (מכילתא בשלח טו:א), ומפני שכל אשה עזר לאיש ובת גילו, ולא יתכן זה שתהיה אשה אחת משישים רבוא שהוא בת גילו לבד שקול נגד ששים רבוא. אבל הגרים שהם חוץ מישראל ואינם בכלל ששים רבוא מישראל, יותר מזדווג למשה בעבור השווי הזה, כי משה נבדל מישראל אינו נכנס תחת מספר ששים רבוא מישראל, וכן הגיורת ג"כ אינה נכנסת תחת מספר ישראל וכו', ע"ש. ובסוף ההקדמה לספר יהושע

כתבנו דכמו שהיה משה רבינו שקול כנגד כל ישראל, כך יהושע היה שקול כנגד כל ישראל (ע' אלשיך א:ב) ע"ש, ומשו"ה גם הוא לא נשא גיורת... שו"ר באהבת יהונתן (הפטרה לפר' שלח) דנתעורר בזה האיך נסב יהושע את רחב, הא אמרו חז"ל לא תנסוב גיורתא. וכתב דאיתא בזוהר דלאו כל הגרים שוים, דלפעמים נשמת ישראל מובלע בין האומות, וזה הגר ישראל ממש הוא. ולפעמים מצינו גר שיש לו נשמה מן האומות העולם והוא 'תחת' כנפי השכינה (ע' רות ב:יב), דאילו נשמת ישראל היא למעלה מכנפי השכינה, ולרחב היתה לה נשמה ונשמתה היתה במדרגה גדולה, והראיה שיצאה ממנה ח' נביאים וכהנים גדולים (מגילה יד:)." (וציין לע"ע בעירות דבש ח"ב דרוש ב', הוצאת מכון אור הספר דף כ"ה ע"א.) והוסיף עוד קצת בהערה שם וז"ל, "עוד טעם למה נשא יהושע את רחב, ע' רמ"ע מפאנו (גלגולי נשמות אות מ') בשם ר"ח ויטל דזהו להיותו גלגל יוסף, ומה שלא לקח אשת אדוניו לקח עתה בהיות שבאתה בגלגל רחב, ובהיותו מבחינת ירח לכן היה בירריחו." (ואפשר להוסיף עוד ע"פ מה שהביא בספר נחלת שמעון (יהושע ח"ב סי' לח:ג) מהאברבנאל (יחזקאל מז:כא-כב) וכפות תמרים (סוכה לח:) דאע"פ דגרים לא נטלו חלק בארץ ישראל כשנתחלקה הארץ בימי יהושע, יטלו עכ"פ לעתיד לבא, ע"ש. ואולי יש ללמוד משם דלעתיד לבא גרים יהשבו עוד יותר כשאר העם וכאחד השבטים ממש, וע'.)

ולמעשה כתב האגרו"מ (אהע"ז ח"ד סו"ס ע"א) ע"פ גמ' הוריות הנ"ל "שליכא שום איסור ושום חשש" לישא גיורת שנתגיירה לשם שמים. אבל הוסיף דכשהיא ראויה להוליד בנים "טוב ליקח יותר בת ישראל שהרי בנים דומין לאחי האם". אמנם כתב בתשו' משנה שכיר (לר' ישכר טייכטאל זצ"ל, אבהע"ז סי' ו') וז"ל, "למדנו (מהמקורות הנ"ל) שכל נפש היפה ירחק נפש עצמו מזה. ובאור הל' תפילין (סי' תקל"א) הביא מדרש ילמדנו (פסיקתא רבתי כב:ה) מכאן אמרו אל תאמין בגר עד עשרים ושתים דורות, הרי דהזוהמה נמשכת עד כ"ב דורות וצריך לרחק מהם. אולם לאו כללא היא בכל מקום, דאם הגיורת היא צדקת יותר מאשת ישראל יש לקרב הגיורת כמבואר בספר חסידים סי' שע"ז ע"ש, וע"ע בחת"ס אהע"ז סי' קי"ג." וז"ל ספר חסידים שם, "כל שיש לו לב טוב ולוקח גיורת שיש לה לב טוב וצנועים וגומלי חסדים ונעימים במשא ומתן, מוטב להתחתן בזרעם מלהתחתן בזרע ישראל שאין בהם אלה המדות לפי שהזרע של גר יהיו צדיקים וטובים". והחת"ס שם איירי בציור שאבי שאבי של החתן המיר דתו, וכתב החת"ס דכיון דהפליג כמה דורות אין בזה חסרון יחוס. אבל אינו דומה לגמרי לעניננו. וקשה לברר כללים גמורים בזה, והכל לפי הענין.

סימן ג' – הזמן המוקדם בשעת הדחק למצות טלית תפלין ק"ש ותפלה

א: לבישת טלית

איתא בשו"ע (יח:ג) דאין לברך על הטלית עד שיוכל להכיר בין תכלת ללבן. אבל כתב הרמ"א ע"פ המרדכי בשם הראבי"ה דיכול לברך אפי' מעלות השחר. והמרדכי כתב דכן המנהג, ונר' דמשו"ה פסק הרמ"א כן. והגר"א הביא עוד סיוע למרדכי מרש"י (מנחות מג:), אבל כתב שלפי פשוטו נר' דלא כמרדכי מהא דתלה הגמ' (מנחות שם וירושלמי ברכות ריש א:ב) זמנו של ק"ש לגבי ציצית, ומשמע בהדיא דמצות ציצית מתחלת משיכיר כמו ק"ש. וע' באגרו"מ (או"ח ח"ד סי' ו' ד') ומה שהשכרעתי) דהסכים לקושיית הגר"א ותמה על המרדכי האיך כתב דציצית נוהגת מעלות השחר משום דזמנו תלוי בראייה, והרי ראייה גופא היא משיכיר, וכמו שהקשה הגר"א. וכתב עוד, דנר' דלגבי ק"ש הפס' שלומדים ממנו שיעור זה של משיכיר אינו אלא אסמכתא בעלמא דנלמד מציצית. אבל מדאו' יכול לקרות מעלות השחר. אבל לגבי ציצית יש מקום לומר דהויא דרשה גמורה ואינו יוצא אף מדאו' אלא משיכיר. ולכן כתב דאין לעשות כפסק של הרמ"א, ומי שצריך להתפלל מוקדם יכול לברך על התפלין (ע' לקמן) ולהתפלל, אבל על ציצית אין לו לברך אלא משיכיר, ואם כבר הסיר טליתו באותו זמן אז יכול הוא לברך בזמן על הטלית קטן וזה יחשב כעין המשך של מצוותו של לבישת טלית בבוקר.

אמנם יש להעיר בזה למעשה. דהנה נר' מבואר במנחת יצחק (ח"ט סי' ט') ושואל ומשיב (תליתאה ח"ב סי' קס"ב) דשיעור משיכיר אינו אלא מדרבנן בין לטלית בין לתפלין. (אע"פ דעיקר דברי השאול ומשיב קאי אתפלין, אבל נר' מבואר מהשאלה דפשוט לו גם טלית.) ונר' שהבינו שהדרשה אינה אלא אסמכתא ולא דרשה גמורה מדאו'. ונראה עוד, דבאמת **שיעור משיכיר אינו אלא זמן של לכתחי'**, אבל בדיעבד ובשעת הדחק העמידו חכמים אדינא דזמנו מעלות השחר וכמ"ש הרי"ף ורמב"ם ושו"ע (נח:ד) לגבי ק"ש (ע' ב ברכות סוף ח:), דאע"פ דלכתחי' נלמד זמנו מזמן ראייה כמבואר במנחות הנ"ל, אבל בדיעבד מהני מעלות השחר. וי"ל דהה"נ ציצית דלא תלו אותה בזמן ראייה אלא לכתחי'. ויש לדייק כן בגמ' עצמה, דהנה איתא בגמ' ברכות (ט:), "א"ר הונא הלכה כאחרים (משיכיר), אמר אביי לתפלין כאחרים לק"ש כותיקין". וכתבו הראשונים שהזמן דציצית דומה לזמן לתפלין, ע"ש ברשב"א ועוד ראשונים הרבה. והנה זמן ותיקין אינו אלא למצוה ולכתחי' (ע"ש בתוס' ועוד), אבל מדינא מותר לקרות ק"ש משיכיר (ואפי' בלא שעת הדחק כ"כ, ע"ע בזה באגרו"מ הנ"ל). ובשעת הדחק יכול לקרות אפי' מעמוד השחר כנ"ל. וכיון דמוכח שמאמר זה בגמ' קאי אלכתחי', י"ל גם לגבי תפלין וציצית שהשוו שניהם לק"ש במימרא שם, דשיעור משיכיר אינו אלא לכתחי', ולא באו כלל לומר דאין מצוה לפני משיכיר. וכן ע"ש בהגה"ה (על הרא"ש שם א:י) דלשונו ד"מצוה" להניח תפלין משיכיר, ויש לדייק בלשונו קצת כמ"ש, דלא איירי אלא בזמן המצוה לכתחי'. (אבל כל זה לא זה מדברי המ"ב על השו"ע הנ"ל יח:ג, וגם השואל ומשיב הנ"ל נר' דהבין דמדינא א"א לברך אלא משיכיר, וצע"ע.)

[וע' תוס' (ברכות ח: וריש ט.) דביאר דאיכא ב' דעות בגמ' שם אם ציצית ותפלין הוא מעלות השחר או מנץ החמה. וקצת העירו עליהם הראשונים (ע"ש ברשב"א וברא"ש) מהמש' מגילה (כ.) דכל מצוות היום מצותן בדיעבד מעלות השחר. וראיתי בשם הגרי"ד זצ"ל (בספר רשימות שעורים על ברכות שם) דתוס' מודי דבדיעבד מהני מעלות השחר, וכוונתו רק לכתחי'. ולפי דבריו מבואר בהדיא דתפלין וציצית מצותן בדיעבד מעלות השחר. אבל באמת ביאור זה בתוס' אינו מוכח, שהרי כתבו התוס' שם דזמן ק"ש הוא משיכיר אבל ציצית ותפלין אינו אלא מזמן הנץ, והרי מבואר בברכות הנ"ל (ט:) דהזמן לציצית ותפלין הוא ג"כ משיכיר כמו ק"ש. אלא מוכח דלפי תוס' הסוגיא דהתם (ח:) פליג אסוגיא דידן (ט:) מפורש בתוס' עצמם (ט.), וכן נר' מפורש בתוס' עצמם (ט.), והסוגיא דהתם דלא כהלכתא. ולכן י"ל דכמו דלפי תוס' הברייתא דהתם (ח:) פליג על סוגיין (ט:), כמו"כ פליג על המש' במגילה הנ"ל וס"ל דכל מצוות היום אינו אלא מנץ החמה, ולברייתא ב' (ע' תוס' ריש ט.) כל מצוות היום וגם ציצית ותפלין זמנם מעלות השחר אף לכתחי'. וצ"ע.]

והנה עיקר שיטת הראבי"ה הנ"ל (שהיא מקור פסקי המרדכי והרמ"א כנ"ל) דיכול לברך על הציצית מעלות השחר אף לכתחי' באמת צ"ב. [ז"ל הראבי"ה הל' מגילה סי' תקע"ע, "נ"ל דאע"ג דמשמע (ממש' מגילה שם) דלכתחי' בעינן עד הנץ החמה (לכל מצוות היום), הני מילי בהני דכתיב בהו יום בהדיא, אבל ציצית לא כתיב ביה יום בהדיא, אלא וראיתם אותם, בראיה תליא מילתא. ומעמוד השחר כשר לכתחי'. וכן עמא דבר. תדע, דהכא הגמ' מייתי לה מדכתיב והיה לנו הלילה למשמר והיום למלאכה, ובריש ברכות קאמר עלה (לגבי זמן ק"ש) אע"פ שאין ראיה לדבר זכר לדבר וכו', אלא טעמא משום דלא כתיב התם (לגבי ק"ש) יום בהדיא אלא בשכיבה וקימה תליה רחמנא, הלכך לאו ראיה גמורה היא אלא זכר לדבר, אבל הכא דכתיב יום גמרינן מינה. הילכך גבי ציצית נמי לא כתיב יום אלא ראיה גמרינן מינה, ולא גמרינן מינה."] שהרי הקשו הפוסקים הנ"ל דזמן ראיה אינו אלא משיכיר ולא מעלות השחר. אמנם נר' לפרש דודאי גם מעמוד השחר יכול לראות כמו דאיתא בהדיא ברפ"ב דתמיד, דגם מקודם לזמן משיכיר כבר האיר פני המזרח (וע' מ"ב נח:יח אם עמוד השחר הוא קצת קודם שהאיר פני המזרח או באותה שעה עצמה). והא דהקשה הגר"א דעכ"פ א"א להכיר בין תכלת ללבן, אין זה קשיא, שהראבי"ה הבין שזהו

לימוד בעלמא לענין ק"ש ומשום דרוב אינשי קמים באותו זמן, אבל ציצית עצמה היא מזמן שיכול לראות, ולאו דוקא משיכיר בין תכלת ללבן וכדומה, וזמן ראייה בעלמא הוא כבר מעמוד השחר. ובאמת הגמ' (מנחות הנ"ל) למדה מציצית רק לק"ש ולא הזכירה הגמ' לימוד לציצית עצמה, ויש להביא מזה קצת ראיה לדברי הראבי"ה דזמן ציצית אינו משיכיר בין תכלת ללבן אלא מעמוד השחר וכמ"ש.

אולם ראיתי מאמר מהגה"ר יחיאל זילבר שליט"א (נדפס באוצרות ירושלים קובץ ע"ח, ד"ה והפוסקים) שהביא כמה ראשונים דנקטו כעיקר כפי' הראבי"ה הנ"ל במש"כ מגילה לחלק בין שאר מצוות וציצית, אבל מבואר בדבריהם דעיקר טענתם רק להוכיח שאינו מעוכב ללבוש ציצית קודם הנץ, אבל לא שמקדימים כ"כ עד עלוה"ש. וזה מקצת לשונו, "באגודה מגילה שם (אות כ"ד) לא הזכיר זמן עמוד השחר אלא אך שאין זמן ציצית מהנץ החמה דתלוי בראיה, וכן מצאתי בספר העיטור הל' ציצית שג"כ כתב כראבי"ה דציצית אף לכתחי' לפני הנץ החמה דלא תלוי אלא בראיה, אלא שמסיים שם דהזמן הוא משיכיר בין תכלת ללבן. ובבית הבחירה (ברכות דף ט') ובארחות חיים (הל' ציצית אות כ"ד) וכל בו (סי' כ"ב) וצדה לדרך (מאמר א' כלל ד' פרק ה') ג"כ פסקו דזמן ציצית הוא משיכיר בין תכלת שבה ללבן שבה." ולכן כתב דאפשר דאף שיטת הראבי"ה הוא כן וז"ל, "וי"ל דלשונם (מרדכי וראבי"ה) לאו דוקא, ועיקר דבריהם לפרש שאין הזמן לכתחי' מהנץ החמה כשאר הדברים שמצוותן ביום בגמ' מגילה שם. ומש"כ כראבי"ה 'ומעמוד השחר כשר לכתחי' וכן עמא דבר', הכוונה שנהגו שלא להכות לזמן הנץ החמה שהוא מאוחר טובא, אבל מעלות השחר עד הזמן דמשיכיר אין אלא הפרש מועט ולא נחתו לזה לקבוע הזמן בדיוק." ונמצא לפי דבריו דאף הראבי"ה והמרדכי לא כיוונו לעלות השחר ממש, אלא קרוב לזה. וכעי"ז מצינו בתוס' (ברכות ח:) דעמוד השחר שהוזכר בגמ' שם (לגבי זמן ק"ש) הוא לאו דוקא אלא הכוונה למשיכיר, ע"ש. (ועכ"פ מבואר דזמנים אלו של עמוד השחר ומשיכיר קרובים טובא ומשו"ה יש מקום לומר אותם שלא בדיוק, וע' לקמן בסמוך.) ועכ"פ עדיין י"ל דכל זה אינו אלא לכתחי', אבל בדיעבד כו"ע מודי דיצא מעמוד השחר וכמ"ש לעיל. וכל הדין של הראבי"ה הוא רק להתיר מעמוד השחר לכתחי', אבל היה פשוט לו (ואפשר לומר כן גם לשאר ראשונים) דבדיעבד יצא מעמוד השחר.

ולדינא, הנה מצינו שהרמ"א הקיל למעשה כמרדכי וראבי"ה, וכמה פוסקים אחרונים כתבו דיכול לסמוך עליו בשעת הדחק. והם הבינו המרדכי כפשוטו, דהיינו מעמוד השחר ממש ולא כהגה"ר זילבר הנ"ל. ואף השו"ע והגר"א דחלקו על הרמ"א, ביארנו מסברא וע"פ לשון הגמ' די"ל דכוונתם רק לכתחי', אבל מודי דבדיעבד זמנם מעלות השחר כמו כ"ש ושאר מצוות היום. (ואף שהשו"ע סתם ולא ביאר כמ"ש בס"נ ח לגבי ק"ש, י"ל משום שהראשונים עצמם סתמו בזה כיון שאינו מפורש בגמ' אלא לגבי ק"ש כמ"ש הרי"ף וראשונים על הגמ' ברכות ח:. והנה השו"ע סי' ל' סתם גם לגבי תפלין אע"פ דהתם נר' ודאי דאינו דרשה גמורה להניח תפלין משיכיר דוקא, דלא כתיב בהדיא בתורה ולא ראיתם אותו לגבי תפלין, ע' היטב באגרו"מ הנ"ל.) ועוד, הרי נר' מבואר בשואל ומשיב ומנחת יצחק הנ"ל דכל עיקר דין דזמנו הנ"ל רק **משיכיר אינו אלא דרבנן ולכן שומעין להקל**. (והא דחשיב ספק דרבנן ולא ספק דאו' של לא תשא, ע' בשואל ומשיב מש"כ בזה. ויש להוסיף לדבריו ע"פ מה שדנו הראשונים ואחרונים במקום שחז"ל גזרו גזירה וכדומה אם הם עקרו המצוה לגמרי או דהשאירו הדין דאו' על מקומו. ולכן מי שקיים המצוה נגד דעת חכמים ובירך עליה י"ל דלא חשיב ברכה לבטלה כלל, עכ"פ מדאו'. [ע' בזה בקובץ בית אהרן וישראל, קובץ קכ"ד עמ' קנ"ב שדן בזה בטוב טעם. וע"ע באחרונים על תוס' סוכה (ג.).] ובפרט בנידון דידן נר' דאין חשש, כיון דע"פ כללי ההוראה יש להקל בדין דרבנן. ולכן אפי' אם בעלמא החשיבוה כברכה לבטלה למי שאינו חושש לדבריהם, אבל הכא י"ל דכו"ע מודי דאין בזה חשש. וע' בזה.) ועוד יש להוסיף דכבר כתבו הפוסקים דלפי שיטת הרא"ש יכול לברך על כסות יום אף בלילה ממש, והשתמשו הפוסקים בשיטתו כסניף להקל (ע' שו"ע סי' י"ח הנ"ל ובמ"ב ועי מאזנים למשפט סי' ג'). ולכן נר' דבשעת הדחק אינו צריך לדחוק את עצמו הרבה, ויש לסמוך על המקילין בזה ולברך מזמן עלוה"ש. ואפי' מי שרוצה לפקפק בכל זה, נר' דעכ"פ יש לסמוך על דעת המקילין בחישוב זמן משיכיר ולדונו כמ"ש הפוסקים בשם הפמ"ג (ע' ביאוה"ל סי' נ"ח ד"ה כמו) דזמנו ו' דקות לאחר עמוד השחר. וודאי יש להקל כמו הפוסקים האחרים שכתבו דמשיכיר הוא כששים דקות לפני הנץ וכמו שכתבו זה בטעמו מנהג ירושלים. וכן ע' במנחת יצחק הנ"ל וז"ל, "שפיר י"ל דעכ"פ אחרי רבע שעה או עכ"פ אף רק 6 מינוט כמ"ש הפמ"ג מזמן (עמוד השחר המבואר בלוחות) כבר הגיע לזמן של כדי שיכיר. כי אף אם יהי' ספק בדבר, הרי מבואר בתשו' שו"מ (הנ"ל) דיש לילך לקולא משום דהוי ספק דרבנן ולקולא ע"ש." (וידוע דקשה לשער לפי ראות עינינו מהו זמן משיכיר, ע' בספר פסקי תשובות סי' י"ח, אבל יש פוסקים שאחזו שיכולו לשער, ולפי דבריהם אפשר דתלוי הדבר לפי ראות עיניהם.)

אבל עדיין יש להעיר בכל זה, שהרי יכול לסלק את עצמו מן הספק ולברך אחר התפלה וכמו שפסק האגרו"מ הנ"ל, ולמה לן להקל ולהכניס ראשינו לספק ברכה לבטלה. אבל נר' דאין זה טענה כ"כ, א', דודאי עדיף לברך קודם המצוה, והרי איירי בשעת הדחק לבעלי בתים שטרודין במלאכתן, ואם ע"פ דין אינו צריך לחוש, אין זה הכנסת עצמו למקום ספק. וב', י"ל סברא כעין מש"כ האגרו"מ עצמו (שם וגם האו"ח ח"א סי' י') דאם נימא לבעלי בתים שלא לברך יראו בעיניהם הדבר כדבר קל וכספק מצוה בעלמא, וזה יכול לגרום להם לזלזל במצוה ועוד שיתרגלו לעשות מצוות בלי לברך ויהי' הדבר קל בעיניהם.

ואף מי שיכול לדחוק את עצמו טובא וללכת למנין מאוחר קצת, אינו נר' שצריך לדחוק א"ע ולהטיל עול על כבד על אשתו ומשפחתו וכו', אלא יוכל להתפלל באופן הגון ובמתינות במנין מוקדם (ומה טוב אם עי"ז גם יוכל ללמוד קצת אחרי התפלה).

<u>ב: הנחת תפלין</u>

איתא בשו"ע (סי' ל') דזמנה משיכיר. אבל נר' לפ' כמ"ש לעיל, דאחר דשיעור זמן זה אינו אלא מדרבנן, ומצותו בדיעבד היא מעמוד השחר כמו ק"ש ושאר מצוות היום, יכול בשעת הדחק להניחם ולברך אף מעמוד השחר. ובפרט כן לגבי מצות תפלין דלא כתיב ראייה בהדיא בקרא ורק אסמכוה אקרא כמבואר בר' יונה הו"ד בב"י שלכתחי' יש להניחן בשעה שיכול לראות חבירו, וכן מפורש בלבוש דקרא זה אינו אלא אסמכתא, ולכן טענת הגר"א נגד שיטת הראב"ה הנ"ל אינה שייכת כ"כ. (אבל מאידך גיסא מש"כ הראב"ה והמרדכי להתיר המצוה לכתחי' מעמוד השחר לא נאמר אלא לגבי ציצית ולא תפלין. והדבר מבואר בהדיא בברכות (ט:) דמצות תפלין לכתחי' משיכיר.)

אבל י"ל לגבי תפלין עוד ענין, שמלבד השאלה של קיום המצוה, הרי אסרו חכמים הנחתם בלילה שמא ישן ויפיח. אבל י"ל דלא גזרו איסור זה מעמוד השחר ואילך דחשיב יום מעיקר הדין. אמנם א"א לפרש כן לפי דעת הלבוש (ואחריו כתבו הפמ"ג ומ"ב) דעיקר הטעם שתקנו מצות תפלין רק משיכיר הוא משום דקודם זמן זה עדיין חשיב לילה לענין מצוה זו ועדיין איכא חשש שמא יישן ויפיח. אולם דבריו מחודשים לכאו', שהרי אחר עלוה"ש כבר חשיב יום מעיקר הדין לכל מצוות היום, ומהיכא תיתי להוסיף טעם לחומרא מה שלא כתבו הראשונים. (וכבר הזכרנו לעיל דברי ר' יונה, והו"ד בב"י וערוה"ש, דשיעור משיכיר בתפלין הוא משום דרשת הקרא דגם לגבי תפלין שייך ענין של "ראייה".)

ועכ"פ נר' דודאי אפשר להקל בשיעור משיכיר וכמ"ש הפוסקים (שו"מ ומנח"י) בהדיא כנ"ל. (אבל ע' מ"ב מ'ל דכתב דאסור לברך קודם משיכיר. ונר' משום דס"ל כלבוש וכמ"ש בהדיא בסי' ל', ולכן אסור להניח קודם משיכיר.)

ואכן מבואר בפוסקים עוד יותר מזה **דאפשר בשעת הדחק להקל אף להניח תפלין ולברך קודם עמוד השחר** אם כבר קם ממטתו לגמרי והולך בדרך, דבכה"ג אין חשש שמא ישן. ע' בזה בראק"א על השו"ע הנ"ל (סי' ל') ע"פ ר' פרץ (והו"ד בביאוה"ל שם). וכבר התיר דבר זה באגרו"מ (או"ה ח"א סי' י' וח"ד סי' ו'), ובפרט לבעלי בתים שאם לא יניחו תפלין בבוקר ובברכה יבאו לזלזל במצוה, ע"ש. (אבל כתב שם דאפשר דת"ח אין לו לברך עד זמנו, וע' קצת שינוי לשונו בשתי התשובות הנ"ל.)

<u>ג: קריאת שמע</u>

מבואר בגמ' (ברכות ט:) דמצוה מן המובחר לקרות ק"ש כותיקין. ועכ"פ נפסק בהדיא בשו"ע דזמנו אף לכתחי' (רק שאינו מצוה מן המובחר) משיכיר, וגם מהני בדיעבד מזמן עלות השחר. ועוד הזכרנו מש"כ האגרו"מ (או"ה ח"ד סי' ו' ד"ה ומה שהכרעתי) דזמן זה של משיכיר אינו אלא מדרבנן, ולכן אף מי שרוצה לקרות מזמן משיכיר אפשר לו להקל בשיעור זה ע"פ תשו' השואל ומשיב ומנחת יצחק הנ"ל דשומעין להקל בזמנים אלו ששיעורם מדרבנן.

אולם יש להעיר למעשה ממש"כ המג"א (נה:ה) דאין לברך ברכת אור יוצר קודם משיכיר, והביאו המ"ב (שם ס"ק י"ז). אבל שהשו"ע שם פסק דיכול לברך, נר' דעכ"פ יש לסמוך לקולא בזמן כשיכיר לפי השיטות המקילין, ויש בזה ספק ספיקא, שמא הלכה כשו"ע ואת"ל כמג"א שמא כבר הגיע זמן משיכיר. וע' בזה.

<u>ד: תפלה</u>

מבואר בגמ' (ברכות ט:) דזמנו לכתחי' הוא מיד אחר הנץ וכותיקין. אבל מי שאינו מתפלל באותו זמן, יש מקום עיון אם זמנו לכתחי' הוא דוקא לאחר הנץ אף שאינו מיד או אם לכתחי' יכול להתפלל אף קודם הנץ. והנה כשנעיין בראשונים לא נתבאר כלל שום עדיפות להתפלל לאחר הנץ (כשאינו מיד אחר הנץ וכותיקין). ויש פוסקים אחרונים דאכן העירו כן, ע' פרי יצחק (סי' ב') ואגרו"מ (או"ה ח"ד סי' ו' ד"ה והנה לולא). אלא שהם כתבו שהדבר מחודש (והאגרו"מ הסתפק ת דינא, ע"ש בסו"ד). ויש לבאר הדבר קצת כמו שנר' מהראשונים. הנה הטור (סי' פ"ט) כתב וז"ל, "זמן תפלת השחר מתחיל משעלה עמוד השחר והאיר פני המזרח היא כנגד תמיד של השחר, ומאותה שעה ואילך הוא זמנה, ומ"מ עיקר מצותה עם הנץ החמה". ומשמע מפשטות לשונו דעיקר **זמנה אכן משהאיר פני המזרח כמו הקרבן תמיד** ואין בזה ענין של בדיעבד, ורק **לכתחי' יש לנהוג כותיקין** כמו שסמכוה אקרא יראוך עם שמש (ברכות ט:). אלא דנחלקו המפרשים קצת אם הארת פני המזרח שוה לעמוד השחר או קצת אח"כ, ע' ערוה"ש (פט:יא-יב) וביאוה"ל בזה. ועכ"פ מזמן קצת אחרי עלוה"ש וכ"ש משיכיר כבר חשיב זמנו לכתחי'. וכ"כ הפר"ח (פט:א ד"ה ואם התפלל משעלה עמוה"ש) וז"ל, "שלשה זמנים יש להתחלת זמן התפלה, והנה עיקר מצותה הוא מהנץ החמה וכו', ולכתחי' יכול להתפלל משעלה עמוד השחר והאיר פני המזרח וכו', ומיהו אם התפלל משעלה עמוה"ש יצא וכדתנן במגילה משעלה עמוה"ש יצא, וגם התמיד אם שחטוהו משעלה

עמוה"ש לא נפסל". ועוד אפשר לדייק כמ"ש מהא דאמרו רז"ל שהקורא עם אנשי משמר לא קיים מצותו כראוי, ולא אמרו כן אלא על ק"ש ולא על התפלה עצמה. (ואף בדעת הרמב"ם אין הכרח לומר דאיכא שום עדיפות לשעה אחר הנץ יותר משעה קודם הנץ, וכמ"ש בפרי יצחק הנ"ל ע"ש.)

והנה אם מתפלל משיכיר מבואר בהדיא בר' ירוחם (הו"ד בב"י סי' פ"ט) דיצא לכתחי', והוא הבין כן מגירסתו בגמ' ברכות הנ"ל. אלא דהב"י הבין דכוונתו לומר דמשיכיר ועמוד השחר זמן אחד הוא ותמה עליו קצת, אבל כבר העירו האחרונים עליו וכתבו דאין זה כוונת ר' ירוחם. כ"כ הדרישה וז"ל, "נר' לדעת ר' ירוחם דודאי משיכיר חבירו ומשעלה עמוה"ש שני זמנים הם וכו', דג' זמנים הם, הרוצה להיות מן הותיקין וכו' יתפללו עם הנץ החמה. ומי שאינו מדקדק כל כך יכול לקרות לכתחי' משיכיר וכו', ומיהו אם התפלל מעלה עמוה"ש נמי יצא". ונמצא מכל זה דמי שאינו יכול להתפלל כותיקין, יכול להתפלל אף לכתחי' משיכיר.

ובחישוב זמן משיכיר שוב י"ל כמ"ש לעיל מהפוסקים דכיון דזמנים אלו אינם אלא מדבריהם יש להקל ולסמוך על דעת המקילין לחשבון כשש דקות אחר עלוה"ש וכ"ש משישים דקות קודם הנץ כמנהג ירושלים שהובא בפוסקים. וכ"ש הכא דנר' ע"פ הנ"ל דכבר חשיב לכתחי' משהאיר פני המזרח שהוא קרוב מאד לעלוה"ש. (אולם יש להעיר דנר' מבואר בכמה פוסקים אחרונים דלא כדברינו, ע' מנחת יצחק ח"ט סי' י' דעדיף טפי להתפלל אחר הנץ אפי' שלא עם הנץ מלהתפלל קודם הנץ. וכן ע' שו"ע הגר"ז ובכף החיים ומ"ב בשעה"צ פט:ח. וצ"ע מכל הנ"ל.)

סימן ד' – שמחה ותפילה על מפלתן של רשעים

א: יש במפלתן "שמחה" אבל אינה "טוב"

איתא בגמ' מגילה (י: ע"פ דהי"ב כ:כא-כב) דקודם שהלכו בנ"י למלחמה שרו לה' על הישועה ואמרו "הודו לה' כי לעולם חסדו", אבל לא אמרו הודו לה' "כי טוב"[1] משום שמפלתן של רשעים אינה נקראת "טוב". והדבר צ"ב למה עכ"פ שרו שירה אחר שאין מפלתן "טוב". ולא עוד, הרי מבואר בקרא שהישועה באה דוקא "בעת החלו ברנה ותהלה", ומשמע בהדיא דראוי לשיר בכה"ג, וצ"ב למה. ונראה מוכח לפרש דאין הקפידה באמירת הלל אלא באמירת "כי טוב". והביאור בזה הוא דאע"פ דאנו צריכים להודות לה' על הישועה שעשה לנו ולשמוח על ריבוי כבוד שמים שבא ע"י מפלתן של רשעים, אעפ"כ חייבין לדעת דבאמת אין זה הטוב הגמור וכמו שיתבאר.

הנה כבר הקשו כל המפרשים בסתירת הפסוקים בענין זה. שהרי מצד א' מבואר במשלי (כד:יז) "בנפול אויבך אל תשמח". ומכח זה ביארו חז"ל (ילק"ש משלי סו"ס תתק"ס) וז"ל, "אמר האלקים... ראויים היו ישראל לקרות את ההלל כל ז' ימי הפסח כשם שקורין ז' ימי החג, ואין קורין אלא יום א' בלבד, ולמה כן אלא בשביל שנהרגו המצרים וטבעו בים שהם שונאי, ואני הכתבתי בנפול אויבך אל תשמח." וכעי"ז איתא בגמ' מגילה הנ"ל, "שאין הקב"ה שמח במפלתן של רשעים", ומשו"ה מנע את מלאכי השרת מלומר שירה בשעה שהמצריים היו טובעים בים. אולם מצד שני מבואר בכמה וכמה מקומות שיש בזה שמחה גדולה וכמאמר הכת' (משלי יא:י) "ובאבד רשעים רנה". וכיוצ"ב איתא בברכות (י.) דדוד המע"ה "ראה במפלתן של רשעים ואמר שירה וכו'. וכן ע' בילק"ש (תהלים רמז תרכ"ז) וז"ל, "אמר ר' ישמעאל יש שמחה לפני הקב"ה כשיאבדו מכעיסיו מן העולם, וכן הוא אומר יתמו חטאים וכו'... ואבד רשעים רנה, ואומר שני רשעים שברת לפני הקב"ה כשיאבדו מכעיסיו מן העולם, וכן הוא אומר יתמו חטאים וכו'... ואבד רשעים רנה, ואומר שני רשעים שברת לה' הישועה, ואמר ואני הנני מביא את המבול מים - ואני ברצון הנני בשמחה וכו'." וכן איתא בתוספתא סנהדרין (פי"ד סו"ה ב) לגבי עיר הנדחת וז"ל, "כשם ששמחה לפני המקום בקיומן של צדיקים כך שמחה לפני המקום באבודן של רשעים שנא' באבוד רשעים רנה". ועוד, הרי בנ"י עצמם אכן שרו שירה על הים (ובמחזור ויטרי סי' רס"ה מבואר ש"זו השירה היא על מפלת אויבינו"). וכיוצ"ב מצינו גם להלכה כמש"כ הרמב"ם (פ"א ה"י, אבל ע' בשו"ע יו"ד שמ:ה) וז"ל, "כל הפורשין מדרכי צבור והם האנשים שפרקו עול המצות וכו' וכן המינים והמשומדים והמוסרין כל אלו אין מתאבלין עליהן, אלא אחיהם ושאר קרוביהם לובשין לבנים ומתעטפים לבנים ואוכלים ושותים ושמחים שאבדו שונאיו של הקב"ה, ועליהם הכת' אומר (תהלים קלט:כא) הלא משנאיך ה' אשנא". וע' בש"ך (שמה:ט) שהביא עוד מקור לדין זה מפס' דאבוד רשעים רנה. והדברים צ"ב.

ובאמת הגמ' עצמה (סנהדרין ריש לט:) כבר חקרה בזה וז"ל, "א"ר אחא בר חנינא, באבוד רשעים רנה... ומי חדי קוב"ה במפלתן של רשעים, הכתיב וכו' שאין הקב"ה שמח במפלתן של רשעים... אמר ריב"ח הוא אינו שש אבל אחרים משיש." הרי לן פשר הדבר הדבר מפורש בדברי הגמ', דאע"פ שאין הקב"ה שש עכ"פ אחרים מותרים לשמוח. אולם הדברים עדיין טעונין ליבון, שהרי בנפול אויבך אל תשמח נאמר לבני אדם ולא"ד כלפי הקב"ה, והבאנו לעיל מהמדרש דמהאי טעמא גופא אין אומרים הלל שלם כל ימי הפסח, הרי לן דאף אחרים אינן מותרין לשמוח. ועוד הבאנו לעיל גם להיפך, שאף לפני הקב"ה יש שמחה כשיאבדו מכעיסיו וכו'. וצ"ב.

אלא נר' דיסוד הענין הוא כהנ"ל ברישא דברינו. דמצד א' ודאי ראוי לשמוח על מפלתן של רשעים, שהרי "מיתתן של רשעים הנאה להן והנאה לעולם" (סנהדרין עא:). דע"י אבוד רשעים נצולין הצדיקים ונתבערו מכשולם ונתרבה כבוד שמים בארץ. אבל מצד ב' מפלתן של רשעים אינה מראה הטוב הגמור של הקב"ה, דודאי היה יותר טוב אם לא היו נענשים כלל והיו שבים בכל ליבם ועושים רצון ה'. ולכן **אין במפלתן של רשעים שמחה גמורה כיון שיש צד קלקול ואינו גילוי של הטוב הגמור של הבורא ית'**. וזהו כוונת הגמ' שהקב"ה אינו שש אבל אחרים משיש, דהיינו דמהמבט של הקב"ה (כביכול) שהוא עצם הדבר אין בזה שמחה גמורה, אבל ממבט של אנשים שהוא המבט המעשי בעוה"ז ודאי שמחה גדולה היא. ולפ"ז שעיקר החילוק אינו בין הקב"ה ובנ"א אלא בין מבט כבוד הגמור לבין מבט מעשית, יש לפרש המדרשים הנ"ל בקל. דהא דאיתא דיש שמחה לפני הקב"ה, היינו דיש להקב"ה שמחה בהצלת ישראל ובאבד הרע מהעולם, אבל לא מיירי שם ממבט הטוב הגמור.[2] והא דאין לנו לגמור את ההלל כל ימי פסח היינו כדי שגם אנו נכיר היסוד הזה ששמחה זו יש לה צד קלקול ואין הנס הזה מראה הטוב הגמור של הש"י. (וע"ע לקמן ענף ד' בביאור הדיון בענין הלל ושמחה בימי הפסח ביתר הרחבה.)

---

[1] צל"ע במלבי"ם בדה"י שם דמפרש לשון כי טוב בפס' שם, וקשה שהרי בזה לא כתיב לשון זה בהאי קרא. ועכ"פ גם מפירושו יוצא שאין רצון ה' בעצם מפלתן וז"ל, "הודו לה' כי טוב, שאינו יוצא כדי להרע לאו"ה רק כדי להטיב ע"י לישראל, כי לעולם חסדו קיים עליהם".

[2] דע, דכל מה דאמרינן שהקב"ה אינו שמח וכיוצ"ב ודאי אין הכוונה לשמחה ממש, דפשוט דלא שייכא אלו דברים אצל הקב"ה. אלא הכוונה היא כלפינו, דהיינו שקלקול אינו מראה מידת טובנו. וע"ע במהר"ל (גו"א בראשית ו:ו סוד"ה ויתעצב) וז"ל, "ואם יאמר, סו"ס הש"י שיש בו כל השלימות

ובאמת הדברים כבר מפורשים בהדיא בהדיא בגדולי המפרשים. ז"ל המהרש"א (סנהדרין לט:), "שהשמחה לפניו הוא החפץ והרצון, וכבר אמר הכת' (י' יחזקאל יח:כג) כי לא אחפוץ במות הרשע כי אם בשובו מדרכו וחיה. וז"ש שלא נאמר כי טוב במפלתן של רשעים, דכי טוב נאמר על הקיום והרצון לפניו." וע"ע במהר"ל בחי' אגדות (סנהדרין שם) וז"ל, "כי השמחה הוא כאשר יש לו שלימות ואז נמצא השמחה, והש"י רצה בבריאתם מפני שהוא עלת הכל... שהש"י רוצה וחפץ במעשיו, ואיך ישמח בהפסד שלהם... לכך הוא אינו שש אבל משיש אחרים, כי לנבראים אחרים הרשעים מצירים ומתנגדים להם ובמפלתן ראוי שישישו לאחרים." ובמק"א (גור אריה במדבר יח:ח) כתב עוד וז"ל, "ואני הנני מביא מבול מים (בראשית ו:יז), שיש שמחה באבדון של רשעים (כ"כ בספרי שם). ונר' דלא קשיא, דודאי אין שמחה לפני הקב"ה בשעת המבול דכתיב (בראשית ו:ו) ויתעצב ה' על לבו, ואיך יתכן לומר שיש שמחה לפניו, אלא הכת' אומר שיש שמחה באבדון של רשעים, דהיינו שאחרים ששים... וכיון שיש שמחה באבוד רשעים כתב אצלו לשון ואני הנני שהוא לשון זריזות, אע"ג דאין שמחה לפניו באבדון רשעים, אין הנני הכתוב לשון שהוא רק שמחה רק לשון זריזות, הזריז לדבר, והזירוז הוא שמחה בכל מקום... מ"מ הוא זריז לדבר שהרי טוב הוא שיאבדו רשעים." הרי לן דהקב"ה בעצמו אינו שש משום שאין הקב"ה רוצה בקלקול והפסד, אבל יש לו זריזות שיש בה הוראת שמחה משום דעכ"פ טוב לאחרים.[3]

ועפ"ז מובן היטב דבנ"י אמרו שירה על הים ולא מלאכי השרת, דבנ"י שרו על ישועתם ואיבוד הרע מן העולם, אבל המלאכים לא היו מותרים לשיר כיון שהם היו רוצים לשיר מכח שמחה כלפי שמיא ולפני ה'.[4] ועוד, המסתכל בשירת הים יראה שהשירה מזכירה גבורת ה', ומלכותו לעולמי עד אבל אינה מזכירה טובו הגדול, וזהו כמ"ש לעיל מהגמ' מגילה דאין אומרים "כי טוב" בהלל על מפלתן של רשעים. ואפשר שזוהי כוונת המהרש"א בסנהדרין שם וז"ל, "במדרש רבה (בשלח כג:ז) אמרו שאמר הקב"ה למלאכים אז ישיר משה ובנ"י תחילה ואח"כ המלאכים (הרי לן דהמלאכים מותרים לומר שירה)... י"ל דשירה דקאמר הכא (דאסורין לומר) היינו הלל אבל לאז ישיר אין לחוש." ויש לפרש דבריו כמ"ש דאז ישיר לא מזכיר אלא טובו וחסדו ית' ושירה על גבורותיו, ע"ש.[6]

ב: אין לשמוח אלא משום ריבוי כבוד שמים וכיוצ"ב שיש במפלתן, והחיוב להכיר הקלקול בשעה שמענישם

כבר הזכרנו הא דמבואר במדרש (ילק"ש משלי) דכיון דאיכא צד קלקול במפלתן של רשעים אסור להרבות בשמחה יותר מדי, ולכן אין אנו גומרים את ההלל כל ימי הפסח כדי להזכיר הצד קלקול הטמון בישועתנו (וע"ע לקמן ענף ד'). ומצינו עוד, דגם עצם השמחה שאנו שמחים במפלתן צריך להיות מפאת הדברים הטובים שיש במפלתן ולא משום גוף ההפסד. זאת אומרת, חייב האדם להכיר דאבדון באמת אינו טוב, ואדם השמח מפאת הקלקול הרי הוא מתנגד לרצון קונו שאינו חפץ במות הרשע. וע' במהר"ל בדרך חיים (אבות פ"ד מ"כ) דביאר הענין היטב וז"ל, "יפה הוא העוה"ז מצד שהוא תיקון לרשעים, כי אין מדה הזאת שהוא מדת הקלקלה יפה כלל, לכך הקב"ה תקן התשובה לאדם בעוה"ז שלא יהא מקלקל הרשע. והא דכתיב באבוד רשעים רנה היינו כשנאבד הרשע יש לו לשמוח מפני כבוד המקום[7], אבל הש"י בעצמו אינו שש במפלתן של רשעים, שהתקלקלה אינה יפה... והכי איתא בפ"ק דמגילה (הנ"ל), מפני מה לא נאמר כי טוב בהודאה זו מפני שאין הש"י שמח במפלתן של רשעים... והיינו טעמא שודאי כאשר הרשעות מסתלק מן העולם יש שמחה וזהו מפני כבוד הש"י ולפיכך יש לשמוח,

---

אין ראוי לומר עליו התעצבות שאין שלימות רק כאשר יש שמחה וחדוה, כי למבין אין זה קשיא, רק ה'עוז והחדוה במקומו', ועל"ז יש התעצבות, והוא יתברך פועל אצל כל א' וא' לפי הראוי", ע"ש עוד.

[3] חז"ל הדגישו דאבוד רשעים הוא טוב "לעולם", וזהו משום שהוא טוב לעולם אבל אינו טוב בעצם. ע' סנהדרין (קיג:) וז"ל, "רשע בא לעולם חרון בא לעולם... רשע אבד מן העולם טובה באה לעולם שנא' ובאבוד רשעים רנה". ובסנהדרין (עא:), "מיתתן של רשעים הנאה להן (פרש"י שאין מוסיפין לחטוא) והנאה לעולם (פרש"י ששקטה כל הארץ)". וכן נר' מעצם הקרא (משלי יא:י), "בטוב צדיקים תעלץ קריה, ובאבוד רשעים רנה", דהיינו שישנה שמחה בעוה"ז בקריה של הצדיק ולא הרשע. וכן ע"ש בראב"ע וז"ל, "ישמחו אנשי קריה", ובאבוד רשעים ירננו". וכן איתא ברלב"ג ועוד.

[4] וע"ז יש לפרש הגמ' (שבת קו.) דשריפת בת כהן נחשבה כקלקול מצד עצם הריגתה, אבל יש בשריפתה גם צד תיקון מפאת ביעור הרע. וז"ל הרשב"א שם, "הבערה גופה דבת כהן קלקול גמור הוא... יש בהם תיקון מצד שהן מתבערין מתוך העדה." וכעי"ז מבואר בעוד ראשונים ע"ש.

[5] אולם יש להעיר מהגמ' מגילה (יד.) דגמרינן חיוב הלל בפורים מהא דאמרו שירה על הים, ומשמע שהם ענין א', וכמ"כ רש"י שם, "הלל נמי נימא, שהוא שירה". וי"ל דודאי ענין א' הם, אלא דהלל של שירת הים שלא הוזכר ביה טובו ית' היה מותר אף למלאכי השרת לאומרו. אבל מש"כ המהר"ל לחלק ביניהם ביסודם עדיין צ"ע.

[6] בענין עיקר יסוד דברינו ראיתי באו"א קצת הובא בספר תהלה ליונה על מס' מגילה (י:) בשם משנת ר' אהרן (ח"ג מאמר שירה על הנס) וז"ל, "שבשירה והלל על הנס יש ב' ענינים, א', ענין הכרת הטוב וההודאה עליו ומזה יוצא ממילא התקרבות להש"י בדביקות וחיזוק באמונה והשגחה ועל"ז אין טענה כלל באבדון רשעים, ב', ענין עוד עצם ההלל ושבח להבורא, ושבח שהוא ענין זו היא התכלית הנרצית מכל הענין. ויש עוד ענין של הלל ושבח מצד חדושי השגות חדשות באמונה ורק להלל ולשבח לבורא, ועל"ז הקב"ה ממית אותם מיד כדי שיהי' להם חלק לעוה"ב. והחיד"א (ברכות י.) די"ל שירה על מפלתן כשמפלתן היא לטובתן של הרשעים שהקב"ה ממית אותם מיד כדי שיהי' להם חלק לעוה"ב. וכתב עוד שם דרק אין לומר שירה בשעת ההפלה גופא, אבל אחר שכבר גמר הקב"ה הנס יש לשמוח. אבל כל תירוצים אלו מוקשים מהמקורות הנ"ל, ומהגמ' עצמה נר' מבואר כמ"ש בפנים.

[7] וכל המיצר לישראל נחשב כנלחם עם ה' עצמו. ע' רש"י (פר' מטות לא:ג) וז"ל, "לפי שעמדו כנגד ישראל נחשבו הם כאילו עמדו כנגד הקב"ה".

אבל הקב"ה אינו שש מפני דסו"ס הוא קלקלה ואין שמחה לכל דבר שהוא קלקלה... והא דכתיב באבוד רשעים רנה היינו היכי שבא האבוד בשביל הרשעות שהיו דנין אותו ב"ד למיתה בשביל רשעותו כדי לסלק הרשעות מן העולם, אבל אם לא היה משום הרשעות רק נפילה אחרת הגיע לרשע אסור לשמוח."

ולכאו' הכרה זו צריכה להדריכנו גם בעת קיום מצות עונשין, כמו בעונשי ב"ד ומחיית עמלק וז' עממין וכיוצ"ב. וכן נתבאר מדברי החזו"א (או"ח נו:ד ד"ה ומ"מ) וז"ל, "**העונש** (ומיירי שם גם בעניישת נכרים) **צריך להעשות מתוך יגון עמוק**, נקי מרגש צרות עין בשל אחרים". ונר' דאפי' במצות מחיית עמלק דמבואר ברמב"ם (עשה קפ"ז והל' מלכים פ"ה ה"ה) שאנו מצווין לשנוא אותם. המצוה היא להרגיש השנאה מפאת רשעותם והתנגדותם לה' וכלל ישראל ולא משום שנאה בעלמא. וחייבין להלחם בם ולהורגם מתוך שמחה של מצוה ולהרבות כבוד שמים ולא משום גאוה והרצון לשלוט באחרים ח"ו.[8]

אולם ע' מגילה (טז.) וז"ל, "כי סליק בעט ביה (פי' מרדכי בעט בהמן בדרך עלייתו לסוס), אמר ליה (המן למרדכי) לא כתיב לכו בנפל אויבך אל תשמח (בתמיה), אמר ליה הני מילי בישראל אבל בדידכו כתיב (דברים לג:כט) ואתה על במותימו תדרוך". לכאו' מבואר בגמ' דפס' דבנפל זה דנבפל אויבך וכו' לא נאמר לגבי אומות העולם. אבל הדברים קשים טובא, שהרי כבר הזכרנו לעיל מהמהדרש (ילק"ש משלי) דקרא זה נאמר אף על המצרים כשטבעו בים. ועוד קשה שהרי הסברנו ע"פ הגמ' במגילה וסנהדרין וכו' דאסור לשמוח שמחה בעלמא במפלתן של רשעים, וא"כ האיך היה מותר למרדכי לבעט בהמן, ואיזה תירוץ הוא זה דהני מילי בישראל.[9]

אבל נר' דבאמת הדברים פשוטים ומבוארים מעצם הקרא שהביאה הגמ' ומעוד כמה וכמה מקומות בתנ"ך שמצינו שבנ"י נלחמו נגד אויביהם והרגם באופנים אכזריים. דודאי אם היינו עושים כן משום הרגשה של גאוה בעלמא היה בזה חטא והוראת מדות רעות, אבל לא זו הדרך שהתורה צוותה לענוש את אויבנו, אלא מעניישים אותם באופן שנר' בחוץ כאכזריות כדי להראות כח השליטה שיש לה' וכח הצדק והטוב מעל כל רשעי עולם. וודאי מרדכי שבעט בהמן עשה כן להרבות כבוד שמים, ומצוה רבה קיים בזה שקדש שם שמים. אבל למדתנו מרדכי הצדיק בתשובתו דאין נוהגין כן אלא ברשעי עכו"ם ולא ברשעי ישראל, דברשעי ישראל אין זה כבוד שמים להתגרות בהם כך משום שיש גם בזה חילול ה' בנפילת איש ישראל ח"ו.

וצריך להוסיף לדברינו עוד הערה חשובה מהחזו"א (הנ"ל) וז"ל, "ובהיות האדם בלתי שלם בתכלית השלמות ומורגז ביצר הרע, לא יחדל מליהיות רחמני ולהתרשל בשעה שמצווה לעשות דין, ואז ניתן לו להשתמש גם בהערת טבעת נקמה תחת פיקוח הדעת שאין הערתו בזה רק לזירוז הדין, וזהו בכל לבבך בשני יצריך". מבואר בדבריו ז"ל דאע"פ דראוי להיות "נקי מרגש צרות עין" וכו', אעפ"כ כיון דלרוב אינשי קשה מאד להשיג טהרת הלב הזה, מותר להם לזרז את עצמם למצוה זו אפי' ע"י "הערת טבעת נקמה" כדי שלא ירחם על הרשעים. וידועה מה שאמרו חז"ל (ילק"ש שמואל סי' קכ"א ועוד) "כל שהוא רחמן על אכזרים לסוף נעשה אכזר על רחמנים", ולכן עדיף להשתמש "בכל לבבך בשני יצריך" מלרחם שלא כדין.

ומי שמשתמש במידת אכזריות לשם לשמים כדי לקיים מצות ה', כתב האור החיים הקדוש (דברים יג:יח) שהבטיחו לו הכת' שלא יוזנק מידותיו עי"ז. דהנה אמר הקרא (יג:טז-יח) בענין החרמת עיר הנדחת, "הכה תכה את יושבי העיר ההיא לפי חרב... ושרפת באש את העיר ואת כל שללה כליל לה' אלקיך... ולא ידבק בידך מאומה מן החרם למען ישוב ה' מחרון אפו ונתן לך רחמים ורחמך והרבך כאשר נשבע לאבותיך." וביאר האוה"ק וז"ל, "כונת המאמר כאן, לפי שצוה על עיר הנדחת שיהרגו כל העיר לפי חרב ואפי' בהמתם, מעשה הזה יוליד טבע האכזריות בלב האדם, כמו שסיפרו לנו הישמעאלים כת הרוצחים במאמר המלך כי יש להם חשק גדול בשעה שהורגים אדם, ונכרתה מהם שורש הרחמים והיו לאכזר, והבחינה עצמה תהיה נשרשת ברוצחי עיר הנדחת. לזה אמר להם **הבטחה שיתן להם ה' רחמים הגם שהטבע יוליד בהם האכזריות.**" וכ"כ הנצי"ב (העמק דבר פר' פנחס כה:יב) לגבי קנאת פנחס וז"ל, "בשביל כי טבע המעשה שעשה פינחס להרוג נפש היה נותן להשאיר בלב הרגש עז גם אח"כ, אבל באשר היה לשם שמים משום הכי באה הברכה שיהא תמיד בנחת ובמדת השלום ולא יהא זה העינן לפוקת לב. וע' כיוצא בס' דברים (יג:יח) ברוצחי עיר הנדחת." (והוסיף הנצי"ב דבאמת מידת השלום הזאת היתה תקועה בלב פינחס כ"כ עד שאכן התרשל לקנאות אח"כ בזמן הראוי. וז"ל, "וכתיב שלום קטיעה, דבמה

---

[8] האיר לי מו"ר ר' מנדל בלכמן שליט"א דברי המשך חכמה (דברים יג:טו) לגבי מצות הריגת עיר הנדחת וז"ל, "לעשות הישר, לא נאמר הטוב, שאין זה טוב לפני השם יתברך במפלתן של רשעים, ולכן לא נאמר טוב – מגילה (י:)". הרי שוב רואים הקרא דעצם מלשון הקרא דעצם המצוה הוא לעשות רק הישר אבל אנו מכירים שאין זה "טוב" להענישם רשעים. וכיוצ"ב מצינו דגם בעת שנעשה דין ברשעים צריכים להתאבל קצת על מפלתן וכמו שהבי"ד שהורגים את רשע מתענים כל אותו יום. וכן ע' באברבנאל (נחלת אבות על אבות ד:יט) שהביא מדרש דנה פירש מאשתו כל ימי המבול, וכתב לבאר שהוא מפאת בנפול אויבך וכו'.

[9] ונ"ל דחוק לפרש דכונת הגמ' כאן היא דוקא באמלק, דלא נר' כן מפשטות הקרא שהביאו. וראיתי הובא בשם הגר"י עמדין זצ"ל בספרו לחם שמים דכתב דבאמת מרדכי דחוי דחייא בעלמא קדחי להמן. ועוד ראיתי הובא בשם הגר"ח קניבסקי שליט"א (הו"ד בקובץ בית אהרן וישראל שנה כ"ב גליון ה' סיון-תמוז תשס"ז עמ' קמ"ד) דגמ' זו באמת פליגא על המדרש המובא לעיל דאין אומרים הלל כל ימי הפסח משום קרא זה דבנפול אויבך וכו'.

שהיה במדת השלום יותר מהראוי שלא קנא בימי השופטים על פסל מיכה ועוד, כמבואר בתנא דבי אליהו ובילקוט שמעוני שופטים, משום הכי כתיב קטיעא נענש, ונמצא דמדת השלום נהפך לו לרועץ".)

ג: במפלתן של רשעים גמורים איכא שמחה אפי' כלפי שמיא

איתא בזוהר הקדוש (פר' נח סא: אות ט"א, הו"ד בצל"ח ברכות סוף ט: ובספר זאב יטרף פסח סי' צ"ו). "לית חדוה קמי קב"ה כזמנא דאתאבידו חייבי עלמא ואינון דארגיזו קמיה, הה"ד ובאבוד רשעים רנה. וכן בכל דרא ודרא דעביד דינא בחייבי עלמא, חדוה ותושבחתא קמי קב"ה. ואי תימא הא תנינן דלית חדוה קמי קב"ה כד איהו עביד דינא בחייבא, אלא תא חזי, בשעתא דאתעביד דינא בחייבא חדוון ותושבחן קמיה על דאתאבידו מעלמא, והני כד מטא ההוא זמנא דאריך לון ולא תאבן לגביה מחובייהו (פי' כשהגיע הזמן, שהמתין להם ולא עשו תשובה מחטאם), אבל אי אתעביד בהו דינא עד דלא מטא זמנייהו דלא אשתלים חובייהו וכו' כדין לית חדוה קמיה על דאתאבידו (פי' אז אין שמחה לפניו, ורע לפניו על שנאבדו). ואי תימא איהו עד דלא מטא זמנייהו אמאי עביד בהו דינא, דהא קב"ה לא עביד בהו דינא עד דלא מטא זמנייהו אלא בגין שמשתתפו בהדייהו דישראל לאבאשא לון (פי' משום שנתחברו לישראל לעשות להם רע)... ובג"כ אעבר מצראי בימא ואובידו שנאיהון דישראל בימי יהושע (פי' ומשום הכי הטביע את המצרים בים וכו')." הרי למדים מדברי הזוהר דכל מה שהסברנו דנפילתן של רשעים אינה טוב ואין הקב"ה שמח בה, אין זה אלא כשמתו "לפני זמנם", דבכה"ג אמרינן שאין הקב"ה חפץ במות המת כי אם בשובו מדרכו וחיה. אבל אחר שכבר נתן הקב"ה לרשע די זמן לשוב ולא שב וכבר הגיע זמנו למות, אז "לית חדוה קמי קב"ה כזמנא דאתאבידו חייבי עלמא". וביאר לי מו"ר ר' משה סתיו שליט"א דאחר שנתנה להם האפשרות לשוב ולא שבו, כבר אין בהם ניצוץ טוב, **וכיון שכולן רע אין במיתתן צד קלקול כלל** ולכן גם מיתתן מראה טובו של הקב"ה.[10]

וכן ע"ע בתנא דבי אליהו רבה (ספי"ח) דחילק בין רשע גמור ורשע שאינו גמור וז"ל, "הרי הוא אומר בנפול אויבך אל תשמח וכו' ולהלן הוא אומר ובאבוד רשעים רנה, הא כיצד יתקיימו שני כתובים הללו... אם אחד מישראל שהוא רוצה לשמוח במפלתן של רשעים באותן המבקשים לעשות רעה לישראל שהם רשעים גמורים מותר לשמוח ברעתן... ברוך המקום ברוך הוא שאין לפניו לא עולה ולא שכחה וכו' לפיכך נבל ברוחו נפל לאחר עשרת הימים... נתן לנבל לעשות תשובה ולא עשה נאמר ויהי כעשרת הימים ויגוף ה' וכו', וכי מה כתיב בענין של אחריו, וישמע דוד כי מת נבל ויאמר ברוך ה' אשר רב את ריב חרפתי וכו'". ונר' כוונתו כמ"ש הזוהר הנ"ל.

ד: שמחה והלל בפסח

כבר הבאנו דברי רז"ל (ילק"ש משלי סו"ס תתק"ס) וז"ל, "אמר האלקים... ראויים היו ישראל לקרות את ההלל כל ז' ימי הפסח כשם שקורין ז' ימי החג, ולמה כן, אלא בשביל שנהרגו המצרים וטבעו בים שונאי, ואני הכתבתי בנפול אויבך אל תשמח." וכ"כ הב"י (או"ח תצ:ד) בשם שבה"ל בשם מדרש הרנינו, ע"ש. וכתבנו דלמדים מזה שאין לשמוח יותר מדי על מפלתן של רשעים כיון שמפלתן אינה מראה טובו הגמור של הקב"ה.

מאידך גיסא, מבואר בכמה דוכתי ד**חלק גדול מהודאתנו להקב"ה בחג הפסח היא מפאת מפלתן של המצריים דוקא**, ויש לציין כמה מהם. א) הנה מאריכין בליל הסדר בהזכרת מפלתן ועונשן של הני רשעים. וכן משבחין ואומרים הלל באותו לילה גופא שהוכו במכת בכורות.[11] ב) נוהגין לומר "שפוך חמתך אל הגויים וכו'" על כוס רביעי קודם קריאת ההלל. וראיתי בהגדה שלמה (להרמ"מ כשר זצ"ל, פר' ל"ג) שהביא ביאורם של הקדמונים למה אמרינן "שפוך חמתך" וז"ל, "לפי שרצה לומר לא לנו (בהלל)... מקדים תחילה לבקש נקמה עליהם"[12]. והביא עוד מהאו"ז וז"ל, "לפי שהזכרנו מצרים פעמים רבות והמזכיר רשע צריך לקללו לפיכך אנו פותחים בשפוך". והמאירי כתב מהירושלמי דד' כוסות כנגד ד' מלכיות שנשתעבדו בישראל, ורמז להשקותם ד' כוסות של תרעלה, ועל כן תקנו בכוס רביעי שפוך חמתך וכו'". (ועוד ראיתי בשם הא"ח בשם הראב"ד ד' כוסות דד' פורעניות שלקו המצרים – מכת בכורים, וטביעת י"ס, ובימי נבוכדנצר, והרביעי לעתיד לבא." וע"ש עוד.) ג) וכן המנהג לשפוך יין מכוס של יין בהזכרת המכות, מבואר בכל הקדמונים דאין בזה

<hr>

[10] וגם בזאב יטרף שם ביאר כיסוד דברינו וז"ל, "אין לשמוח בנפילת האויב בעוד שיש לו זמן לעשות תשובה ולהתהפך להיות אהוב, ואפי' אם בנפילתו נצולים ישראל מאיתו, אין הצלתם מטילה עליהם רק חובת שירה על גבורותיו של פועל ישועתם, אך עדיין נמנעים מלהלל לו על טובו וחסדו מפני שאין גומרים את ההלל אלא על גילוי טוב וחסד של מעלה... אולם... כד אשתלים זמנא דאריך לון ולא תבו... כל כה"ג ליכא שיור מדת טובו וחסדו ית' דכבר כלה קצם של רשעים ותו לא מתארך להם אף."

[11] וכן ע' במכילתא (פר' בשלח ריש פר' שירה) ע"פ פס' בישעיה (ל:כט) דגם בפסח שרו שירה באותו לילה.

[12] ועוד הביא שם מהגדת צרפת ע"ד שמעינו לעיל מהמהר"ל (דרך חיים על אבות) בענין כוונתנו בשמחה על מפלתן וז"ל, "ועם כל זה, לא יעשה זה למעננו כי אם לתת כבוד לשמו".

ענין של מיעוט של שמחה משום מפלתן של רשעים[13], אלא אדרבה רצוננו בזה שתבא חמת ה' על שונאינו ולא עלינו ח"ו (מהרי"ל יט:א), והשפיכות הן כנגד חרבו של הקב"ה והמלאך הממונה על הנקמה. ויש נוהגים לזרוק מן הכוס באצבע לרמז על מה שנא' אצבע אלקים היא (ע' דרכ"מ או"ח תעג:יח). ובביאור הגר"א (גליון לשו"ע שם) הביא טעם לזה ע"פ הירושלמי דד' כוסות הן כנגד הפורעניות שהקב"ה עתיד להשקות את אומות העולם כנ"ל. ומכל זה נר' כמ"ש דנכלל בהודאתנו לה' על הצלתנו גם הודאה על מפלתן של שונאינו. וכמו שמבואר דשירת המלאכים בקריעת י"ס אינה מפאת הצלת כלל ישראל בלבד אלא דיש בה גם ענין של שמחה על מפלתן של רשעים ומשו"ה לא היו מותרים לשיר, וכן הלל בשעת מלחמה (בדבה"י הנ"ל) לא קאי על ההצלה לבדה אלא הבינו חז"ל דיש בה גם משום שמחה על מפלתן, כמו"כ השמחה בשעת הצלה שיש בה גם הפלת רשעים, נכלל בעצם השמחה גם הודאה על מפלתן של שונאינו ואין לחלק. וא"כ צ"ב דברי המדרש הנ"ל שכתב שאין אומרים הלל כל ימי הפסח משום שאין לשמוח על מפלתן של רשעים, והרי עינינו רואות שכן שמחים על מפלתן של המצרים.

ועוד צ"ב מכל הנ"ל, שהרי כבר הבאנו הא דמבואר בכמה מקומות דאכן שרו שירה והלל על מפלתן של רשעים וכדאיתא בגמ' (ברכות י.) דדוד המע"ה במפלתן של רשעים ואמר שירה שנא' יתמו חטאים מן הארץ וכו'", ובגמ' מגילה וסנהדרין הנ"ל דבנ"י שרו לה' על מפלתן של רשעים כמאמר הכת' (דהי"ב כ:כא-כב) "ויעמד משררים לה' ומהללים להדרת קדש וכו' ואומרים הודו לה' כי לעולם חסדו". וכבר הקשה כן המהרש"א (ברכות סוף ט:). וכתב דאכן טעמא דגמ' (ערכין ריש י:) מסתבר יותר, דאין אומרים הלל בשאר ימי הפסח משום שאין הימים חלוקים בקרבנותיהם (ולא דמי לסוכות דכל יום חלוק בקרבנותיו וכל א' וא' כחג בפני עצמו דמי כמ"ש רש"י תענית כח:), ע"ש. אבל דברי המדרש צ"ב.[14]

וראיתי הובא ממשנת רבי אהרן (מאמרים ח"ג עמ' ג') דכתב להוכיח מהגמ' ערכין הנ"ל דאמירת הלל הוא "או מטעם חג או מטעם נס". וע"פ"ז כתב לפרש סוגיין וז"ל, "ולפ"ז צריך ב' טעמים אהא דאין גומרין את הלל בשביעי של פסח, דהא דאינן חלוקין בקרבנותיהן הוא טעם מספיק על ענין החג, דמטעם חג אין צריך לגמור רק ביום ראשון, אבל מטעם הנס של קריעת י"ס יגמרו את ההלל בז' של פסח, ועל זה צריך לטעם המדרש דמעשי ידי טובעין בים וכו', ע"ש עוד. אבל לכאו' אין זה מספיק, שהרי מצינו שאכן אמרו הלל על נס של מפלתן של רשעים וכמ"ש.

ולכן נלע"ד דודאי אמרינן הלל על מפלתן של רשעים, וכוונת המדרש אינה אלא להסביר למה לא בפסח צוה הקב"ה שיהי' שמחה יתירה כמו שיש בחג הסוכות. ועל זה תירץ המדרש דשאני פסח שיש בה גם קלקול לרשעים ולכן אין להלל ולשמוח יותר מדי כמו בסוכות. דהיינו דאע"פ דהלל יום א' ודאי אמרינן, אבל להוסיף הלל לכל יום ויום כבר אינו ראוי. ועוד, באמת לא מיירי המדרש בשביעי של פסח דוקא, אלא כוונת המדרש להסביר מאי שנא חג הפסח בכללותו מחג הסוכות שמצינו בו שמחה יתירה. וכן מבואר בהדיא בילקוט (פר' אמור סי' תרנ"ד) וז"ל, "אתה מוצא שלש שמחות כתיב בחג (הסוכות)... אבל בפסח אין אתה מוצא שכתוב בו אפי' שמחה אחת, למה... בשביל שמתו בו המצריים. וכן אתה מוצא כל ז' ימי החג אנו קורין בהן את ההלל אבל בפסח אין אנו קורין את ההלל אלא ביו"ט הראשון ולילו, למה, משום בנפל אויב וכו'." הרי לן בהדיא דאין כוונת המדרש להוסיף טעם לאמירת הלל ולדחותו, אלא כוונת חז"ל בזה רק להסביר טעמא דקרא למה לא צוה הקב"ה שמחה יתירה עם הלל בכל יום כמו שצוה בסוכות. ולפ"ז אין בזה סתירה כלל לדברי הגמ' ערכין הנ"ל אלא הוספת טעם, דגם חילוק קרבנות של כל יום ויום של סוכות מראה החידוש וריבוי שמחה שיש בכל יום של חג הסוכות, ובפסח זה חידוש ליכא, וביאור ענין זה נכלל בג"כ בשאילת המדרש.[15]

---

[13] אולם ראיתי הובא בשם האברבנאל בזבח פסח שהשפיכות הן כדי למעט בשמחה קצת מטעמא דבנפול אויב אך תשמח. אבל בדקתי בזבח פסח ולא מצאתי פי' זה, וצע"ע.

[14] ולא נר' לחלק בין שירה והלל, שהרי שירה מבואר בגמ' מגילה (יד.) דענין א' הם ונלמדים זה מזה, ע"ש. וכן מבואר בערכין הנ"ל וברמב"ן (השגות לספה"מ שרש א', עמ' ל"ו במהו' פרנקל). אמנם ע' בשו"ת חוות יאיר (סי' רכ"ה) דהוכיח דתרי מיני שירה איכא ואין לשון שירה שוה בכל מקום, ע"ש. ולפי"ז אפשר לומר דשירת דוד המלך לא היה חשוב כהלל ממש, וכן באמת העלה החו"י שם. אולם בפס' בדבה"י הנ"ל איתא בהדיא לשון הלל.

[15] ובאמת בירושלמי (סוכה ה:א, ריש כב:) איתא עוד טעם אחר וז"ל, "ר' יונה בשם רבב"ח, כל זמן שהתחיל בחליל, כנגד הלל כל ימי הגמ' נוהג. ריבר"ב בשם רבב"מ למה קורין את ההלל כל שבעת ימי החג (ופי' קרבן העדה - בפסח אין קורין אלא בי"ט הראשון בלבד), כנגד הלולב שהוא מתחדש כל שבעה." וע"ע בילקוט פר' אמור הנ"ל דכתב עוד טעם דהחילוק לענין מצות שמחה דבפסח נידונין על התבואה ואין להרבות בהלל בשעת דין. הרי לן כמה וכמה טעמים לריבוי שמחה של חג הסוכות דאינה שייכת בפסח, ואין שום סתירה בין המאמרים אלא הוסף טעם א' כמ"ש.

אולם במהרי"ל (מנהגים סדר התפילות של פסח אות ט) מבואר כהבנת האחרונים הנ"ל דטעם דמעשה ידי וכו' נאמר על יום ז' דוקא. וז"ל, "גומרין ההלל בשני ימים הראשונים של פסח, והלל אומר בדילוג כמו בר"ח... לפי שבשביעי טבעו המצריים ואמר הקב"ה מעשה ידי טובעים בים ואתם אומרים שירה. וא"ת עדיין ביום ז' וח' לא נימא אבל בחול המועד נימא, לא קשה דאז הוי חול המועד חשוב משביעי שהוא יו"ט. ורש"י יהיב טעמא שאין גומרין הלל בחול המועד דפסח מפני שנאמר כאלה תעשה ליום שבעת ימים ואין חילוק בקרבנות משא"כ בח"ה דסוכות. (וכ"כ הט"ז תצ:ג ולבוש ס"ק ד'.) [ועכ"פ מהא דהביא טעמא של רש"י כטעם אחר (כדאיתא בגמ' ערכין הנ"ל) מבואר דהבין דהמדרש חולק על הגמ' משא"כ לפי ר' אהרן הנ"ל, ע"ש.] וכן מבואר מהא דלפי המהרי"ל בעצם היה ראוי לקרות ההלל ע"פ הגמ' הנ"ל, אבל נר' דאף דעת

ולפי דברינו מיושב עכ"פ חצי הלל כל ימי הפסח. דבאמת מפאת מפלתן של רשעים אמרינן בעלמא אפי' הלל
שלם, ורק הכא דכבר אמרנו הלל ביום א' אין מפריזין על המדה לגמור ההלל בכל יום. ובאמת אין זה אלא זכר בעלמא
למפלתן, דהיינו שמזכירים במקצת שאין השמחה שלימה כיון שהצלה זו אינה מראה טובו הגמור של השי"ת וכמ"ש, אבל
ודאי שמחה מיהא איכא[16]. וע' באמת בפוסקים (דרכ"מ סי' ת"ץ) שנחלקו הראשונים לגבי שביעי של פסח אם אמרינן "זמן
חירותינו" כשאר ימי הפסח או אם אמרינן "זמן שמחתנו". וביאר הדרכ"מ הטעם לומר זמן שמחתנו וז"ל, "לפי שהיו שמחים
שטבעו בים". והביא דכבר הוזכרה סברא זו במהרי"ל (סדר התפילות של פסח אות ה'), אלא דהמהרי"ל כתב דאין המנהג
כן, וכן פסק הרמ"א. אבל בדרישה נר' דפסק דאכן אמרינן זמן שמחתנו מהאי טעמא. ורואים מזה דבאמת מפלתן הויא טעמא
לשמוח, ורק לא אמרינן הלל כדי לעשות זכר בעלמא וכמ"ש. ואפי' לפי המנהג דאמרינן זמן חרותנו, לא נר' מהפוסקים הנ"ל
דנחלקו בסברא זו, אלא נחלקו רק אם ראוי יותר לומר זמן חרותנו כשאר ימי הפסח, ע"ש.[17]

אולם אף לפי דברינו ודאי אין מפלתן נקראת "טוב", וכבר הבאנו לעיל שמשו"ה נמנעו בנ"י מלומר הודו לה' "כי טוב" על
מפלתן של רשעים. וא"כ באמת קשה האיך אמרינן "הודו לה' כי טוב" בהלל (בין בהלל שלם שביום א' ובין בחצי הלל בשאר
ימי הפסח).[18] ועוד קשה מהא דאיתא במס' סופרים (יח:ב) וז"ל, "וביו"ט האחרון של פסח [אומרים] הלל הגדול, ואיזהו הלל
הגדול, הודו לה' כי טוב הודו לאלקי האלהים וכו' (תהלים קל"ו)". הרי מנהג קדום היה לומר הודו לה' "כי טוב" דוקא באחרון
של פסח (משום דהזכיר הנס על הים), ולכאו' מנהג קשה הוא כיון דמפלתן של רשעים אינה נקראת טוב, ואנחנו אפי' ממעטים
קצת בהלל מהאי טעמא[19].

ואולי י"ל דההלל שאומרים בחג אינו נר' לעין כ"כ דקאי על מפלתן של רשעים שהרי עיקרו הוא לשמוח לפני ה' ולהתקרב
לה' ביו"ט. והא דאין אומרים הלל שלם הוא רק שיהי' היכרא בעלמא למפלתן של רשעים וכמ"ש. אבל לא משום שכל מילה
ומילה של ההלל באמת מיירי במפלתן ממש. ודוקא הלל בשעת מפלתן וכשאינו יו"ט נחשב כשירה ישירה על מפלתן, ובכה"ג
אין לומר "כי טוב".

ה: שמחה והלל בפורים

המהרי"ל אינה סותרת עיקר דברינו, והא דאין אומרים הלל משום מעשה ידי וכו' הוא רק משום שכבר אמרנו הלל בפסח ביום ראשון, אבל ביום
ראשון אכן נכלל בהלל גם משום מפלתן של רשעים וכמ"ש.

אמנם ע' בכל בו (סי' נ"ב) דנר' קצת כהבנת משנת ר' אהרן דצריך גם טעם הגמ' וגם טעם המדרש וכמ"ש וז"ל, "ויש נותנים טעם בדבר לפי שפסח
כל הימים שוים בקרבנותיהם ולפיכך אין מברכין אלא על יום ראשון ושני שגם הוא ספק ראשון, אבל בשביעי אע"פ שהוא יו"ט קדש, מפני שהשוטבע פרעה
וכל חילו בים בו ביום על דרך שאמרו ז"ל בקשו מלאכי השרת לומר שירה לפני הקב"ה השיב להם מעשי ידי טובעים בים ואתם אומרים שירה לפני
לפיכך אין קורין אותו אלא בדילוג". אולם יש להקשות עליו כמו שהקשינו על המשנה דר' אהרן. ולכן נר' דגם הוא מודה לעיקר יסוד דברינו דבעלמא
אמרינן הלל על מפלתן של רשעים. ודוקא הכא דכבר אמרנו הלל פעם א' בפסח ראשון לא אמרינן הלל עוד פעם בשביעי של פסח אע"פ דאיכא מחייב
בפנ"ע בשביל נס דקריעת י"ס, דכיון דכבר אמרנו הלל בפסח אין להרבות יותר מדי משום מפלתן. וע"ע בכל בו שם דהביא עוד טעם שאין אומרים
הלל כל ימי פסח ובמאי חלוק ממסכות וחנוכה וז"ל, "ויש נותנים טעם אחר והוא דכיון דחג המצות לית ביה חובת מצה רק לילה ראשונה ושניה לפי
שבשאר ימים אפשר ליה בפירות או בפת אורז ודוחן וכיוצא בהן לפיכך אין מברכין על ההלל רק בב' ימים הראשונים שהם חובת מצה שהיא עקר
מצות היום אבל בחג שכל שבעת הימים צריך שישב בסוכה וירבד לישב בסוכה בכל עת שיכנס לישב בה צריך שיברך שיכנס על ההלל ויגמור אותו בכל
יום... וגם בח' ימי חנוכה ראוי לברך על כל הימים לגמור לפי שבכל יום היה הנס הולך וחזק." הרי מבואר בדבריו דהנס הנוסף של קריעת י"ס אינו
טעם מוחלט לחייב עוד הלל, ואפי' בלי הטעם של מעשה ידי וכו' הלל אמרינן הלל אפי' על מפלתן של רשעים. ורק בשביעי של פסח שכבר אמרנו הלל ואין כאן נס וחג
חדש שיש לגמרי אז י"ל דממעטים בהלל קצת משום מפלתן של רשעים.

[16] ואפשר שיש להוסיף לזה קצת ע"פ מה שראיתי בספר ירח למועדים (לר' ירוחם אלשין שליט"א, פסח סי' נ') בשם הגר"ח (הו"ד במקראי קודש
ימים נוראים ס"ח) וז"ל, "שהשאיר הגר"ח על הגמ' ערכין דאין אומרים הלל בראש השנה משום שספרי חיים וספרי מתים פתוחים לפניו, הלוא אמרו
שיר של יום בר"ה. ותירץ הגר"ח דדין אמירת הלל דלהלל דלא שאני בעין שיהא שמחה שלימה, ובר"ה אין השמחה שלימה לכן אין מוכשר לומר בו הלל
משא"כ לענין שיר של יום אין צריך שמחה שלימה, ושמחה מיהא איכא בר"ה." (ע' רמב"ם הל' חנוכה ג:ו והל' יו"ט ו:יז). ולפי דברי הגר"ח זצ"ל
אפשר להוסיף עוד הוכחה לדברינו מהא דנוהגין לומר חצי הלל בפסח ולא בר"ה, שהרי נר' דאף חצי הלל קרוב הוא לשמחה שלמה ואעפ"כ אומרים
אותו כל ימי הפסח, ורק בר"ה דספרי חיים וספרי מתים פתוחים לפניו אין אומרים הלל כלל. וע' בזה. (אבל בספר ירח למועדים כתב לבאר באו"א
לגמרי על פי דרכו.)

[17] וע' בחק יעקב (תצ:ט) דכתב כעין דברינו וז"ל, "וכתב בשכ"ג סי' תפ"ו, וקשה דא"כ למה לא אמרי' משום מעשי ידי וכו' עכ"ל. ובאמת לק"מ,
דדוקא ההלל לומר שירה לפני הקב"ה כאלו יש שמחה לפניו אין אומרים משום מעשי ידיו וכו' אבל אומרים זמן שמחתנו שיש באבוד רשעים רנה
וכדאיתא להדיא בחילוק זה ס"פ א' דיני ממונות (סנהדרין לט:)." הרי מבואר דנקט החק יעקב כיסוד שיסדנו לעיל דהקב"ה אינו שש
אבל מה שנר' מדבריו דאמירת הלל דינה כמו "שירה לפני הקב"ה כאלו יש שמחה לפניו", דבר זה לא נר' וכמ"ש לעיל מהא
דמצינו בכמה דוכתי דבאמת אומרים הלל על מפלתן של רשעים. ודוקא הכא לא אמרינן ומטעמא שהסברנו.

[18] שו"ר בחוות יאיר (סי' רכ"ה) דהקשה קושיא זו וכתב לתרץ וז"ל, "ואע"פ שאומרים בו הודו לה' כי טוב וכמ"ש, מ"מ הואיל דקרינן ומדלגין אין לפניו ית' כאן שמחה שלימה.
הודו לה' כי טוב דע"כ לא נאמר שם כי טוב לפי שאין שם שמחה הקב"ה שמח וכו', מ"מ הואיל דקרינן ומדלגין אין לפניו ית' כאן שמחה שלימה. אבל אין תירוצו
נר' כ"כ, שהרי נר' מהגמ' שעיקר ההקפדה הוא על לשון "כי טוב" וכמ"ש. ומה שאין גומרין את ההלל כדי שלא יהי' השמחה שלימה לכאו' אינה
מועיל כלום לעיקר ההקפדה.

[19] ואפשר שזהו באמת כוונת סוף ההלכה במס' סופרים שם וז"ל, "ונהגו העם לומר הלל הגדול אע"פ שאינו מן המובחר", וע' בזה. ועכ"פ
המנהג במקומה עומד.

איתא בגמ' מגילה (יד.) דמעיקר הדין היה ראוי לומר הלל בפורים אלא דלמעשה אין אומרים אותו משום דאין אומרים הלל על נס שבחו"ל ועוד טעמים, ע"ש. ולהד מ"ד קריית המגילה גופא נחשבת כהלל. (ולא עוד, אלא דדנו כמה פוסקים במי שאין לו מגילה אם י"ד הלל ממש. יע"ש במאירי דחידש כן, וע"ע באחרונים הו"ד בספר תהלה ליונה שם.) הרי לן בהדיא דאע"פ דבפורים יש בו משום מפלתן של רשעים, אעפ"כ שמחים בו שמחה יתירה וגם יש לקרות בו את ההלל. וע' גמ' מגילה (טז:) דקרי למגילת אסתר שירה על מפלתן של רשעים, ע"ש היטב ובחי' הר"ן. וכן ע' במחזור ויטרי (סדר פורים סי' רנ"ד) וז"ל, "ונר' שאומרים שיר מזמור לאסף כדי לסמוך שיר ממפלתן של רשעים למגילה שהיא מפלתן של רשעים". ומשמע **שהשמחה בפורים וגם קריאת המגילה דדינה כהלל במקצת ישועתנו אינן מפאת ישועתנו בלבד אלא גם משום מפלתן של רשעים דוקא.**

והדברים מפורשים בהדיא במקצת ראשונים ריש מס' מגילה. דאיתא בגמ' שם (סוף ב.) די"א דבזמה"ז אין מקדימין הקריאה ליום הכניסה. והביאו הראשונים גירסת הירושלמי (פ"א סוה"ד [ו:]). ע"ש בגירסת הפני משה וציון ירושלים ע"פ הראשונים בביאור טעמא דמילתא. וז"ל המאירי שם, "ויש גורסין הואיל ומסתכנין בה, וכך היא שנויה בברייתא (ע' תוספתא א:ג) ובתלמוד המערב, ומפרשין הטעם הואיל וישראל מסתכנין עכשיו בקיום דתותיהם, והשונאים מתעוררים עליהם כשרואין אותן מתמידים בשמחה על נקמתם, תקנו שלא לפרסם בשמחה יותר מן הראוי ודיה בשעתה. ואע"פ ששמחת חנוכה נמשכת שמונה ימים, אותה שמחה של נס השמן היתה, ולא ניצוח האויבים." וכ"כ בכל בו (הל' פורים סי' מ"ה) וז"ל, "ואע"פ שזכרון נס חנוכה עושין ח' ימים ולא חששו לה, אפשר לומר לפי שאותה מצוה היא לזכרון הנס של שמן לא לזכרון נס נקמת האויבים. אבל זה שהוא לזכרון נקמת האויבים יש לחוש שלא יקנאו על זה." וכ"כ בארחות חיים (הל' מגלה ופורים סי' כ"ב). וכן איתא במכתם, והוסיף עוד בזה"ל, "שמא ישמעו ויקנאו על רוב שמחתנו לאידם ולנקום נקמתינו מהם". והנמו"י שם כתב וז"ל, "שיש במגלה ספור מפלת אויבים משא"כ בחנוכה וביו"ט".

וכן ע' בלשון בתפילת על הנסים, דלגבי פורים לא הוזכר בהדיא ענין הישועה ורק נכתב קלקול הרשעים (משא"כ לגבי חנוכה דכ"כ ג"כ ענין הישועה "ולעמך ישראל עשית תשועה גדולה וכו'"). וכן הברכה דאמרינן אחר קריאת המגילה איתא, "הרב את ריבנו והדן את דיננו והנוקם את נקמתנו וכו'". (ואע"פ דחותמים "הא-ל המושיע", נר' משאר הברכה דמדגישים דוקא הנקמה דוקא בגויים שעשה הקב"ה בשבילנו, ע"ש. וכן עע"ש בשיר "אשר הניא" ששרים אחר קריאת המגילה.)[20]

וכיוצ"ב כבר הזכרנו לעיל הא דאיתא בגמ' מגילה (טז.) דבעט מרדכי בהמן, וכשתמה עליו המן דהכתיב בנפול אויבך אל תשמח, אמר ליה מרדכי דהני מילי בישראל אבל באומות העולם כתיב ואתה על במותימו תדרוך, ע"ש. הרי לן בהדיא דענין בנפול אויבך אל תשמח לא נאמר לגבי נפילת המן. (אלא דהסברנו לעיל ע"פ המהר"ל דשמחה זו צריכה להיות מפאת ריבוי כבוד שמים דוקא, ע"ש.)

הרי מבואר מכל הנ"ל דודאי שמחים משום מפלתן של רשעים, רק דצריך ג"כ לזכור שאין זה הטוב הגמור וכמו שנתבאר. אולם ע' במשך חכמה (פר' בא יב:טו) דנר' לכאו' להיפך מדברינו. וז"ל בקיצור, "כי כל העמים בדתותיהן הנימוסיות יעשו יום

[20] ובאמת כד נעיין במגילת אסתר יראה מהפסוקים דעיקר הישועה כבר באה ליהודים זמן הרבה קודם פורים, ושמחת פורים בא גדר היא מפאת מפלתן של הרשעים דוקא. דהנה מיד אחר ששלחו האגרת השניה כבר שמחו בנ"י כדכתיב (ח:טז-יז) "ליהודים היתה אורה ושמחה וששון ויקר וכו' שמחה וששון ליהודים משתה ויום טוב". וכשבא יום י"ג באדר בפסוקים (ט:א-ד) דפחדו האויבים ולא רצו לשלוח יד ביהודים, ואעפ"כ (שם פס' ה) "ויכו היהודים בכל אויביהם מכת חרב והרג ואבדן ויעשו בשנאיהם כרצונם". הרי נר' שלא היו היהודים בסכנה באותה שעה, אלא תפסו היהודים רשות המלך כהזדמנות להנקם מאויביהם ולמחות עמלק מכל שאפשר. וכן כשביקשה אסתר יום נוסף להרוג את שונאיהם בשושן (ט:יג) נר' שלא היה אז סכנה נוכחית, אלא רצתה אסתר עוד אפשרות להלחם באויבים.

ועוד נראה מחז"ל והמפרשים דהחל גדול דשמחת פורים נקבע ע"פ נקמה בגויים והקידוש ה' שבא ע"י מחיית הרע, ולא"ד משום הצלת ישראל גרידא. דהנה מצינו ענין מחיית עמלק (שעניננו מחיית הרע ואין עיקרו הצלה) בכמה דינים שנוהגין לפורים (כגון "שבת זכור" ועוד, וע' מגילה ז.). וכן ביארו כמה ראשונים (ע' ברטב"א ומאירי וספר המאורות וכו' ב' ריש מס' מגילה וער"ן) דהטעם דדנים כרכים המוקפין חומה מימות יהושע בן נון משום שהוא היה הראשון שנלחם בעמלק ולכן ראוי לקבוע יום הפורים ע"י יהושע. וכן נר' שהמלחמה שנלחמו בנ"י באותו זמן היה מדין מצות מחיית עמלק ממש. דהנה ע' בתרגום (ט:טז) שהשונאים היו בכלל עמלק. וע' רבינו בחיי (שמות יז:טז) דפי' הא דכתיב "ובזה לא שלחו את ידם" (ט:י, ט:טו) משום שנהגו איסור הנאה בשלל עמלק, ומבואר דהשונאים שנהרגו בשושן ביום י"ד היו מעמלק. אלא דחילק בזה בין המלחמה ביום י"ד והמלחמה של יום ט"ו וז"ל (ט:טו), "הנה על המלחמה של היום הראשון נאמר (ט:ב) שנקהלו היהודים בעריהם בכל מדינות המלך אחשורוש לשלוח יד 'במבקשי רעתם' וכן לקמן (ט:טז) נאמר לשון זה 'ועמד על נפשם', שמלחמתם היתה מלחמת קיום והצלה לעצמם מכל מבקשי רעתם. אבל בפס' זה במלחמה בשושן ביום השני לא נאמר לשון זה, כי אותם העמלקים שנשארו כבר לא היו באותה העת 'מבקשי רעתם' בפועל של היהודים, לאחר שעיקר אנשיהם כבר נהרגו." וביאר שם עוד דלכן טעמא שהוסיפו להרוג הוא משום מצות מחיית עמלק. וע"ע בפס' ט:טז שם מה שדייק עוד שמלחמה זו היתה לשם מצות מחיית עמלק. (ויש לע' בנוגע לענין זה בהא דדנו האחרונים בענין מצות מחיית עמלק אם זהו דוקא דין ב"עמלק" או דבאמת כל צוררי היהודים יש להם דין של עמלק במקצת. וע' בספר נחלת שמעון ספר יהושע ובספר ימי פורים ועוד. ועוד יש לדון אם קיימת המצוה בזמן דליכא מלך. ע' בספר נחלת שמעון ספר יהושע ובספר ימי פורים ועוד. וראיתי במאמר מהגא' ר' אהרן יפהן זצ"ל הו"ד בסו"ס תהלה ליונה ד"ה שלא גם להיראים בני דהציווי הוא רק במלך, מיהו קיום מצוה יש גם ע"י מלך".)

אבל ע' ברמב"ם בסוף הקדמתו למשנה תורה (אחר מנין המצוות) שכתב וז"ל, "תקנו וצוו לקרות המגלה בעונתה כדי להזכיר שבחיו של הקב"ה ותשועות שעשה לנו והיה קרוב לשועינו כדי לברכו ולהללו וכדי להודיע לדורות הבאים שאמת מה שהבטיחנו בתורה כי מי גוי גדול אשר לו אלקים קרובים אליו וכו'". ונר' מזה שעיקר היום נקבע משום הישועה. וכן נר' מבואר בגר"א במאירי מגילת אסתר (ט:טז) וז"ל, "ועשה אותו יום (י"ג) משתה ושמחה, כי ביום י"ג היתה להם צרה גדולה כי היו יראים שמא יעמדו כנגדם וייהרגו הם, אבל עכשיו שאיש לא עמד בפניהם עשו היום משתה." וצע"ע.

הנצחון יום מפלת אויביהם לחג חג הנצחון, לא כן בישראל, המה לא ישמחו על מפלת אויביהם ולא יחגו בשמחה על זה, וכמ"ש בנפל אויבך אל תשמח... הרי דאדם המעלה אינו שמח בנפל אויבו משום שהשמחה רע בעיני ה', הלא הרע בעיני ה' צריך לשנאתי. ולכן לא נזכר בפסח חג המצות כי בו עשה במצרים שפטים, רק כי הוציא ה' את בנ"י ממצרים, אבל על מפלת האויבים אין חג ויו"ט לישראל... וכן בנס פורים לא עשו יו"ט ביום שנתלה המן או ביום שהרגו בשונאיהם, כי זה אין שמחה לפני עמו ישראל, רק היו י"ט הוא 'בימים אשר נחו מאויביהם'... שלכן לא היה חושש לקנאה את מעוררת עלינו בין האומות (ע' מגילה ז.) וברש"י 'שאנו שמחים במפלתן'), שאין השמחה רק על המנוחה לא על יום ההרג בשונאיהם וכו'." ולכא' דבריו קשים מכל הנ"ל. ועכ"פ עיקר מה שכתב דקבעה התורה החג על שם הישועה ולא על שם מפלת האויב, אכן משמע כן מהפסוקים שהביא. ולכן נר' דאף אם חלק גדול מהשמחה הוא מפאת מפלתן של רשעים וכמ"ש, אעפ"כ אינו ראוי לקבוע עצם החג על שם זה כיון שאין זה הטוב הגמור וכמ"ש. ומשו"ה קבעו החג על שם דבר הטוב בעצמו שהוא רבוי כבוד ה' ועליית עם ישראל.

ו: תפילה להמית רשעים

איתא בברכות (ז.), "ההוא צדוקי דהוה בשבבותיה דריב"ל, הוה קא מצער ליה טובא בקראי, יומא חד... סבר כי מטא ההוא שעתא (המסוגלת לקללו) אלטייה, כי מטא ההוא שעתא ניים (ולא יכול לקללו). אמר ש"מ לאו אורח ארעא למעבד הכי, ורחמיו על כל מעשיו כתיב, וכתיב גם ענוש לצדיק לא טוב." הרי לן דכיון שהקב"ה מרחם אף על רשע גמור כצדוקי שכופר בתושבע"פ ואין לו חלק לעוה"ב, לכן אין לנו לקללו ולהביא מיתתו. וכיוצ"ב מצינו בברכות (י.) וז"ל, "הנהו בריוני (פרש"י פריצים) דהוו בשבבותיה דר"מ והוו קא מצערו ליה טובא. הוה קא בעי ר"מ רחמי עלייהו כי היכי דלימותו, אמרה ליה ברוריא דביתהו מאי דעתך משום דכתיב יתמו חטאים, מי כתיב חוטאים חטאים כתיב[21]... אלא בעי רחמי עלייהו דלהדרו בתשובה... בעא רחמי עלייהו והדרו בתשובה." הרי שוב מבואר דכמו שהקב"ה אינו חפץ במות הרשע אלא בשובו מדרכו וחיה (וכמו שמצינו לעיל שהקב"ה אינו אוהב השחתה שאין זה "טוב"), כמו"כ תפלתינו צריכין להיות על דרך זו[22].

אבל כבר העירו התוס' (ברכות ז.) וז"ל, "ההוא צדוקי וכו' ולא מעלין (וא"כ קשה למה זה ראוי לקללם והרי מותר להורידם לבור), היינו בידי אדם, אבל בידי שמים לאו אורח ארעא להעונשם ולהטריחם ולהורגם בידי שמים שלא כדרך בני אדם." ונר' כוונתם כמ"ש בתוס' (ע"ז ד:) וז"ל, "כי לא היה לו לדחוק בידי שמים ולהעניש מי שאינם רוצים להעניש." והוסיף בתוס' ר' אלחנן שם וז"ל, "דהוי כעין מכחיש פמליא של מעלה ודוחק להעניש בידי שמים מה שאין רצון שמים להעניש, אבל כשהורגו בעצמו בידים אין דוחק לפני השמים להעניש כלום[23]." ויש לבאר דאין לנו להכניס עצמנו לכבשי דרחמנא (חשבונות הנתסרין), שהקב"ה יודע היטב מה דינו של כל בנ"א והוא יכול לרחם על הרשעים עד לבסוף ולהביא הצלת הצדיקים כהרף עין. אבל אנחנו מצווין לנהוג כפי מה שעינינו רואות ואסור לנו לרחם על אכזרי וכמ"ש רז"ל (ילק"ש שמואל רמז קכ"א הנ"ל ועוד) "כל שהוא רחמן על אכזרים לסוף נעשה אכזר על רחמנים". ולכן אם הקב"ה נותן הרשע בידינו מותר לנו להורגו, אבל להכריח להקב"ה (כביכול) להביא מיתתו לאו אורח ארעא.

אמנם יש להקשות על הגמ' הנ"ל מברכת המינים שאנו מתפללים בתפלת שמו"ע ג' פעמים בכל יום על מפלתן של רשעים. אולם ע"פ במהר"ל בדרך זו אף תפלה דפי' הנ"ל, **דאין אנו מתפללין על מפלתן אלא שיעשו תשובה**. וז"ל בקיצור (באר הגולה, סוף באר ז', עמ' קמ"ט-ק"נ), "הרי לך (ע"פ גמ' ברכות י. הנ"ל)... אף שהוא רשע אין להתפלל עליו שימות מאחר שאפשר שישוב מחטאו, א"כ למה יתפלל עליו שיהי' נאבד מאחר שהאדם מעשה ידיו של הש"י לכך אין ראוי זה... וא"כ איך אפשר שהם עברו על דברי הזהרת עצמם (ותקנו בברכת המינים להתפלל שימותו). רק כי התפילה היא כך, 'אל תהא תקוה' שלא יהי' תקוה להם שיהיו עוד במציאות רק יסורו מן העולם, ורצו לומר שלא יהיו עוד אנשים כאלו בעולם רק יחזרו מן מעשיהם. 'וכל המינים כרגע יאבדו', שלא תהיה דעת מינות בעולם ואז יהיו המינים נאבדים מן העולם... 'וכל אויבי עמך מהרה יכרתו' פי' יכרתו שלא יהיו עוד אויבים לעמך ולא תהי' מלכות זדון בעולם. אבל על מפלתן של מלכות אף על

---

[21] ע"ש בתוס' הרא"ש ובמהרש"א דאע"פ דפשטות הקרא מיירי בחוטאים ולא בחטאים, וכ"כ המלבי"ם עה"פ שם וכמבואר בפס' ריש תהלים, וגם בגמ' עצמה דרשו לענין חוטאים וכדאיתא להלן בגמ' שדוד המע"ה אמר שירה על מפלתן של רשעים באמירת מזמור זה, ואעפ"כ כיון דמשני קרא בדיבוריה יש לדרשו גם לדין זה שאין להתפלל על מיתתן של חוטאים.

[22] וכן ראיתי בשם מדרש הנעלם (בראשית פר' ק"ה) וז"ל, "אמר רבי, מצוה לו לאדם להתפלל על הרשעים כדי שיחזרו למוטב ולא יכנסו לגיהנם... ואמר רב אסור לו לאדם להתפלל על הרשעים שיסתלקו מן העולם."

[23] וע' בספר סדר יעקב (ע"ז שם) שהביא לע"ע בענין זה במושב זקנים לבעלי התוס' (שמות ב:יד) וע"ש מה שהעיר עליהם. וע"ע מה שציין למאירי גיטין ז' ע"א (ד"ה הוזכר).

מלכות זדון אין התפלה כלל... וכל הדברים שנזכרו אין מדבר מן מפלתן רק שיסיר הש"י הדבר הרע הזה מלבם ויחזרו בתשובה."[24]

אבל לכאו' לא כן משפטות לשון חז"ל וכמה מפרשי התפלה דנר' דמיירי ברשעים עצמם. וע"ד באבודרהם בפירושו לברכת המינים (הודפס ברבעון תורני צפונות, תמוז תשמ"ט, שנה א' גליון ד' עמ' י"ח) וז"ל, "למשומדים אל תהי תקוה שלא תהיה להם שום תקוה עוד בעוה"ז וגם לעוה"ב לפי שנידונים לגיהנם לדורי דורות. וכ"כ רבינו יהודה ב"ר יקר רבו של הרמב"ן גם בפירושו, וכעי"ז כתבו עוד כמה מפרשים. ובשבולי הלקט (ענין תפילה סי' י"ח) כתב מקור קדום לתפלה זו שנר' דמיירי במפלתן ממש וז"ל, "כשטבעו המצריים בים פתחו מלאכי השרת ואמרו בא"י מכניע זדים". וכן איתא באוצר המדרשים (איזנשטיין, תפלת שמונה עשרה) וז"ל, "כשטבעו המצריים בים פתחו מלאכי השרת ואמרו בא"י שובר אויבים ומכניע זדים". וכעי"ז איתא בעוד מפרשים ומדרשים (הו"ד באנציקלופדיה תלמודית ח"ד ערך ברכת המינים) שי"ח הברכות שבתפלה נסדרו לפי המאורעות שבסדר עולם, ובענין ברכת המינים כתוב וז"ל, "כשהחליש יהושע את עמלק ואת עמו לפי חרב פתחו מלאכי השרת ואמרו בא"י שובר אויבים ומכניע זדים... כשעמד המן הרשע על ישראל וקלקל הקב"ה עצתו והשיבו גמולו בראשו אמרו בא"י שובר אויבים ומכניע זדים. כשבנה שלמה את בית המקדש והתפלל לפני הקב"ה ואמר ושפט את עבדיך להרשיע רשע לתת דרכו בראשו אמרו בא"י שובר אויבים ומכניע זדים."

ובאמת כבר הקשו מקצת מהראשונים קושיית המהר"ל הנ"ל ותרצו באו"א. וז"ל האבודרהם (שם עמ' כ'), "וא"ת האיך אנו מקללין בתפילתנו המינים והמשומדים, הא אמרינן בפ"ק דברכות (ז. הנ"ל) וכו' לאו אורחא דארעא למעבד הכי וכו'. וי"ל דכי קאמר לאו אורחא דארעא למעבד הכי הני מילי לקללו שבא לידי כליון אבל בקשה שאני." ובהערות שם הביא כעי"ז מפי' ר' יהודה ב"ר יקר וז"ל, "היינו דוקא לעונשו בהכרח כי התם בכרבלתא דתרנגולא או בכשפים והשבעות, אבל יכולים להתפלל שלא ייטב להם, ואם לא ישמע התפלה יחדל." וביאור הדבר איתא בראבי"ה (ברכות שם סי' ט"ז) וז"ל, "וצריך אדם שלא יכוון בשעה שהקב"ה כועס להעניש דמי חבירו... מפני שהוא כהורגו בידים שאז בברור נענש. אבל בענין אחר שפיר דמי היכא דלית ליה דינא בארעא, וכעין תפלה למשומדים וכמו שנמצא בספר תהלים (פר' ק"ט) שקלל דוד אויביו." **הרי לן דתפלה בעלמא שיאבד הרשע מותרת** (ולפי הראבי"ה אף לקללו מותר כשאינו בשעה המיוחדת לקללות)[25], **אבל לקללו ולהתפלל לה' באופן שיהרגו בודאי אינו ראוי**, דשמא רצון ה' הוא להאריך לו ואף ולתת לו עוד זמן לשוב.

אולם עדיין צ"ע מהגמ' הנ"ל (ברכות י.) דמבואר דראוי להתפלל שישובו הרשעים, ואינו ראוי להתפלל על מפלתן של רשעים אפי' כשאין התפלה באופן שיהרגן ה' בודאי. ואפשר לפרש דודאי עדיף שישובו, ואכן מתפללים שיעשו כן. אבל מוסיפין דאם יקרה שאינם שבים יש להם עכ"פ למות כדי שלא יעשו עוד עול. וכן קצת נר' מהמשך דברי האבודרהם הנ"ל וז"ל, "וכל המינים כרגע יאבדו... ודוקא אם לא ישוב שאם חזר לטוב מקבלים אותו בתשובה שאין לך דבר שעומד בפני התשובה." ואפשר דכוונתו להדגיש ענין זה, דלא איירי ברכה זו אלא באלו רשעים שאינם רוצים לשוב וודאי לא ישובו בזמן קרוב, אבל ודאי עדיף לן שישובו. ואע"פ שאין אנו מזכירים תשובת הרשעים בפרט בברכה זו, לכאו' הם נכללים בברכת השיבנו דכבר נאמרה קודם לברכת המינים בשמו"ע. ואכן דייקו מקצת מהמפרשים בלשון כמה נוסחאות של ברכת המינים דאיכא קצת זכר בעצם הברכה לגמ' הנ"ל. הנה כתב בפי' עיון תפלה (הו"ד בסדור אוצר התפלות) וז"ל, "וכל הרשעה כרגע תאבד, כ"ה גי' הגר"א וכו' על שם 'יתמו חטאים' ולא לומר 'עושי רשעה'. וכן אנו מתפללים בברכת קדושים ה' לר"ה ויו"כ 'וכל הרשעה כולה כעשן תכלה', וכן סובבות רוב תפלותינו על מפלת הרשעה לא על מפלת הרשעים, כמו בעלינו לשבח 'על כן נקוה לך וגו' להעביר גלולים וכו', אבל עובדיהם יתנו לבם לשוב אל השי"ת." הרי לן דודאי עיקר רצוננו הוא שישובו החוטאים, אבל בברכה זו אמרינן דאם לא ישובו אז יש להם עכ"פ ליאבד מן העולם ולא להמשיך קלקולם ולקלקל אחרים.

והנה כל זה הוא תירוץ א' של האבודרהם. אבל אח"כ הוסיף עוד תירוץ לעיקר הקושיא מגמ' ברכות הנ"ל (ז.) וז"ל, "אי נמי דמשום צערא לאו אורח ארעא למעבד הכי כדאיתא התם דקאמר מצערי ליה, אבל אנו בתפילתנו *לכבוד הבורא* אנו מתכוונים מפני שכופר בו." הרי לן **דאדם שכוונתו לכבוד שמים ולא להנאת עצמו כלל יכול להתפלל אף על איבוד רשעים.** וכך היתה כוונת מסדרי ברכת המינים. ויסוד הזה נתבאר היטב בכמה אחרונים. הנה ז"ל הראי"ה קוק זצ"ל (עולת ראיה ח"א עמ' רע"ח) לבאר למה שמואל הקטן נבחר לכתוב ברכה זו (ע' ברכות סוף כח:), "כל הברכות של התפלה שהן מלאות חסד ואהבה ראוי לתקן כל חכם הראוי למעלה רוממה כזאת... אבל ברכה זו של התפלה, שבתוכה אצורים דברים של שנאה ומשטמה, והאדם האשר הוא אדם, א"א כלל שלא תמצא בקרבו איזו שנאה טבעית לאויבי נפשו ורודפי עמו, צריכה היא לבא דוקא ממי

---

[24] שו"ר בספר שובה ישראל (ח"ב עמ' קל"ז) שדייק בעוד מקצת אחרונים (יערות דבש דרש ב', וע"ש עוד) כדברי המהר"ל הנ"ל. אבל הסיק שם כמ"ש לקמן בסמוך וז"ל, "מ"מ מפשטות הלשון של נוסח הברכה לא משמע כן".

[25] ובאמת נר' לפרש כן גם בדעת האבודרהם, דנר' מדבריו דעצם תפלה זו נחשב כקללה. וז"ל, "ומלכות זדון זו מלכות רומי... ולכך תקנו לקללה בתפלת שחרית וערבית וכו'." וכן הוכיח בספר שובה ישראל (עמ' קל"ז) מר' יונה ברכות כ"ט ק"ד. (ובאמת צ"ע דאף בלשון המהר"ל מבואר דחשיב קללה דקרי לה "קללת המינים", והרי הוא ס"ל שמתפללים שישובו ולא שיאבדו, וע' בזה.)

שכולו טהור וקדוש לה', שתשכונת השנאה הטבעית אין בלבבו כלל... ע"כ עמד שמואל הקטן ותקנה, ורק הוא באמת ראוי לה, כי הוא אשר דרש תמיד בנפול אויבך אל תשמח. והוא כשיתעורר לתקן ברכה למינים לא תמצא בה כי אם רגשת לב טהור לתכלית הטוב האמתי הכללי." וכ"כ בספר שפתי חיים (ביאורי תפלת שמו"ע עמ' קנ"ח), והוסיף הא דביארו חז"ל (הובא בתוי"ט אבות ד:יט) מדוע נקרא שמואל הקטן "לפי שהיה מקטין את עצמו... וכשמת אמרו עליו הי חסיד הי עניו", וז"ל, "דוקא שמואל הקטן בגודל ענוותו היה ראוי לחבר ברכת המינים בכוונה טהורה לאבדן הרשעים כדי שיתגדל כבוד הש"י ולא מתוך מניעים אישיים של שמחה עצמית בנצחון אנוכית על אויביו". וכ"כ איתא בספר משנת ישראל על אבות (ד:יט) וז"ל, "אין דומה נקמה ושמחה לשם שמים ושמחה שלא לשם שמים. ושמואל הקטן בעצמו תיקן לומר ג' פעמים ביום ברוך אתה ה' שובר אויבים ומכניע זדים וכו' היה גם בנפול אויבך אך תשמח."[26]

וי"ל עוד, דאפי' אם בדרך כלל אינו ראוי להתפלל שיאבדו שום בנ"א ואפי' כשהם רשעים, אעפ"כ **שאני הכא שאנו מוכרחים לעשות כן כיון שהם מזיקים לרבים.** וכ"כ בספר שובה ישראל (מאת ר' אברהם וויינפעלד זצ"ל, ח"ב עמ' קל"ט) וז"ל, "יקשה לפ"ז (דאפי' רשעים גמורים יכולים לחזור בתשובה) מדוע תיקנו להתפלל שיאבדו... והנלע"ד דכשנעיין בל' הרמב"ם ריש פ"ב תפילה שכתב וז"ל, 'מימי ר"ג רבו האפיקורסין בישראל והיו מצירין לישראל ומסיתין אותן לשוב מאחרי ה', וכיון שראה שזו צרכי מכל צרכי בנ"א עמד הוא ובית דינו והתקין ברכה אחת וכו', ע"כ. נר' מזה ברור שכל זמן שהיו האפיקורסין מיעוטים נחבאים אל תוך כליהם ולא התערבו בין בנ"י, לא צרו להם ולא הסיתו אותם, אע"פ שגם אז בודאי הם מכשול לכלל ואם יש כח בידינו יש להרגין כנ"ל, עכ"ז אם אין בידינו לסלקם וצריכים אנו לתפילה נכון להתפלל שיהי' באופן היותר טוב והשב לב עובדיהם לעבדך. אבל בעת אשר רבו האפיקורסין והצירו את ישראל והסיתו אותם מאחרי ה' עד שהיה סכנה עצומה לכלל ישראל דלא ליתי לאמשוכי אבתרייהו אז אין מקום להתפלל על תקנתם אלא שבמהרה יאבדו, ע"כ תיקן ברכת המינים. וע"ש בכ"מ שכת' בשם ה"ר מנוח וז"ל, 'כדי שימנעו העם לטעות להמיר ולצאת מכלל הדת תקנו להודיע שאין למומרים תקנה', ע"כ. וע' בפי' רבינו יהונתן הכהן מלוניל מביא מהנמצא בכל הדפוסים הישנים בפי' רש"י שעיקר ברכת המינים תקנו נגד כת יש"ו והנוצרי שלימדה להפך דברי אלקים חיים ע"ש. גם מזה משמע כמו שכתבנו שאלמלא לא היה חשש שיטעו אחריהם לא היו מתקנין להתפלל שימותו אלא שישובו, אבל מחמת סכנת כלל ישראל תקנו כן, כי טוב לדאוג בעד טובת הכלל מלדאוג על תקנת האפיקורסין. וע' בספר לחם שמים להגא"י ר' יעקב עמדין זצ"ל על אבות פ"ב מי"ב שכת' וז"ל, 'וכן הוא אומר במקום אחר יתמו חטאים ולא חוטאים, ואפי' את המין לא רצה ריב"ל לקלל, אך לא כל המינין שוין', ע"ש. וי"ל שהחילוק הוא כנ"ל בין אם הוא מין בפנ"ע או אם הוא רוצה למשוך אחרים אחריו כמ"ש. ולפי"ז לק"מ מה דאמרה ברוריא יתמו חטאים ולא חוטאים אפי' הי' מין, כי מעיקרא דדינא כן הוא כנ"ל וכו', אבל מעת אשר נתרבו האפיקורסים ונעשו לסכנה לכלל ישראל חז"ל שינו ותיקנו להתפלל על מיתתם כנ"ל ודו"ק.[27]

ועוד יש להעיר, דהנה כבר הזכרנו לעיל כמה דוגמאות שנר' מבואר שמתפללים להקב"ה שינקום נגד שונאי ישראל (כגון הא דאמרינן בליל פסח "שפוך חמתך וכו'", וכן עוד). ונראה דבכה"ג כו"ע מודי דראוי להתפלל על מפלתן של רשעים, דשאני התם דאיירי **ברשעי אומות העולם שהם מצירים לישראל מדור דור**, והם רשעים גמורים כגון עמלק וכיו"ב דמצוה לשנאם ולהלחם ולהכחידם נגדם (ע' רמב"ם ושא"ר לגבי מצות זכירת מעשה עמלק). וראיתי בספר שובה ישראל (הנ"ל עמ' קל"ו) דכתב כעין חילוק זה בשם כמה אחרונים וז"ל, "בספר דינא דחיי (לאוין רי"א) איתא וז"ל, שעכו"ם מצוה לקללו דכתיב שם רשעים ירקב. ודבריו מובאים בברכי יוסף (חו"מ סי' כ"ו ס"א)." אבל עע"ש שהעיר מתוס' ברכות (ז. הנ"ל) דכתבו דכופר מישראל חמור מעכו"ם לענין זה. אבל נראה דיש לחלק בין עכו"ם בעלמא לבין רשעי אומות העולם שנלחמים באופן תמידי נגד ה' ועמו.

---

26 ועיקר החילוק הזה הוא על דרך מש"כ המהר"ל ועוד מפרשים הנ"ל שאין לשמוח על מפלתן של רשעים אלא לכבוד ה' ולא להנאת עצמו כלל.

27 וע' בספר שומע תפלה (לר' ישעי' בראווער, ח"ב פר' נ"א אותיות י"ח, כ"ו-כ"ח) שהביא כעי"ז מר' צדוק הכהן (צדקת הצדיק אות ע"א) ועוד מפרשים. ובאמת כעין סברא זו כבר נזכרת בתוס' הרא"ש על הגמ' ברכות שם (י.) וז"ל, "יהא בעי רחמי עלימתו, גם ענוש לצדיק לא טוב ואפי' בצדוקין, שמא היו מצערין אותו יותר מדאי או שמא היו רשעים יותר מדאי". ואע"פ דנר' מהגמ' דאפי' בכה"ג טענת ברוריה היתה צדקת יותר, י"ל דכשהרשעים גם מזיקים לרבים אף ברוריה היתה מודה. וע"ע במאירים שם. וע' בספר חסידים (סי' תרפ"ח) וז"ל, "מי שמחטיא את הרבים וחלה אין מתפללים עליו שיתרפא... אין מתפללים עליו שיעשה תשובה כי לא יועיל." ובמקו"א (סי' תס"ו) כתב וז"ל, "אם החזן מתפלל על החולה שמסיק לבריות אין לענות אמן אחריו." וע' ר' בחיי (ריש פר' קרח טז:ד) על הא דכתיב "וישמע משה ויפל על פניו" וז"ל, "ואולי בנפילת אפים זה העניש משה לקרח ולכל עדתו, ומכאן למד ר' אליעזר שהעניש לר' גמליאל בנפילת אפים כמ"ש בסוף פר' הזהב (ב"מ נט:)".

סימן ה' – איסור אכילה ועשיית מלאכה קודם שחרית

יש לע' במי שקשה לו לילך למנין מוקדם (שצריך לעזור לאשתו בטיפול הבנים או משום שזמנו ללמוד תורה ביישוב הדעת הוא רק באותו זמן ואינו יכול ללמוד הרבה אם הוא הולך לשחרית מוקדם וכל כיוצ"ב), האם יש מקום להתיר לו לעסוק במלאכות קצת (טיפול בבנים, לימוד התורה וכו') ואולי גם לאכול ורק אח"כ להתפלל.

א: נסיעה ועיסוק במלאכה וכו'

והנה בענין לימוד ונסיעה ועיסוק במלאכה וטיפול בבנים וכו' קודם התפלה נר' דאיכא כמה צדדים להקל.

א) לכאו' מבואר בהדיא במג"א (שלב:ח) להתיר כשיש לו מנין קבוע וכיוצ"ב וכמ"ש הפוסקים לגבי מנחה (ע' פסקי תשובות שם ועוד). שהרי המג"א (ע"פ המהרי"ו) כתב בפירוש להשוות מלאכות לפני שחרית ומנחה (וע"ע מ"ב פט:יט דגם איסורן שוה). ונר' הטעם דכיון דיש לו מנין קבוע (או שומר וכיוצ"ב) אין חשש שמא יפשע ולא יתפלל. וכן הוא מנהג כמה וכמה קהילות בארצות הברית להתפלל שחרית בשבת בשעה תשע בבוקר, ועד אותו זמן הרי כולם מתעסקים בבניהם ובלימודם וכו', ולא שמענו אוסרים בזה.

ב) ואין בזה משום "צדק לפניו יהלך וכו'" (ברכות יד.) כיון דאינו מדחה התפלה משום צרכיו אלא משום מצוה או איזה אונס. וראיתי בספר ידי כהן קונטרס שיח אברכים (סדר א' הע' א') שהביא דברי הפוסקים להתיר טיפול בילדים קודם התפלה וז"ל, "שו"ת אול"צ (ח"ב פמ"ה סעי' כ), ואף שאסור להתעסק בצרכיו קודם התפילה כמבואר בשו"ע (פט:ג), מ"מ טיפול בילדים חשיב לצורך מצוה, ולעסוק בצורכי מצוה מותר קודם התפילה כמ"ש בפר"ח (שם ס"ק ו). וכ"כ בהליכות שלמה (תפלה פ"ב סעי' ו') בשם הגרשז"א זצ"ל דה"ה להכנת ארוחה עבורם שהרי ודאי מוטל עליו לעזור לבני ביתו ולגמול עמהם חסד, ובכך חשיב כצורכי שמים." וע"ע שהביא עוד כמה פוסקים שהתירו לקנות אוכל קודם התפילה עבור הילדים וכל כיוצ"ב.

ג) ובפרט כשהאדם מתפלל ברכות לעצמו קודם שעוסק במלאכה יש להצטרף גם מש"כ הרמ"א (פט:ג), ע"ש.

וע"ע בקובץ אור ישראל (קובץ ל"ב עמ' ס"ב) שהאריך להצדיק מנהג הרבה אנשים לנסוע למקום עבודתם קודם התפלה.

ב: אכילה ושתיה

אבל בענין אכילה ושתיה החמירו הפוסקים טפי. דהנה אע"פ דמנהג העולם להקל באיסור זה קודם מנחה ומעריב וכמ"ש המג"א הנ"ל (וע"ע פסקי תשובות הנ"ל וכן בספר שיח הלכה סי' פ"ט אות י"ז), לא הקילו הפוסקים כה"ג באיסור אכילה קודם שחרית משום דחמירא טפי מהטעם דאיתא בברכות (י): דיש בזה משום גאוה נגד ה' ר"ל וגם הסמיכוהו רז"ל אקרא דלא תאכלו על הדם ע"ש. וכיון שאין האיסור משום שמא יפשע וכו', לא כתבו להתיר ע"פ המהרי"ו במג"א הנ"ל. ועוד מזה הוכיחו הפוסקים (ע' ביאוה"ל פט:ג ד"ה וכן) מגמ' ברכות (ריש כח:) דעדיף להתפלל ביחידות מלאכול קודם התפלה ולהתפלל בציבור, ע"ש. ומוכח מגמ' שם דאע"פ שאינו מתאחר תפלתו משום עסקיו אלא משום שהגיע הזמן שהצבור מתפללים, עכ"פ אין לאכול קודם התפלה ולמלאות תאותו וצרכי גופו קודם שמתפלל. ועוד החמירו כמה פוסקים (ע' יביע אומר ח"ה כב:ה) ע"פ הזוהר שלא לאכול אפי' זמן הרבה קודם עלוה"ש בשעה שא"א להתפלל כלל, דאין איסור זה מפאת חשש שמא יפשע וכו' אלא משום שאין לו לטפל בצרכי גופו קודם שמתפלל לה'. (משא"כ איסור מלאכה וכו' דנר' מהפוסקים הנ"ל שאינו מפאת עצם העסק בצרכי עצמו קודם התפלה, אלא משום שמדחה עבודת התפלה מפני מלאכת עצמו. אבל אם אינו מדחהו ע"י עסקיו וגם אין חשש שמא יפשע יש להקל וכמ"ש.)

ועכ"פ נר' להביא בזה כמה צדדים להקל גם לענין אכילה קודם שחרית, עכ"פ בשעת הדחק.

א) הנה **הרמב"ם ושו"ע נר' דהשוו בין איסור מלאכה ואיסור אכילה קודם שחרית**, ודלא כחילוק הנ"ל. וז"ל הרמב"ם (הל' תפלה פ"ו ה"ד). "אסור לו לאדם שיטעום כלום או שיעשה מלאכה מאחר שעלה עמוד השחר עד שיתפלל תפלת שחרית. וכן לא ישכים לפתח חבירו לשאול בשלומו קודם שיתפלל תפלת שחרית. ולא יצא לדרך קודם שיתפלל." וכעי"ז בשו"ע (פט:ג) וז"ל, "אסור להתעסק בצרכיו או לילך לדרך עד שיתפלל תפלת שמונה עשרה, ולא לאכול ולא לשתות". וכן דייק הערוה"ש (פט:כ) דנר' דהרמב"ם למד איסור מלאכה מהקרא של 'ואותי השלכת אחרי גויך' (ברכות י: הנ"ל) לגבי איסור אכילה קודם שחרית שהוא דרך גאוה. ומשמע דגדר אחד יש לכל הני דינים. ולכן כמו שיש להקל לענין מלאכה **כשאינו מאחר תפלתו משום רצונו בלבד אלא משום איזה צורך מצוה או אונס וכשאין חשש שמא יפשע**, כמו"כ אפשר להקל גם לענין אכילה קודם שחרית. והיינו דכמו דאיסור מלאכה ויציאה לדרך וכו' הנלמדים מפסוקים (ברכות יד. הנ"ל) לא נאמרו אלא כשמדחה התפלה משום צרכי עצמו, כמו"כ לא אמרו דאכילה נחשבת כגאוה וכו' אלא כשמדחה תפלתו משום תאות אכילה. אבל מי שאינו מתפלל משום שלא הגיע זמן שהצבור מתפללין או משום איזה מצוה, אין אכילתו נחשבת כגאוה

ואין בו משום לא תאכלו על הדם. והא דאיתא בגמ' (כח: הנ"ל) דאסור לאכול אפי' כשלא הגיע השעה שהצבור מתפללין, י"ל דהתם איירי כשיש חשש שמא יפשע ואין לו שומר וכו'. (ובאמת נר' דמוכח לומר כן, שהרי איירי שם לענין תפילת מוסף ומנחה, והרי לא שייכי הני לאיסור לא תאכלו על הדם, ולא אסרו אלו אלא משאר טעמים הנ"ל שמא יפשע וכו'.)

ב) והנה עיקר הסברא דאין איסור אכילה אלא כשיש לו חיוב להתפלל והוא מדחהו משום אכילה כבר נר' מהראשונים בענין אכילה קודם עלוה"ש. ע' בתשו' להורות נתן (ח"א סי' ה' אות ט') וז"ל, "מבואר ברשב"א ברכות (י:) דבאכל קודם זמן תפלה ליכא משום השלכת גויך... נר' דס"ל דהגאוה היא בעצם האכילה והשתיה ולא במה שבטנו מתמלא, וע"כ כל שאוכל טרם הגיע זמן התפלה ליכא משום גאוה." וכן נר' לפי פשוטו מכל הפוסקים דפסקו כן מעיקר הדין (אלא דכתבו הפוסקים דראוי לאדם ברי' וחזק להחמיר כדעת הזוהר שלא לאכול אפי' קודם עלוה"ש ולבא לפני בוראו כעני רעב לפני אדונו, ע' יבי"א הנ"ל ועוד). ולפי"ז י"ל דאכילה קודם שהגיע השעה שהצבור מתפללין שוה לאכילה קודם עלוה"ש שלא הגיע זמן תפלה כלל.

ג) כתבו הפוסקים (פט:ג-ד) להתיר אכילה ושתיה **למי שרעב ואינו יכול לכוין בתפלתו**. וביארו המפרשים ההיתר (ע' מ"ב שם ס"ק כ"ב) משום שאינו אוכל דרך גאוה אלא משום בריאות ולמצוה. ומאותו טעם שהקילו הרבה בזה ונהגו לאכול ולשתות תמיד קודם תפלה כדי שיוכלו לכוין היטב בתפלתם, וכתבו דבזמן הזה נתמעטו הלבבות ואינם יכולין לכוין היטב קודם האכילה. ע' שו"ת שב יעקב (סי' ח'), וע' בקובץ אור ישראל (קובץ ל"ב עמ' נו-סא) לרשימה של ספרי חסידות ופוסקים שכתבו להקל. ומעין אותו טעם י"ל גם בנידון דידן, שהרי הוא מתאחר בדרך גאוה אלא משום צורכי מצוה או אונס אחר.

וכן דברתי בא' מפוסקי זמננו דאין לחייב להטריח את האדם את עצמו ואת אשתו להתפלל מוקדם בזמן שאינו רעב, אלא כיון שעוסק בצרכי מצוה ובדברים הנצרכים וכשהגיע זמן תפלה כבר רעב מותר לו לאכול קודם התפלה. וגם אין לחייבו להתפלל ביחידות קודם שיאכל, דעינינו רואות שתפלה ביחידות אין כוונתה רצויה וגם מקצרין בה, ועדיף טפי להתפלל בצבור ובישוב הדעת אחר שיאכל קצת. ואע"פ שהמ"ב כתב דעדיף להתפלל ביחידות, כבר דחינו הראיה והבאנו כמה צדדים להקל בזה. וע"ע בשו"ת ארץ צבי (פרומר, ח"ב סי' ב') דדן בשאלה זו וכתב טעם להתיר לכוין כעין הנ"ל וז"ל, "ולכאו' יש להעיר דכיון דאיתא בשו"ע דאם אינו יכול לכוין מותר לו לאכול קודם התפלה כדי שיוכל לכוין, וא"כ דה"ה דמותר לאכול קודם התפלה כדי להתפלל בצבור, כיון דאיתא בכמה מקומות בשו"ע (סי' ק"א סעי' א') דהיום אין אנו יכולים לכוין כראוי, ובש"ס תענית (ח.) דתפלה בלא כוונה מתקבלת דווקא בצבור ולא ביחיד ע"ש. וא"כ תפלה בצבור מועיל כמו כוונה בתפלה ושניהם בפלס א' הן, תפלה ביחיד בכוונה ותפלה בצבור בלא כוונה. וא"כ אפשר לומר דכמו דמותר לאכול קודם התפילה כדי שיוכל לכוין כמו"כ מותר לאכול כדי להתפלל בצבור." (אבל עע"ש דכתב לדחות דאין סברא זו מוכרחת.)

ובשו"ת מהר"י שטייף (סי' מ"א, מצויין בשש"כ ח"ב פר' נ"ב הע"ב מ' מ"ח) האריך קצת בענין זה והסיק לקולא וז"ל, "וע"ד ששאל בעניין אכילה קודם תפלה איזה עדיף, אם להתיר לאכול קודם התפלה כדי להתפלל עם המנין או להתפלל ביחיד ולאכול אח"כ. הנה מסברא הי' להקדים שיתפללו ביחידות, כי תפילה בצבור בודאי אינה אלא מעלה מדרבנן אבל לאכול קודם התפלה עכ"פ אסמכוהו על קרא דכ' לא תאכל על הדם וכו' וחמיר טובא כדאמרו ז"ל אחר שהתגאה זה קיבל עליו עול מלכות שמים. ואפי' לדעת הכוזרי דס"ל דתפלה בצבור היא מן התורה ועדיף, מ"מ לא שייך לומר דתפלה בצבור תדחה ל"ת דרבנן וכו' דקיי"ל דבעינן בעידנא. וכאן עובר על ל"ת שמדרבנן קודם שמקיים העשה... אמנם כל זה אם יש איסור בזה לאכול קודם התפלה, אבל מאחר דקיי"ל באו"ח סי' פ"ט סעי' ג' דלצורך רפואה אין כאן משום גאוה ואינה בכלל הלאו דלא תאכלו על הדם דהרעב והצמא הם בכלל חולים ומותרים לאכול קודם התפלה וכו', בכה"ג אין כאן כלל משום דלא תאכלו על הדם, וא"כ עדיף טפי להתיר לאכול גם קודם התפלה ולהשתדל להתפלל בצבור." אלא דפקפק קצת בזה למעשה והסיק דאין לעשות כן בקביעות וז"ל, "וכיון שעושה כן להבריא גופו לרפואה אין כאן בית מיחוש כלל. ואולי יש להחמיר שלא לאכול אלא לשתות משקאות של חלב הרבה, וגם בזה לא ינהגו כן בקביעות. ושוב אין לחוש למה שחושש הרב ר' רפאל הורוויטץ שליט"א שלא ירגילו לנהוג כן גם בעת בריאותם, מאחר שלפעמים ימנעו עצמם מלאכול קודם התפלה יהי' להם זה להיכר שלא להרגיל כן בזמן בריאותם."

והוסיף המהר"י שטייף עוד סברא להקל וז"ל, "ונר' עוד עפ"י שכ' שם בסעי' ב' דאע"ג דאסור לשאול בשלום קודם התפלה מ"מ כל שכבר התחיל לומר הברכות אין לחוש כ"כ, א"כ י"ל דה"ה לענין האיסור דלא תאכלו על הדם, כל שכבר התפלל עד שכבר פסוקי דזמרה וכבר קרא ק"ש של קרבנות וקיבל עליו עול מ"ש שוב אין בזה משום גאוה וכו', דהא קיבל עליו עול מ"ש קודם האכילה." ואע"פ דרוב פוסקים (ע' ביאוה"ל פט:ג ד"ה ולא לאכול, וע' עינים למשפט ברכות י: ד"ה כל האוכל) כתבו דאין לאכול עד שיתפלל ק"ש ושמו"ע כראוי, יש להצטרף סברא זו בשעת הדחק. (וע' בביאוה"ל הנ"ל דהזכיר סברא זו אבל כתב כן להחמיר וז"ל, "נ"ל דאפי' מי שמוכרח לאכול לרפואה קודם התפלה יקרא עכ"פ קריאת שמע קודם.")

וודאי עדיף טפי אם יכול להקטין רעבתו ע"י טעימה בעלמא וכיוצ"ב, דכבר דייקו כמה פוסקים בהא דנאמר האיסור בגמ' בלשון "לא תאכלו" ולא הוזכר איסור "טעימה" בהדיא בגמ' שם. וגם בשו"ע איתא לשון אכילה ושתיה. ואכן ע' שאילת יעב"ץ (ח"א סי' מ') שכתב דלא אסרו טעימה. וכן ע' בספר הליכות שלמה (תפלה רפ"ב) דכתב דאפי' מי שמותר לאכול קודם תפלה משום בריאותו עדיף לאכול רק מעט אם יוכל. וכן דייק בספר פסקי תשובות (סי' פ"ט הע' 223) מהנמו"י דלא אסרו אלא אכילת כזית. וע"ע בספר עינים למשפט (ברכות י: אות ג') דדייק ממקצת ראשונים דאפשר דלא אסרו אלא מידי דמשכר. (אבל הרמב"ם הנ"ל נר' בהדיא דאסרו אף טעימה בעלמא, וע' ברכות כח: דאיתא לשון טעימה אבל לא להלכה. וע"ע בתשו' יביע אומר ח"ה סי' כב:א דכתב לדחות שיטת היעב"ץ הנ"ל. וע' בקובץ אור ישראל ל"א ע"מ' צ"ג כמה פרטים בזה, וע"ע בקובץ אור ישראל ל"ב עמ' מ"ט.)

כתב הרא"ה (ברכות יא.) וז"ל, "שמעינן דכל היכא דאפסיקא הלכתא כחד מרבנן כד נמי דאפשיטא הלכתא ואיכא מאן דפליג עליה אסור למיעבד כאידך אפי' לחומרא וחייב למעבד כהתירא דהאיך דאפשיטא הלכתא כותיה. וטעמא דמילתא משום דמחזי כחולק על רבותיו." וכעי"ז איתא בתשו' הרשב"א (ח"א סו"ס רנ"ג) וז"ל, "אם היה רב א' במקומם ולמדם הן הולכים אחר דבריו... והנה במקומו של ר' אליעזר כורתין עצים (בשבת) לעשות פחמין לעשות אזמל ולא מיחו בידם חכמים לפי שהן עושין כדברי רבם. ובמקום רבם אילו יעשו שלא כדבריו יקלו בכבוד רבם במקומו." והוסיף הריטב"א (שבת קל. ד"ה והיו) דשייך בזה גם מצות לא תסור וז"ל, "במקומו (של ר' אליעזר) היו עושין כמותו לא תסור מן הדבר אשר יגידו לך ימין ושמאל". הרי לן דמי שנפסק ההלכה כותיה (בין בשביל כל ישראל ובין בשביל אותו מקום בפרט) **חייב לשמוע אליו משום דשייך גביה מצוה מיוחדת של כבוד**. וכתבו הראשונים הנ"ל דדינו כמו רבו, ומי שאינו נוהג כמותו הרי הוא כחולק עליו. (וכתבו הפוסקים בהדיא דאסור לנהוג שלא כהוראת רבו אפי' לקולא וכדאיתא במג"א (סג:ב) בשם המהרש"ל (ב"ק פ"ז סי' מ"א) וז"ל, "אם מחמיר בפני רבו ורבו מיקל, מנדין אותו עביד לשם שמים, ואפי' אין פשוט כ"כ להתיר לא יחמיר נגד דברי רבו אם אין שיש לו ראיה לסתור דבריו". וענין זה חמור מאד וכמ"ש רז"ל שהחולק על רבו כחולק על השכינה, ע' רמב"ם הל' ת"ת פ"ה ה"א. ואע"פ דמשמע מהמג"א דמותר לנהוג דלא כותיה כשהוא אינו בפניו, י"ל דרב העיר ומי שנפסק הלכתא כותיה חמירי טפי משום דכך נפסק הדין להכלל כולו.) ונראה לבאר יסוד דין **כבוד זה שהוא כדי לחזק הסמכות והכח של רבו והבית דין.**

וכעי"ז מצינו גם בנוגע לכבודו של כל רב דעלמא. דהנה אמרו רז"ל (ע"ז ז.) "הנשאל לחכם וטימא לא ישאל לחכם ויטהר". וביאר הר"ן (שם ב. בדפ"ה) טעמא של דבר וז"ל, "מפני כבודו של ראשון, ועוד כדי שלא תראה תורה כשתי תורות הללו אוסרים והללו מתירים", עע"ש. (ואפי' הראשונים שפי' הגמ' שם באו' משום שויה חתיכה דאיסורא, אפשר דמודי דאיכא גם משום כבוד, ע"ש היטב בלשון הריטב"א ועוד ראשונים.) ואפשר לבאר דהטעם שהצריכה התורה להקפיד כ"כ על כבוד הרב על דרך מש"כ הר"ן עצמו אח"כ. דדיינו דכמו שצריכין ליזהר שלא תראה תורה כשתי תורות, כמו"כ צריכין להקפיד על כבוד דיינים כדי שלא יזלזלו אינשי בענין הוראה דרך כלל ותראה תורה כחוכא ואטלולא.

ובאמת מבואר בעוד כמה דוכתי דחוץ מכבוד ת"ח (ואיסור ביזוי ת"ח) ישנו עוד דין מסויים של "כבוד דיין". ואפילו יימצא דיין שאינו ת"ח חייבין עכ"פ לכבדו מפאת מעמדו וכמו שיתבאר.

הנה ראיתי דבר נאה בספר גבורת יצחק (לר' אברהם סורוצקין, סנהדרין יד: ד"ה ושופטיך) וז"ל, "הרמב"ם בפכ"ו מהל' סנהדרין ה"ב כתב שהמקלל אחד מישראל לוקה אחת, ואם קלל דיין לוקה שתים, ואם קלל נשיא לוקה שלש (ומקורו במכילתא, וכן איתא במס' סופרים סופ"ד). ובה"א שם כתב הרמב"ם שנשיא אחד ראש סנהדרי גדולה או המלך. וצ"ע, דבשלמא אם מקלל ראש סנהדרי גדולה דהוי גם דיין שפיר לוקה שלש, אבל בכהאי גוונא שמקלל המלך שלא הוי דיין למה ילקה שלש. ומצאתי שכבר נתעורר בזה המנח"ח (עא:ב) ונשאר בצ"ע. ונ"ל דהנה באמת יש רשות למלך לשפוט ולענוש העם עפ"י דיני ומשפטי המלכות וכמבואר ברמב"ם בפ"ג מהל' מלכים. והנה אמרינן שופטיך זה מלך, דכתיב במשפט יעמיד ארץ. הרי דיש למלך תורת ושם שופט. וע' ברמב"ם פ"ב מהל' סנהדרין ה"ה וז"ל, מלכי בית דוד אע"פ שאין מושיבין אותם בסנהדרין יושבין ודנין הם את העם, עכ"ל. הרי דהמלך דן את העם ויש עליו שם שופט. ולפ"ז שפיר הוי בכלל הלאו דאלהים לא תקלל, ומשו"ה המקלל מלך לוקה שלש." ואע"פ דיתכן שהמלך אינו ת"ח, אעפ"כ הרי סו"ס כיון שיש לו דין של דיין (מפאת כח הוראתו בעניני הוראת שעה וכדומה), לכן חייב על קללתו מפאת חיוב קללת דיין. ומוכח דאיכא כבוד מיוחד לדיין שאינו ת"ח מדין חכם. (ובעיקר הדין ע"ע במנח"ח שם דנקט כפשוט דצריך דיין סמוך, ולכן התקשה בענין מלך אם משכחת כלל מלך שיהיה סמוך, ע"ש. אבל מסתימת לשון הרמב"ם וסיעתו משמע דכל נשיא בכלל ואפי' אינו סמוך, ומשמע כהסבר הנ"ל. וע"ע בספר מנחה חדשה (מצ' עא:ב ד"ה ובעיקר) דהביא מהאו"ת כשיטת המנח"ח, אבל כתב דמדברי הברכי יוסף נר' דכל דיין קבוע בעירו בכלל זה ואע"פ שאינו סמוך.)

ונר' להסביר הענין ע"פ שורש האי איסור גופא וכמ"ש הרדב"ז (מצודת דוד מצ' תקנ"ו), והוא על דרך מש"כ לעיל וז"ל, "טעם המצוה מבואר לפי הפשט, כי המלך או הנשיא או הדיין מעמידין העולם והישוב המדיני כדאיתא **'מלך במשפט יעמיד ארץ'**. ואם ינתן רשות לכל א' לבזות ולקלל את השופטים הנה יהרס הדת ומשפט הארץ יפול, כי יהיו דבריו נבזים ובלתי נשמעים, ואיש את רעהו חיים בלעו." והוסיף עוד טעם ע"ד הסוד וז"ל, "ועל דרך הסוד, כבר כתבנו למעלה כי הסנהדרין הם דוגמא [של] סנהדרי גדולה של מעלה... ולכן הוציא הכתוב מצוה זו בלשון 'אלקים [לא תקלל]' שהיא אזהרה גם למברך [למחרף] כלפי מעלה."

ומצינו היסוד הזה בעוד מקומות הרבה. הנה ע' סוף הוריות (יג:) דמשמע דכבוד נשיא גדול מכבוד שאר ת"ח אף כששאר ת"ח גדולים טפי מהנשיא. וכן עע"ש (בסוף העמ') דמשמע דחשיבותא דאביו של אדם מסייע ליה לימנות כאב בי"ד אע"פ

שהוא עצמו אינו גדול משאר החכמים. (אבל ע' רמב"ם הל' סנהדרין פ"א ה"ג דמבואר שהאב שבי"ד גדול בחכמה משאר הדיינים. וכן ע' הוריות ד: ותוס' סנהדרין טז: ד"ה אחד בענין מופלא שבבי"ד דמשמע כן. אבל נר' דעדיין יתכן שהוא שוה לאחרים ואעפ"כ כבודו גדול טפי משום מעמדו וכמ"ש.) וגם לענין ראש ישיבה מצינו בגמ' שצריך לכבדו ביותר משום עצם מעמדו. וכדאיתא בחולין (קלד:) דשייך גביה ענין "גלדהו משל אחיו" וכמ"ש רש"י שם וז"ל, "ממונה ראש ישיבה יכול לקדם ולזכות שהרי ישיבה עליו (תלמיד אחר) לגדלו ולהעשירו". וכן ע' סוף הוריות (יד.) בענין רבה ור' יוסף. ומשמע דאפי' ראש ישיבה שאינו גדול בחכמה משאר חכמים צריך לכבדו טפי משום עצם מעמדו. וע"פ האי סברא יש עוד לבאר ענין "זילותא דבי דינא", דמצינו בכמה דוכתי (ע' ב"ב לב., סוטה כה. ועוד) דאיכא הקפדה שלא יצטרכו בי"ד לחזור על עצמם אפי' במקום שלא טעו, והרבה כיוצ"ב. וטעמא משום שצריך שבי"ד יראו חזקים וכבודם מעולה כעין מלכות, דמלך במשפט יעמיד ארץ וכמ"ש. (אבל אין דיניהם כמלך ממש שהרי הם יכולים למחול על כבודם. וע' בחי' הר"ן (סנהדרין יט:) שכתב חידוש בענין זה וז"ל, "מאי דאמרה תורה דבעלי דינין בהעמדה משום כבוד ב"ד הוא, והם יכולין למחול", עכ"ש. ואיכא עוד כיוצ"ב.) ולכאו' נר' לפי כל הנ"ל שהחכמים הממונים על הכלל ועל עדי הכשרות וכדומה, כולם חייבים לכבדם משום עצם מעמדם אפי' אם אינם גדולים בחכמה יותר משאר ת"ח.

ויש להוסיף דנר' דיש לדיין ומנהיג הדור סייעתא דשמיא מיוחדת, לא"ד משום ריבוי חכמתו אלא משום עצם משרתו כמנהיג לכלל. וכעי"ז ראיתי הובא מספר חוט המשולש (על קורות ותולדות מרן החת"ס) שאמר החת"ס כך, "דע כי בכל דור ודור מעמיד הקב"ה איש על העדה להאיר להם הדרך ולהתיר הספיקות שלהם. ויען כי רובם ככולם שואלים דבר ה' מפי, נר' בעליל כי מן השמים מסכימים לזה. וב"ה למדתי כפי הצורך וכוונתי בלתי לה' לבדו, ע"כ איני חושד להקב"ה שיכשלני ח"ו ובודאי יסכים יסכים להוראתי. ואם הראיה לפעמים אינו אמת, מכל מקום הדין אמת הוא." (וקצת נ"ל דמשו"ה כל העם צריכים כפרה אף כשחטאו ע"פ שגגת בי"ד וכמבואר בקרא (שלח טו:כו), "ונסלח לכל עדת בני ישראל וכו' כי לכל העם בשגגה". וזהו אף למ"ד יחיד שעשה בהוראת בי"ד פטור, ואף לר"מ (בהוריות ו.) דב"ד מביאים הקרבן ולא הציבור. ויש לבאר משום דבי"ד הגדול שהם הממונים על הכלל יש בשגגתם פגם בכלל כולו, שהרי זכות הכלל היתה צריכה להוסיף סייעתא דשמיא להוראתם. והא דזכות הכלל לא הגינה עליהם סימן הוא לחסרון בכלל כולו.) ולפ"ז י"ל דאע"פ שהדיין עצמו אינו חכם גדול ואינו ראוי מצד עצמו לכבוד גדול, אעפ"כ ראוי אליו הכבוד משום ריבוי סייעתא דשמיא שיש לו.

איתא בספרי (סו"פ שלח, וכעי"ז איתא בגמ' ברכות יב:), "לא תתורו אחרי לבבכם זו מינות וכו' ואחרי עיניכם זו זנות". ויש לע' בדעת הרמב"ם בביאור מצוה זו, שהרי בספה"מ (ל"ת מ"ז) מנה שני ענינים אלו כמצוה א' וז"ל, "היא שהזהירנו שלא לתור אחרי לבבנו עד שנאמין דעות שהם הפך הדעות שחייבתנו התורה... והוא אמרו יתעלה וכו' אחרי לבבכם זה מינות. ואחרי עיניכם זה זנות וכו' רוצה באמרו אחר זה זנות המשך אחר ההנאות והתאוות הגשמיות והתעסק המחשבה בהן תמיד." אבל במשנה תורה פסק הרמב"ם מצוה זו רק ע"ז והרחיב דבריו רק לגבי איסור "אחרי לבבכם זו מינות". אבל כמעט ולא כתב כלום בענין החלק השני "אחרי עיניכם זו זנות". וז"ל (פ"ב ה"ג), "כל מחשבה שגורמת לו לאדם לעקור עיקר מעיקרי התורה מוזהרין אנו שלא נעלה אותה על לבנו ולא נסיח דעתנו לכך ונחשב ונמשך אחר הרהורי הלב... ועל ענין זה הזהירה תורה ונאמר בה ולא תתורו וכו', כלומר לא ימשך כל אחד מכם אחר דעתו הקצרה וידמה שמחשבתו משגת האמת. כך אמרו חכמים אחר אמרו לא תתורו אחר לבבכם זו מינות ואחרי עיניכם זו זנות." ולכאו' **צ"ב מדוע ביאר הרמב"ם בהלכותיו האיסור של מינות בהרחבה, אבל האיסור של "אחרי עיניכם זו זנות" לא ביאר כלל**, ורק בסוף דבריו הזכיר זה בקיצור איסור ולא ביאר עניינו. וגם בשאר דוכתי במשנה תורה לא הגדיר הרמב"ם איסור זה כלל (ורק הזכירו בקיצור בהל' תשובה, אבל מבואר מדבריו גם שם שאין כוונתו להגדיר עיקר עניינו, וע' לקמן).

ועוד צ"ב בהא דכבר העירו המפרשים למה מנו הרמב"ם והרמב"ן מצוה זו כמצוה אחת ולא שתים. וז"ל ספר מצות המלך (ל"ת מ"ז ריש ענף ג'), "הקשה במשנת חכמים, הובא במנ"ח מצ' שפ"ז, לדעת הרמב"ן דאיסורים הנפרטים בלאו אחד אינן נמנים במצוה אחת אלא כל איסור נמנה ללאו בפני ע', א"כ למה לענין לא תתורו שימנו לב' לאוין יעו"ש. וכן הקשה בספר נתיב מצותיך לה"ר שאול הכהן הספרדי עמ' ק'. ובאמת כבר קדמו התשב"ץ בזוהר הרקיע לאוין סי' ק"ו להקשות כן אף לדעת הרמב"ם, 'וקרוב הוא למנותן שתים, שענינם חלוק, זה מינות וזה זנות, והכתוב חלקן באמרו אחרי לבבכם ואחרי עיניכם, ולא אמר אחרי לבבכם ועיניכם.' (ועי"ש בספר מצות המלך מש"כ לבאר שיטת הרמב"ם וז"ל, "היסוד הני לאוין הוא שלא לתור אחר מחשבתו, דהיינו שלא יהא מחשבתו הפקר לחשוב כל מה שעולה על דעתו בלי גבול... והיינו לא הזנות עצמה אסרה תורה כאן וגם לא המחשבה לזנות אסרה התורה כאן, אלא גוף המחשבה הוא שאסרה התורה, שלא יהא חפשי לחשוב כל מה שעולה על דעתו... מעתה ב' הענינים ה'אחרי לבבכם' וה'אחרי עיניכם' חדא מצוה הן. ודבריו נעמים, אבל נלע"ד דאינן מייישבין דברי הרמב"ם, וצ"ע.)

ונראה לבאר **שהרמב"ם הבין דלאו זה של "אחרי עיניכם זו זנות" הוא באמת מצוה כוללת שאינה נמנה למצוה בפנ"ע**, וכהני מצוותיו שכתב הרמב"ם בספה"מ (שורש ד') דאינן נמנין כלל למצוות בפנ"ע. וז"ל שם, "הנה יבואו בתורה צוויין ואזהרות אינם בדבר רמוז אבל יכללהו המצות כולם, כאילו יאמר עשה כל מה שצויתיך לעשות והזהר מכל מה שהזהרתיך ממנו... ואין פנים למנות הצווי הזה מצוה בפני עצמה שהוא לא יצוה לעשות מעשה מיוחד... וכבר טעו [אחרים] בשרש הזה ג'כ עד שמנו קדושים תהיו מצוה מכלל מצות עשה. ולא ידעו כי אמרו קדושים תהיו, והתקדשתם והייתם קדושים, הם צוויים לקיים כל התורה, כאילו יאמר היה קדוש בהיותך עושה כל מה שצויתיך בו ונזהר מכל מה שהזהרתיך ממנו. ולשון ספרא קדושים תהיו פרושים תהיו, רוצה לומר הבדלו מן הדברים המגונים כולם שהזהרתי אתכם מהם." ונר' לבאר דגם מצות "לא תתורו אחרי עיניכם" היא כמו מצות "קדושים תהיו", וענין שניהם (לפי דעת הרמב"ם בפי' ענין "זנות" דהכא) הוא שלא יהיו שטופים בתענוגי העולם (וכמ"ש הרמב"ן בריש פר' קדושים בביאור מצות קדושים תהיו), וענין זה כבר ידוע משאר מצות התורה כגון מצות והלכת בדרכיו שפסק הרמב"ם בריש הל' דעות (פ"א ה"ד ועוד), ומצוה זו אינה מוסיפה כלום. ולכן **לא מנה הרמב"ם עיקר מצוה זו אלא משום מצות "אחרי לבבכם זו מינות" שהיא באמת מלמדת חידוש דין** דאסור להרהר מחשבת כפירה וכדומה וכמ"ש הרמב"ם בהל' ע"ז הנ"ל.

[אמנם הערנו לעיל דהזכיר הרמב"ם מצ' זו בעוד מקום אחד (הל' תשובה פ"ד ה"ד), ולפום ריהטא נר' דאכן יש במצוה זו חידוש דין ודלא כמ"ש. וז"ל, "החמשה [דברים] העושה אותן אין חזקתן לשוב מהן לפי שהן דברים קלים בעיני רוב האדם ונמצא חוטא והוא ידמה זה אינו חטא. ואלו הן... ג', המסתכל בעריות, מעלה על דעתו שאין בכך כלום שהוא אומר וכי בעלתי או קרבתי, והוא אינו יודע שראיית העינים עון גדול שהיא גורמת לגופן של עריות שנא' ולא תתורו אחרי לבבכם." אבל באמת נר' פשוט דאין כוונת הרמב"ם לומר דזה המקור לאיסור הסתכלות בנשים, שהרי עיקר איסור הסתכלות בנשים פסק בהל' איסו"ב (פכ"א הל' א'-ב') ולא הזכיר פס' זה כלל, ואדרבה משם משמע דנלמד מקרא אחרינא משום לא תקרבו לגלות ערוה. וז"ל, "לא תקרבו לגלות ערוה, כלומר לא תקרבו לדברים המביאין לידי גילוי ערוה... ואסור לאדם לקרוץ בידיו וכו' לאחת מן העריות... ואפי' להריח בשמים שעליה או להביט ביפיה אסור... והמסתכל אפי' באצבע קטנה של אשה ונתכוון ליהנות כמי שנסתכל במקום התורף." הרי מבואר דהסתכלות בנשים נאסר בכלל קריבה לעריות ולא נתחדש משום לאו דלא תתורו וכו'. (וכ"כ באגרו"מ אהע"ז ח"ד סי' ס', אבל ע' באגרו"מ אהע"ז ח"א סי' נ"ו ובמפרשים אחרים שנפלפלו בביאור דעת הרמב"ם, וצ"ע.) ועוד, הרי כבר כתב הרמב"ם בעצמו בספה"מ הנ"ל דהא דאמרו רז"ל "אחרי עיניכם זו זנות"

אין הכוונה לזנות ממש אלא ל"המשך אחר ההנאות והתאוות הגשמיות והתעסק המחשבה בהן תמיד", וקשה ללמוד עיקר איסור הסתכלות מלאו זה דאיירי בהתעסקות בתענוגים דרך כלל. אלא נר' דהרמב"ם הזכיר פסוק זה בהל' תשובה שם משום דקרא זה מפורש דאיכא איסור לתור אחרי העינים אף כשאינו מתקרב ממש להערוה. וכן הוא דרך הרמב"ם בכמה דוכתי בהלכותיו להוכיח דבריו מקרא המבואר ביותר אפי' כשאותו פס' אינו המקור המדויק. ואכן הרמב"ם לא הזכיר סוף הפס' (דהיינו "אחרי עיניכם") כלל, ולא כתב אלא הפס' של "אחרי לבבכם" דאיירי במחשבת ע"ז שאינה שייכת להכא, ונר' בעליל שהרמב"ם לא כתב כאן המקור המדויק. ועוד יש להעיר שהרמב"ם שם איירי אפי' באיסורים שאינם מפורשים בקרא כגון המתכבד בקלון חבירו והחושד בכשרים, ולכן אינו קשה מה שהרמב"ם אינו מביא עיקר מקור האיסור בתורה, שהרי איירי שם אפי' באיסורים שאין להם מקור מפורש בתורה כלל.]

Essay #8 – The Jewish Politician – Are we to scoff at evil or work with it?

Jewish leaders from time immemorial have had to grapple with the proper way to deal with evil and evildoers: should they stand staunchly against them, fighting defiantly for what is right, or should they dance with the devil, playing the political scene with pragmatic finesse? Indeed, we have seen various great leaders of *Klal Yisroel* take different stances on this issue (due largely to varying situations determined by time and place), and our Rabbis offer essential guidelines that can help us navigate various scenarios.

On the one hand, our Rabbis warn against openly antagonizing evildoers[1]. The Gemara[2] sometimes permits even *flattering* evildoers for various political reasons. On the most basic level, these sources teach us that antagonizing our opponents will only make matters worse. The Torah instructs us to act with *sechel*, conscientiousness and wisdom, and it would be most unwise to provoke the enemy. On a deeper level, battling head-on against evil may indicate an indignant rejection of a Heavenly warning to repent. In our current imperfect (pre-Messianic) world, Hashem sometimes allows evil to prosper in order to punish or test us[3]. We may not disregard and ignore the punishment; we must accept the challenges thrust upon us and work with them to better ourselves. In a similar vein, the Rabbis[4] explain that Moshe Rabbenu afforded honor even to the evil Pharaoh. He recognized that kings and leaders, as evil as some may be, are mere pawns of G-d[5]. "Kingship is given directly by Hashem… and it is an honor to Hashem to afford His kings honor"[6].

Nevertheless, our Rabbis[7] inform us that there are some situations in which battling evil head-on is in fact permitted and even correct. One such instance involves a completely righteous person (*tzadik gamur*), who is permitted to antagonize evil. A *tzadik gamur* merits extra help from Above. Such a great individual is allowed to stand up fearlessly for truth, not needing to take the precautions required of most other leaders. On a deeper level, Rav Yitzchak Hunter zt"l[8] explains that a regular person merely *knows* (cerebrally) that "success" afforded evildoers is only temporary and that they will eventually suffer severe consequences. But a completely righteous person *lives* (experientially) with this outlook. And more, a *tzadik gamur* views the evildoer's current "success" as nothing more than a façade. He understands that, in truth, every act of evil only buries the evildoer deeper and deeper in eternal damnation. Since the *tzadik gamur* lives with such an outlook, his bold stance against evil is not cavalier grandstanding or reckless bravado, but a natural response based on his exalted view of the world around him. We can add that the *tzadik gamur*'s blatant confrontation with evil cannot be perceived as a lowly man trying to take control of a situation against the strong hand of Hashem, for the *tzadik gamur* does not at all identify the evil as prevailing! That is, for most people, in order for the Heavenly sign (sent in the form of an evildoer) to affect them, they need to acknowledge the existence of the evil and accept Hashem's punishment. By doing so, they enable themselves to focus on their own repentance while handling the success of the evildoer with caution, stealth, and wisdom. The *tzadik gamur*, on the other hand, peers above the smokescreen and sees nothing of which to be scared. The *tzadik gamur* certainly responds with teshuva as well, but he does not feel any fear of the evil while doing so.

Mordechai *HaTzadik* was one such completely righteous person. R. Eliyahu Dessler zt"l[9] explains (based on the *Maharal*) that Mordechai shunned evil and would never allow himself to grant evil any honor or success. As a descendant of Binyamin who never bowed to Esav, Mordechai refused to bow to Haman (and even went

---

[1] See *Berachos* 7b and *Megilla* 6b: "אם ראית רשע שהשעה משחקת לו אל תתגרה בו" (if you see an evildoer prospering, do not antagonize him).

[2] *Sotah* 41b

[3] See commentaries on *Berachos* 7a regarding the famous question why good things happen to bad people etc. (See a list of sources in Artscroll edition ibid. note 50.) This discussion also relates to *Berachos* 5a which tells us that the proper response to affliction and hardship is *teshuva*; see commentaries on that Gemara.

[4] *Shemos Rabba* 5:15. See also *Nachalas Shimon* (*Melachim* 1 vol. 2 ch. 51).

[5] It should be noted that Hashem only "utilizes" these evil kings as "pawns" if the kings themselves choose on their own free will to act in this evil manner. See Rambam (*hil. Teshuva* 6:3,5).

[6] *Eitz Yosef* on *Shemos Rabba* ibid.

[7] See *Berachos* and *Megilla* ibid. See also *Einayim LaMishpat* on *Berachos* ibid. along with other commentaries.

[8] *Pachad Yitzchak* Purim 9:2. See also R. Mattisyahu Solomon *Shlit"a*'s *Matnas Chaim* (*Moadim*; Purim #11, pg. 202) for further elaboration. A similar idea is offered by *Chidushei HaGra* and *Meromei Sadeh* on *Berachos* ibid.

[9] *Michtav Me'Eliyahu* (vol. 2 pg. 130); see also *Pachad Yitzchak* ibid. 9:3.

out of his way to openly display his rejection of Haman[10]). And it was this very boldness that ultimately brought the Jewish nation to repentance and Haman to his demise.

Yet the Jewish nation initially resented Mordechai for his insolence, for putting them in grave danger and acting in a manner they perceived as irresponsible[11]. And, in fact, Mordechai's defiance is not the prescribed approach for most people[12]. Indeed, Yaakov Avinu, whose attitude toward life's assorted challenges serves as a paradigm for his descendants to follow[13], did not choose Mordechai's approach, but rather bowed to Esav[14]. R. Aryeh Leib Malin zt"l[15] draws upon various Midrashim[16] to prove that Yaakov's submission to Esav was a terrible compromise of ideals (for which *Klal Yisroel* suffered at the hands of the Romans), but, somewhat paradoxically, also a precedent that directs us throughout our exile. On the one hand, Yaakov was forced to create the appearance of evil triumphing over good, which is itself a horrific disgrace of Hashem and His holy Torah. But on the other hand, Yaakov Avinu's spiritual and physical preparation for his meeting with Esav empowered *Klal Yisroel* throughout history to bow to evil when circumstances demanded, as tragic as this necessity may be.[17]

R. Aryeh Leib adds the following essential point:

כל מה ששלח לו 'עבדך יעקב' לא היה אלא הנהגה בחיצוניות, שכך צריך להתנהג, אבל בודאי בפנימיותו לא היה ליעקב שום הכנעה, אלא שהיה מוכרח לעשות כן... אבל בפנימיות ודאי שאסור שיהיה שום הרגשה של השפלה.[18]

That which Yaakov referred to himself (when speaking to Esav) as 'Yaakov, your servant' was only a front, and he acted this way only out of necessity. But certainly Yaakov did not feel this way inside; he was merely forced to act this way… It is surely forbidden to harbor any feeling of abasement (towards evildoers).

R. Hutner zt"l[19] beautifully articulates this same idea. He explains that the outward flattery that we afford the enemy is, in its essence, simply an outward expression of an inner mockery of that individual: " חניפה מבחוץ ולעג מבפנים".

There are some rare occasions and some unique individuals who may follow Mordechai's open and bold example, but in most situations, we need to handle the political scene with caution and discretion. Yet even as we cooperate with those who oppose our values and principles, we must take care to never lose sight of the idea that the primary response to evil has nothing to do with physically battling the evil. We must focus on fixing the personal and communal sins that stand as the root cause for the "success" of evil. And more, even as we play the political game, R. Aryeh Leib's words must serve as a crucial directive: while we may sometimes be required to flatter the evildoers, our inner chamber can never change. The Jewish politician is constantly aware that G-d calls the shots, that the Torah reigns, and that the success of evil is a mere façade. Such an outlook will steer our minds and souls toward bettering ourselves and our relationship with G-d and hopefully bring us to a point in history when we do not need to toy with politics at all.

---

[10] See *Maharal* and Midrash quoted in *Michtav Me'Eliyahu* ibid. who derive this point from the wording of the Megilla itself.

[11] See *Megilla* bottom of 12b and Midrash quoted in *Michtav Me'Eliyahu* ibid.

[12] See Rabbenu Yonah (*Shaarei Teshuva* 3:199) who codifies the Talmudic sources cited above that permit affording honor to and even flattering evildoers in order to protect oneself.

[13] The Jewish nation is referred to as *Bnei Yisroel* and *Kehillas Yaakov*, i.e. the sons and congregation of Yaakov. The Gemara (*Taanis* 5b) states, "Yaakov Avinu did not die"; Yaakov Avinu lives on forever through his nation (see *Gur Aryeh* end of *Parashas Vayechi*). Yaakov represents the characteristic of everlasting truth (as the *Pasuk* in *Micha* 7:20 states, "*titein emes l'Yaakov*") and the "middle road" that guides us throughout history; see *Z'ev Yitrof* (*Succos*) at length along with numerous other commentators.

[14] Even though Yaakov Avinu was also an exceedingly righteous man, the Rabbis explain that he was afraid that perhaps he nonetheless was not great enough to merit escape from Esav; see *Berachos* bottom of 4a "*shema yigrom ha'chet*".

[15] *Mi'Toraso shel HaGaon Rebbe Aryeh Leib, Maamar #2*

[16] *Bereishis Rabba* 75:5,11

[17] *Ramban*, beginning of *Parashas Vayishlach*

[18] *Mi'Toraso shel HaGaon Rebbe Aryeh Leib* pg. 149

[19] *Pachad Yitzchak* Ibid. See also *Matnos Chaim* ibid.

Essay #9 – Does Keriyas Shema depend on "sleeping and awaking" or "night and day"?

Rabbi Ranan Amster

לעילוי נשמת לאה בת מאיר ע'ה (Lydia Gutman)

1. Reciting Shema before nightfall

The Torah in Parashas V'eschanan (Devarim 6:7) states the following:

"ושננתם לבניך ודברת בם בשבתך בביתך ובלכתך בדרך **ובשכבך ובקומך**"

*"And you shall teach them to your sons and discuss them when you sit in your house, and when you walk on the way, and **when you lie down and when you rise up**."*

The Rabbis teach us that the last two words ("ובשכבך ובקומך", bolded above) teach us the commandment to read the Parasha of Shemah twice a day. The Gemara (Berachos 10b) records the disagreement between Beis Shamai and Beis Hillel regarding how to interpret this Pasuk. Beis Shamai is of the opinion that the Pasuk teaches us the **position** by which one should recite Shema. According to Beis Shammai, when reciting Shema at night, one should read it lying down and when reciting it in the morning one should read it standing up. Beis Hillel disagrees and interprets the Pasuk as teaching the proper **time** to recite Shema. At night, it is recited when people are going to sleep and in the morning it is recited when people are waking up.

Following along with the opinion of Beis Hillel, the Mishnah in the beginning of Berachos (2a) records a disagreement regarding regarding the correct time to recite Shema:

1) R. Eliezer holds that one can recite Shema at night, from "tzeis hakochavim" (nightfall) through the first third of the night, when people are "going" to sleep (see Rashi).
2) Rabban Gamliel holds that one can Shema from nightfall until the next morning ("alos hashachar"), as he understands the Pasuk as referring to the time when people are sleeping, not necessarily when people are *going* to sleep.[1]
3) The Chachomim hold that one can recite Shema from nightfall until midnight. (See Rabbenu Yonah for interpretation of this opinion.)

The Rishonim (Rashi, Tosafos, etc.) relate that the prevelant custom was to recite Shema before nightfall, and they therefore ask the obvious question: how are we allowed to follow this custom since it seems to clearly contradict all of the opinions in the Mishnah?

Rashi (2a) answers that we fulfill the mitzvah of Keriyas Shema through the Shema that we say before bed which is well after nightfall. We say Shema in Shul before nightfall, not in order to fulfill the mitzvah but based on the Yerushalmi that states that one should say some Divrei Torah before Shemoneh Esrei. Keriyas Shema in this context merely serves as the "Divrei Torah" and has nothing to do with fulfilling one's obligation to recite Shema.

Tosafos (2a) disagree for a number of reasons, including the fact that the Gemara (5a) implies that the only reason one recites Shema before bed is to protect from the "mazikim" (evil spirits etc.), and it has nothing to do with fulfilling one's obligation to recite Keriyas Shema twice daily. In addition, Tosafos point out that according to Rashi one should have to say a beracha before reciting Shema before bed since (according to him) that is the main fulfillment of the mitzvah, but the custom is not to make any such beracha. (Tosafos assume that the berachos of Keriyas Shema function as "birchos hamitzvah" of Keriyas Shema, but this point is subject to debate in Rishonim.)

Based on these questions and others, Tosafos maintain that the main fulfillment of the obligation to recite Shema is performed in Shul before nightfall. To answer the original question how the mitzvah could be

---

[1] Alternatively, one can suggest that even according to R. Gamliel the time for reciting Shema is dependent on "going to sleep", but since *some* people go to sleep as late as the following morning, one can still recite Shema until that point. This needs further research.

fulfilled before nightfall, Tosafos write that we follow the opinion of Rabbi Yehuda (recorded on 26a) that one could daven Mincha before "plag haMincha" and then Maariv after "plag haMincha". (The Chachamim disagree and hold that one could daven Mincha all the way until Shekiya but can daven Maariv only after nightfall or Shekiyah.) Since we follow R. Yehuda that after "plag haMincha" one can daven Maariv since it is halachically considered "night", therefore one can also recite Shema at that point.

The Rosh (1:1) questions Tosafos' opinion. The Rosh asks: what does R. Yehuda's opinion have to do with the time for Keriyas Shema?! Reb Yehuda is discussing the time to daven Maariv and what is considered "night" with respect to Tefilla, whereas the time for Keriyas Shema is simply dependent on when people go to sleep, which is certainly not until nightfall!

2. Is Keriyas Shema based on "sleeping and awaking" or "night and day"?

To answer this question and to understand the disagreement between Rashi and Tosafos, one could suggest as follows:

As stated above, the obligation to recite Shema both during the day and again at the night is sourced in a Pasuk in V'eschanan that states that Shema is recited "בשכבך ובקומך", "when you lie down and when you rise up". However, one can understand this command in one of two ways:

1) The entire obligation is based on when people are going to sleep and waking up. The fact that it is day or night is somewhat irrelevant, for the timing is entirely dependent on the time for waking and sleeping, as the simple understanding of the Pasuk indicates.

2) The obligation is really based on when it is considered "day" and "night"; the Torah merely utilizes the language of "בשכבך ובקומך" as a "siman" (indication) to define whether it is day or night, but the halacha is not truly dependant on the time for going to sleep or waking up.

Support for the second possibility can be found in the words of the Rambam (beginning of hil. Keriyas Shema 1:1) who states as follows:

"פעמים בכל יום קוראין קריאת שמע בערב ובבקר. שנאמר ובשכבך ובקומך, בשעה שדרך בני אדם שוכבין, **וזה הוא לילה**, ובשעה שדרך בני אדם עומדין **וזה הוא יום**."

"We are obligated to recite the Shema twice daily - in the evening and in the morning - as the Torah states, '...when you lie down and when you rise' - i.e., when people are accustomed to sleep - **this being the night** *- and when people are accustomed to rise -* **this being daytime**."

When quoting the source for the obligation to recite Shema during the day and night, the Rambam does not simply quote the Pasuk but goes out of his way to say that *"when you lie down"* means "night" and *"when you rise"* means "day". It seems clear that the Rambam interprets the words "בשכבך ובקומך" according to the second interpretation above.

This may also explain the debate between Rashi and Tosafos. Rashi understands the halacha according to the first interpretation above and holds that the obligation is dependent on the time for sleep (not night and day). Therefore, Rashi opines that it is impossible to fulfill ones obligation before nightfall, for people are not yet "going to sleep". Tosafos, however, clearly are of the opinion that the obligation to recite Shema depends upon "day" and "night". Therefore, one can recites Shema even before nightfall once it is halachically considered "night" (according to Reb Yehuda).

3. The applicability of Keriyas Shema throughout the day

Based on the above, one can further understand the words of the Rambam (hilchos Keriyas Shema 1:13) who states the following:

"הקורא אחר שלש שעות ביום אפילו היה אנוס לא יצא ידי חובת קריאת שמע בעונתו, אלא הרי הוא כקורא בתורה, ומברך לפניה ולאחריה **כל היום** אפילו איחר וקרא אחר שלש שעות."

*"One who recites Shema after the end of the third hour, even if he was unavoidably detained, does not fulfill his obligation to recite the Shema at its proper time. Rather, his reading of Shema is equivalent to studying Torah. [Nevertheless] he can recite the blessings for Shema at any point **all day**, even if he delays and recites it after the third hour."* (This opinion of the Rambam is subject to a debate, as many Rishonim are of the opinion that one does not recite the berachos of Keriyas Shema after the fourth hour of the day.)

The Kesef Mishneh asks the following question: Why must the daytime Shema be read before the end of the third hour of the day; just as the obligation to recite Shema at night lasts throughout the night because the entire night is a "time of lying down", so too, one should be permitted to recite the daytime Shema throughout the day, since the entire day is "a time of being awake"!? The Kesef Mishneh answers that according to Torah law one can indeed fulfill his obligation of reciting Shema all day long; the obligation to recite Shema before the end of the third hour of the day is only Rabbinic. The Kesef Mishneh continues that it is for this reason that one may recite the berachos for Keriyas Shema throughout the day, for the Torah obligation applies all day long.

Most Acharonim, however, disagree with the Kesef Mishneh. The Magen Avraham (58:7) asks three questions against him:

1) There is no proof from the fact that one can say the berachos after three hours, for the berachos of Shema are not intrinsically linked to the mitzvah of Keriyas Shema, but represent a seperate prayer. **(Potential answer:** The Magen Avraham's assumption is subject to a debate amongst the Rishonim/Acharonim. The Kesef Mishneh clearly holds that they are indeed linked to the mitzvah of Keriyas Shema; see Tosafos on 2a who seem to imply this as well.)

2) If the Kesef Mishneh were correct, one would be allowed to say the berachos *all day*, not only through the fourth hour of the day. **(Potential answer:** The Rambam indeed holds that one can say the berachos all day.)

3) If the Kesef Mishneh were correct, then Keriyas Shema would not be considered a "time-bound mitzvah" because there would not be a time that one would be exempt from Keriyas Shema, yet the Gemara explicitly states that Keriyas Shema is indeed a time-bound mitzvah from which women are exempt. **(Potential answer:** One can argue that the obligation to recite Shema during the day is distinct from the obligation to recite Shema at night, and both are therefore considered "time-bound" even though the individual is obligated in the mitzvah throughout the day and night; see Shaagas Aryeh.)

The Magen Avraham therefore answers the Kesef Mishneh's questions differently, explaining that the difference between the night Keriyas Shema (which can be recited throughout the night) and the day Keriyas Shema (which can only be said within the first hours of they day) is based on the wording of the Pasuk itself. The word "בשכבך" means when people are "lying down" (not necessarily *going to* lie down), which occurs the entire night, whereas the word "ובקומך" means when people are "getting up", which only occurs in the first hours of the day.

One could suggest that this disagreement between the Kesef Mishneh and the Magen Avraham is part of the debate between Rashi and Tosafos, as described above. According to the Magen Avraham, the time to recite Shema is bound by the meaning of the words "בשכבך ובקומך", like the first interpretation above (Rashi). The Kesef Mishneh, however, opines that Keriyas Shema depends on "day" and "night", as explained in the second interpretation above (Tosafos). This could also be the opinion of the Rambam and can explains why the Rambam rules that one can say the berachos of Keriyas Shema throughout the day – because, as the Kesef Mishneh explained, the mitzvah according to the Torah applies all day, not only when waking up.

4. Is there a distinction between the timing of Tefilla and Keriyas Shema?

The Pri Chadash (siman 58) quotes the Kesef Mishneh and raises a proof against him from the following Gemara (15a):

"רב חסדא לייט אמאן דמהדר אמיא בעידן צלותא, **והני מילי לק"ש אבל לתפלה מהדר**."

"R. Chisda cursed anyone who went looking for water at the time of prayer (and so delayed his prayers). ***This applies to the recital of Shema, but for Tefilla one may go looking.****"*

Rashi explains that the distinction in the Gemara between Keriyas Shema and Tefilla is that Keriyas Shema has a set time according to the Torah, and he should therefore not go looking for water because he may miss that time. Tefilla, on the other hand, does not have a set time, and he can pray the entire day so there is no prohibition to look for water. The Pri Chadash points out that this Gemara explicitly contradicts the Kesef Mishneh, because according to the Kesef Mishneh there should be no difference between Keriyas Shemah and Tefilla since both can be recited all day according to Torah law.

Indeed, Tosafos on that very Gemara (ד"ה אמאן) have a different text of the Gemara (they do not have the sentence in the Gemara that is bolded in the text above) and learn that in truth there is no difference between Keriyas Shema and Tefilla.

According to that which we have explained above, Rashi and Tosafos are each consistent with their own opinion in this disagreement as well. Rashi holds like the first interpretation listed above, that the timing for Keriyas Shema depends upon "going to sleep and rising", and he likely agrees with the Magen Avraham that the time for daytime Keriyas Shema is only until the third hour of the day, even according to Torah law. Tosafos, however, understand that Keriyas Shema depends on "daytime" (like Rambam and Kesef Mishneh), and they therefore see no difference between Tefilla and Keriyas Shema, for both of them apply all day according to Torah law.

Essay #10 – Kaddish D'Rabbanan: What is it and when is it said?

Dr. Jonathan Mazurek

לעילוי נשמת מאיר שלום בן אברהם מנחם ז'ל (Myron Mazurek)

ולעילוי נשמת משה נטע בן נפתלי הלוי ז'ל (Morris Lewinter)

The Gemara (Berachos 3a) relates a famous story about R. Yosi who was once travelling and needed to daven in one of the destroyed buildings (churvos) of Yerushalayim. Upon concluding his Tefilla, he encountered Eliyahu HaNavi who chastised him for davening in such a potentially dangerous environment. Eliyahu then asked him what sound he heard when he was inside the dilapidated building. R. Yosi responded that he heard a Heavenly voice (Bas Kol) lamenting the plight of the destroyed Beis HaMikdash and the exiled Jewish people. Eliyahu responded that this Heavenly voice repeats this refrain three times a day, as well as every time Jews gather in shuls and study halls (Batei Midrash) and recite "Yehei Shmei HaGadol Mevorach".

In this context, Tosafos[1] discuss the proper meaning and significance of "יהא שמיה רבא" (the most lofty part of Kaddish) and raise the question as to why Kaddish is recited in Aramaic as opposed to Hebrew. Tosafos initially entertain the explanation that it is based on the notion that the heavenly angels do not understand Aramaic.[2] Since Kaddish is such a beautiful and lofty prayer, we do not want the angels to become jealous of our privilege to praise Hashem in such an exalted fashion, so we recite it in a language that they do not understand. Tosafos reject this explanation, as there are many wonderful prayers that we recite in Hebrew, and we are nevertheless unconcerned about arousing the jealousy of the heavenly angels.

Tosafos instead offer the following explanation based on Gemara Sotah (49a). The Gemara states:

"אין העולם מתקיים אלא אסדרא דקדושתא ואיהא שמיה רבא דבתר אגדתא."

[Since the day that the Beis Hamikdash was destroyed] the merit upon which the world continues to endure stems from the recitation of Kedusha (recited in the prayer "ובא לציון") and the recital of "יהא שמיה רבא" that follow the learning of "Aggada".

Tosafos explain that since this "Kaddish D'Rabbanan" was typically recited after a community-wide learning session (derasha) to an audience that was not entirely fluent in Hebrew, Kaddish was therefore recited in the vernacular, Aramaic, so that all in attendance would understand the prayer.

This insight of Tosafos as to the origin of Kaddish in general and Kaddish D'Rabbanan in particular raises the question as to what situations require the recitation of Kaddish D'Rabbanan. Kaddish D'Rabbanan (Kaddish with a special insert praising those who learn Torah diligently) was established to be recited after a session of learning was completed. The question that is discussed in the Rishonim and further elucidated in the Acharonim is: what qualifies as "Torah learning" that necessitates a Kaddish D'Rabbanan?

The term used in the Gemara Sotah to describe Kaddish D'Rabbanan is "יהא שמיה רבא דבתר אגדתא". Should this be taken literally, and refer to the sections of Torah Sheba'al Peh (the Oral Torah) that we colloquially refer to as "Aggadeta" (anecdotal or non-Halachic aspects of the Torah), or does it refer to Rabbinic texts in general?

Rashi, explaining Gemara Sotah (ibid.) writes that this Kaddish was established to be recited after the "*hagadah* that the *Darshan* would *doresh* in front of the public gathering every Shabbos". Similar to Tosafos, Rashi refers to the custom of having a public address for the entire community on a weekly basis. From Rashi's words, however, we may be able to glean a further insight. According to Rashi, in order for Kaddish D'Rabbanan to be recited, the public address must include Aggadic material ("*hagadah*") that incorporates a *derasha*, an in depth explication of a *pasuk*. Without such exegetical analysis, it is possible that, according to Rashi's opinion, a Kaddish D'Rabbanan should not be recited.

---

[1] ד"ה ועונין

[2] Sotah 33a; Shabbos 12b

The position of the Rambam is the subject of discussion[3], as he seems to contradict himself in various places. In his Seder HaTefillos (recorded at the end of Sefer Ahavah), the Rambam writes: "If ten or more Jewish men engage in Torah Sheba'al Peh, even in Midrash or Aggadeta, when they conclude, one of them says the following Kaddish...". It seems apparent from this quote that *any* part of Torah Sheba'al Peh, both those that are Halachic in nature as well as those that are merely Aggadic or Midrashic, necessitates a Kaddish D'Rabbanan. Yet the Rambam in his commentary on the sixth chapter of Pirkei Avos, commenting on the supplemental Beraisa of "Rabbi Chananya ben Akashya says," writes that "we recite the Mishnah of 'Rabbi Chananya ben Akashya says' at the conclusion of each chapter of Pirkei Avos because Kaddish D'Rabbanan is only said after *hagadah* and not following the learning of Mishnah." In this source, the Rambam is clear that only those parts of Torah Sheba'al Peh that are Aggadic in nature (and possibly only those that also include a *derasha* from a Pasuk, such as the Beraisa of "Rabbi Chananya ben Akashya") are subject to a Kaddish D'Rabbanan, while those sections of Torah Sheba'al Peh that are Halachic are not.

Various explanations have been proposed to try to explain this apparent contradiction.[4] The Magen Avraham[5] writes that the when the Rambam in Seder HaTefillos states that Kaddish D'Rabbanan is said after learning Torah Sheba'al Peh, he must be referring to a situation where, following the study, a Beraisa or Mishnah containing a derasha from a Pasuk is added, like we do after reading "Bameh Madlikin" (on Friday night) or "Ein K'Elokeinu" (on Shabbos morning).

Alternatively, one can resolve this "contradiction" by pointing out that the Rambam did not write the aforementioned commentary on Pirkei Avos, and there is therefore no contradiction at all. The last chapter of Pirkei Avos is not actually part of the original five chapters of the Masechta (Tractate). Rather, this chapter (referred to as "Kinyan Torah") originated as a Beraisa and was appended to the first five chapters of Pirkei Avos in order to fulfill the custom of reciting a chapter of Pirkei Avos each week on the six intervening Shabbosos between Pesach and Shavuos. The earliest published editions of the Rambam's commentary on Pirkei Avos included a commentary to this additional chapter with the Rambam's name attributed to it.[6] But some of the commentators on Pirkei Avos note that the commentary that was initially attributed to the Rambam was not actually written by him.[7] In fact, a manuscript from Paris, at the conclusion of the fifth chapter of Pirkei Avos states, "here concludes the commentary of the Rambam for this Masechta that was translated from Arabic to Hebrew by Rabbeinu Shemuel ben Tibon". Hence the Rambam in his commentary on Pirkei Avos does not contradict himself in Seder HaTefillos, as the commentary on the "final chapter" of Pirkei Avos was not written by the Rambam at all![8] Consequently, the Rambam's position stands as recorded in Seder HaTefillos that Kaddish D'Rabbanan can be recited upon the conclusion of learning any aspect of Torah Sheba'al Peh, whether it is Halachic, Aggadic or Midrashic. Indeed, Rav Soloveitchik, explaining the Rambam's position, states that the whole purpose of saying Kaddish D'Rabbanan is to praise the Rabbis and their students, for they represent the continuity of the mesorah (tradition) in Klal Yisrael. It is therefore fitting to recite the Kaddish on any part of Torah Sheba'al Peh.

Who then is the commentator of the Beraisa of "Rabi Chananya ben Akashya" that states that Kaddish D'Rabbanan is only recited on Aggadah with a derasha? Manuscripts seem to indicate that this commentary is actually Rashi. If so, Rashi is consistent with his opinion as recorded in his commentary to the Gemara in Sotah. In both places Rashi writes that Kaddish D'Rabbanan is recited upon the conclusion of learning a piece of Aggadeta that also includes a derasha from a Pasuk.

---

[3] Be'er Sheva, Sotah 49a
[4] Be'er Sheva ibid.; Machatzis Hashekel (OC 54:3); Birkei Yosef (OC 55:5); Aruch Hashulchan (OC 55:5).
[5] OC 54:3.
[6] Naples, 1492 edition.
[7] Maharal (in Derech HaChaim) attributes the commentary to Rashi. Maharatz Chayes (Imrei Binah, Siman 16, printed in Kol Kisvei Maharatz Chayes vol. 2 pg. 966) states that the commentary on the sixth perek of Pirkei Avos is neither Rashi nor the Rambam, but another later commentator.
[8] Similarly, the Be'er Sheva, Sotah 49a, writes that the comment on the Mishnah of "Rabbi Chananya ben Akashya" was recorded in the Rambam's name by a mistaken student.

Practically, the application of this discussion is subject to dispute among the Acharonim. The Magen Avraham[9], as mentioned above, states that Kaddish D'Rabbanan should be recited only after concluding with a piece of Aggadah that includes a derasha from a Pasuk. The Aruch Hashulchan[10] disagrees, ruling like the Rambam in Seder HaTefillos, that Kaddish D'Rabbanan can be recited upon the conclusion of learning *any* aspect of Torah Sheba'al Peh, even Halachic matters. The Chafetz Chaim, in his Beiur Halacha[11], states that Kaddish D'Rabbanan is only recited after learning Torah Sheba'al Peh, but not after reading Pesukim of Torah Shebichsav (the "Written Torah"). However, when discussing the Halacha in his Mishnah Berurah[12], the Chafetz Chaim concludes with the opinion of the Magen Avraham, that Aggadah is indeed required.

While it seems that the accepted practice is to recite Kaddish D'Rabbanan only after learning a piece of Aggadah with a derasha (in accordance with the view of the Magen Avraham), there seems to be a very common exception to this rule. Following the daily recitation of Korbanos, "איזהו מקומן" and "ר' ישמעאל אומר", we recite "יהי רצון מלפניך... שיבנה בית המקדש במהרה בימינו..." and then conclude with Kaddish D'Rabbanan. The problem with this practice is that the pieces of Torah Sheba'al Peh that were recited prior to this Kaddish were all Halachic in nature and do not contain Aggadah or a derasha. Thus, reciting Kaddish D'Rabbanan at that point would seemingly contradict the ruling of the Magen Avraham. The Shulchan Aruch HaRav[13] writes that concluding with the "יהי רצון מלפניך..." provides ample reason to recite the Kaddish D'Rabannan. Some later Acharonim[14] explain this reasoning of the Shulchan Aruch HaRav by positing that the "יהי רצון" is actually a quote from Pirkei Avos and is therefore non-Halachic in nature, akin to the learning of Aggadah. Other authorities[15], however, question the authenticity of this statement by the Shulchan Aruch HaRav, as it is published in parentheses.

Interestingly, the Beiur Halacha[16] does not count the Kaddish D'Rabbanan said after "ר' ישמעאל אומר" in the list of Kaddeishim that must be allocated amongst the various mourners in shul (though he does list the Kaddish D'Rabbanan said after "Bameh Madlikin" on Friday night). In fact, a student of the Chafetz Chaim in the Radin Yeshiva is quoted as saying that no Kaddish D'Rabbanan was recited in the Yeshiva after "ר' ישמעאל אומר".[17] It is possible that the Chaftez Chaim is ruling in accordance with the opinion of the Magen Avraham (as quoted in the Mishnah Berurah) that Kaddish D'Rabanan should only be recited after learning a section of Aggada with a derasha of a Pasuk, and it should indeed not be said after the recitation of "ר' ישמעאל אומר".

---

[9] OC 54:3
[10] OC 55:5
[11] OC 155 (ד"ה ויקבע). This seems consistent with the Rambam in Seder HaTefillos.
[12] OC 54:9
[13] OC 54:4
[14] R. Yitzchak Satz, "Kaddish achar beraisa R. Yishmael", Yeshurun 1997, pg. 553.
[15] Kuntrus Hashulchan, Introduction
[16] OC 132
[17] R. Yitzchak Satz, ibid. pg. 555.

Essay #11 – When is it imperative to daven in shul as opposed to one's home?

Dr. Jonathan Dobkowski

The Gemara (6a) quotes a Beraisa in the name of Abba Binyamin that states: "אין תפלה של אדם נשמעת אלא בבית הכנסת"; a person's prayers are only heard in a *beis haknesses (shul)*. Abba Binyamin derives this ruling from a pasuk in Melachim (8:28) which states, "לשמוע אל הרנה ואת התפלה", explaining that "*Tefilla*" should be said in a place where there is "*Rina*" (song), namely a shul, where the tzibur davens "*shiros v'tishbachos*", praises to Hashem, in singsong and harmony.

The essential question remains: how are we to understand Abba Binyamin's statement?

1) Is it the *makom* (place) itself (i.e. the beis haknesses) which causes one's tefillos to be heard?
2) Or is the significance of the beis haknesses not due to the *makom*, but due to the *tzibur* of ten or more people who gather together to daven there?

According to the first option (1), a person must attend a shul in order for his tefillos to be heard even when no tzibur is present (i.e. a person came very late to shul and is forced to daven alone). But according to the second option (2), only when there is a tzibur of ten or more does a person need to make sure to daven in a beis haknesses, but when there is no tzibur davening, there is no difference between davening alone in one's house and davening alone in shul.

Indeed the Gemara appears to read like the first opinion. For the Gemara states: "*במקום רנה שם תהא תפלה*"; in a *place* of "rina" there should be Tefilla. It seems that the key is the *makom*, even if there is no tzibur.

The Rambam (hil. Tefilla 8:1), according to the opinion of the Kesef Mishneh and Lechem Mishneh, seems to understand in accordance with the first option: whether one is davening alone or with a tzibur, one must daven in a beis haknesses. These are the words of the Rambam: "אין תפלתו נשמעת בכל עת אלא בבית הכנסת"; Tefilla is only heard, at all times, in a beis haknesses. It is interesting to note that the Rambam adds the words "בכל עת", *at all times*. The Lechem Mishneh explains that if a person davens by himself, but with kavana and during the time when the tzibur is davening, his tefillos are certainly heard. However, if a person davens alone during a time when there is no tzibur davening (i.e. "בכל עת", at *all* times), then his tefilla is only heard if recited in a beis haknesses.

The Tur (OC 90:9), however, writes: "לא יתפלל אדם אלא בבית הכנסת *עם הצבור*, דאמר ר' יוחנן אין תפלתו של אדם נשמעת אלא בבית הכנסת". The Tur learns that only the unique quality of *tefilla b'tzibur* needs to be recited in a beis haknesses in order for it to be heard, but a *tefilla b'yachid* is heard equally in one's home and in a shul.

Printed in Great Britain
by Amazon